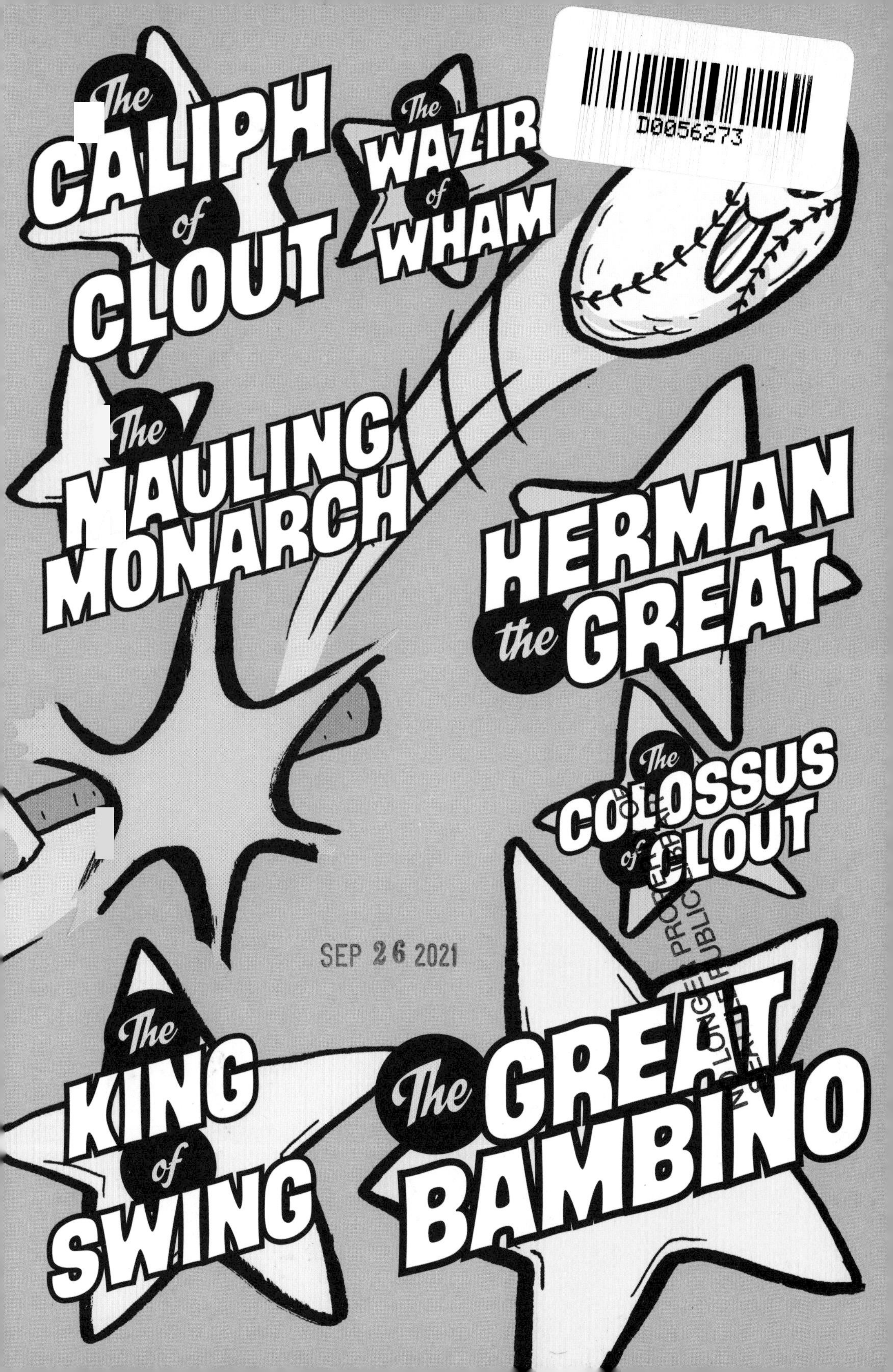
The CALIPH of CLOUT
The WAZIR of WHAM
The MAULING MONARCH
HERMAN the GREAT
The COLOSSUS of CLOUT
The KING of SWING
The GREAT BAMBINO

SHOW ME HISTORY!

BABE Ruth

BASEBALL'S All-Time BEST!

BY
JAMES BUCKLEY JR.

ILLUSTRATED BY
KELLY TINDALL

LETTERING & DESIGN BY
COMICRAFT

COVER ART BY
IAN CHURCHILL

PORTABLE
PRESS

SAN DIEGO, CALIFORNIA

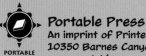

Portable Press
An imprint of Printers Row Publishing Group
10350 Barnes Canyon Road, Suite 100, San Diego, CA 92121
www.portablepress.com • mail@portablepress.com

Printers Row Publishing Group is a division of Readerlink Distribution Services, LLC. Portable Press is a registered trademark of Readerlink Distribution Services, LLC.

Correspondence regarding the content of this book should be addressed to Portable Press, Editorial Department, at the above address. Author or illustration inquiries should be addressed to Oomf, Inc., www.oomf.com.

Publisher: Peter Norton
Associate Publisher: Ana Parker
Developmental Editor: Vicki Jaeger
Senior Product Manager: Kathryn C. Dalby
Production Team: Jonathan Lopes, Rusty von Dyl

 Created at Oomf, Inc., www.Oomf.com
Director: Mark Shulman
Producer: James Buckley Jr.

Author: James Buckley Jr.
Illustrator: Kelly Tindall
Colorist: Shane Corn
Lettering & design by Comicraft: John Roshell, Forest Dempsey, Sarah Jacobs
Cover illustrator: Ian Churchill

Library of Congress Cataloging-in-Publication Data

Names: Buckley, James, Jr., 1963- author. | Tindall, Kelly, illustrator.
Title: Babe Ruth: baseball's all-time best! / James Buckley Jr.; Kelly
   Tindall, illustrator; John Roshell, letterer and designer;
   Ian Churchill, cover artist.
Description: San Diego, CA: Printers Row Publishing Group, [2020] |
   Audience: Ages: 8-12. | Audience: Grades: 4-6.
Identifiers: LCCN 2019017029 | ISBN 9781645170716 (hbk.)
Subjects: LCSH: Ruth, Babe, 1895-1948--Juvenile literature. | Ruth, Babe,
   1895-1948--Comic books, strips, etc. | Baseball players--United
   States--Biography--Juvenile literature. | Baseball players--United
   States--Biography--Comic books, strips, etc.
Classification: LCC GV865.R8 B83 2020 | DDC 796.357092 [B] --dc23 LC
record available at https://lccn.loc.gov/2019017029

Printed in China

24 23 22 21 20   1 2 3 4 5

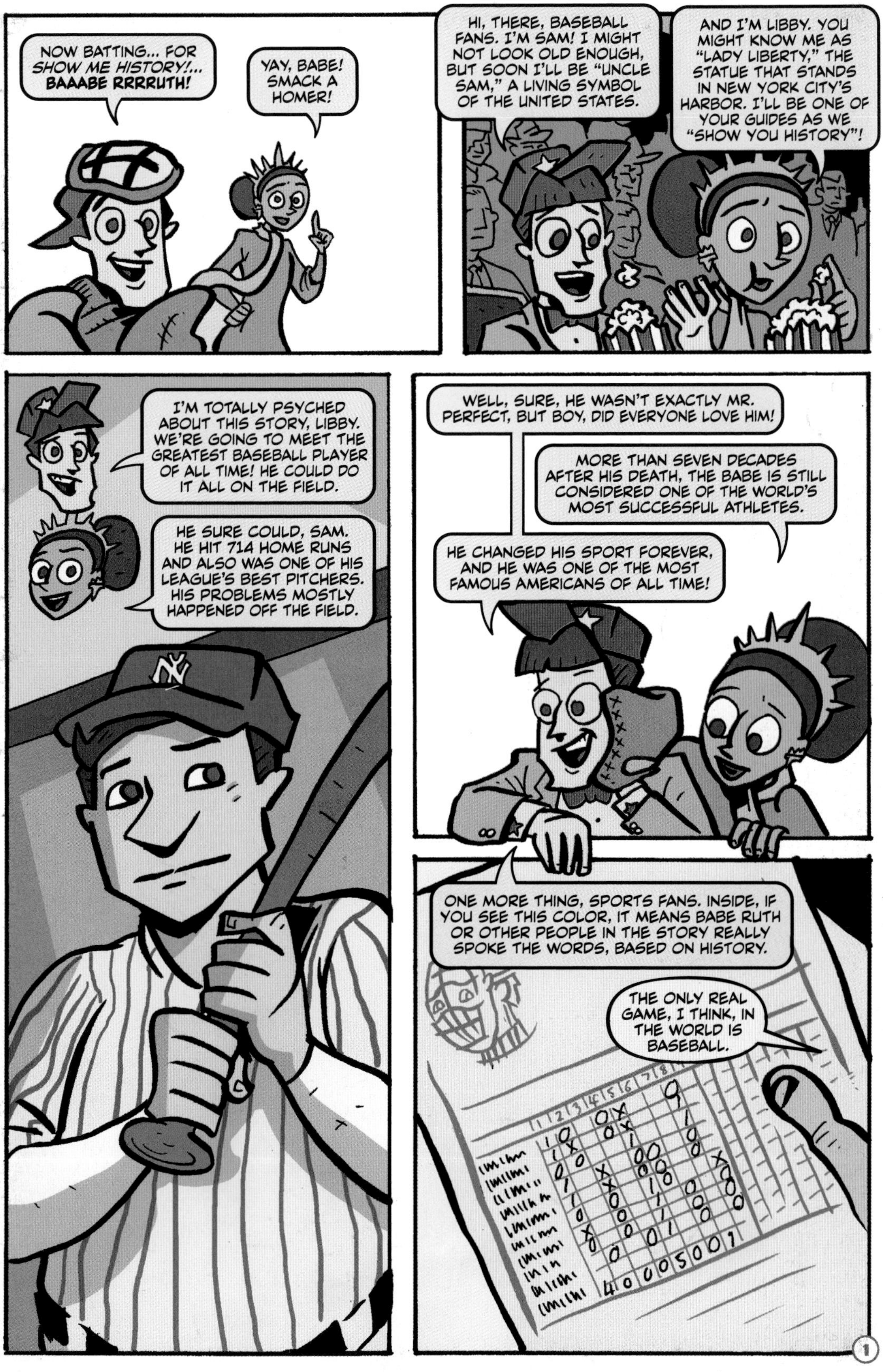
NOW BATTING... FOR *SHOW ME HISTORY!*... **BAAABE RRRRUTH!**
YAY, BABE! SMACK A HOMER!
HI, THERE, BASEBALL FANS. I'M SAM! I MIGHT NOT LOOK OLD ENOUGH, BUT SOON I'LL BE "UNCLE SAM," A LIVING SYMBOL OF THE UNITED STATES.
AND I'M LIBBY. YOU MIGHT KNOW ME AS "LADY LIBERTY," THE STATUE THAT STANDS IN NEW YORK CITY'S HARBOR. I'LL BE ONE OF YOUR GUIDES AS WE "SHOW YOU HISTORY"!
I'M TOTALLY PSYCHED ABOUT THIS STORY, LIBBY. WE'RE GOING TO MEET THE GREATEST BASEBALL PLAYER OF ALL TIME! HE COULD DO IT ALL ON THE FIELD.
HE SURE COULD, SAM. HE HIT 714 HOME RUNS AND ALSO WAS ONE OF HIS LEAGUE'S BEST PITCHERS. HIS PROBLEMS MOSTLY HAPPENED OFF THE FIELD.
WELL, SURE, HE WASN'T EXACTLY MR. PERFECT, BUT BOY, DID EVERYONE LOVE HIM!
MORE THAN SEVEN DECADES AFTER HIS DEATH, THE BABE IS STILL CONSIDERED ONE OF THE WORLD'S MOST SUCCESSFUL ATHLETES.
HE CHANGED HIS SPORT FOREVER, AND HE WAS ONE OF THE MOST FAMOUS AMERICANS OF ALL TIME!
ONE MORE THING, SPORTS FANS. INSIDE, IF YOU SEE THIS COLOR, IT MEANS BABE RUTH OR OTHER PEOPLE IN THE STORY REALLY SPOKE THE WORDS, BASED ON HISTORY.
THE ONLY REAL GAME, I THINK, IN THE WORLD IS BASEBALL.

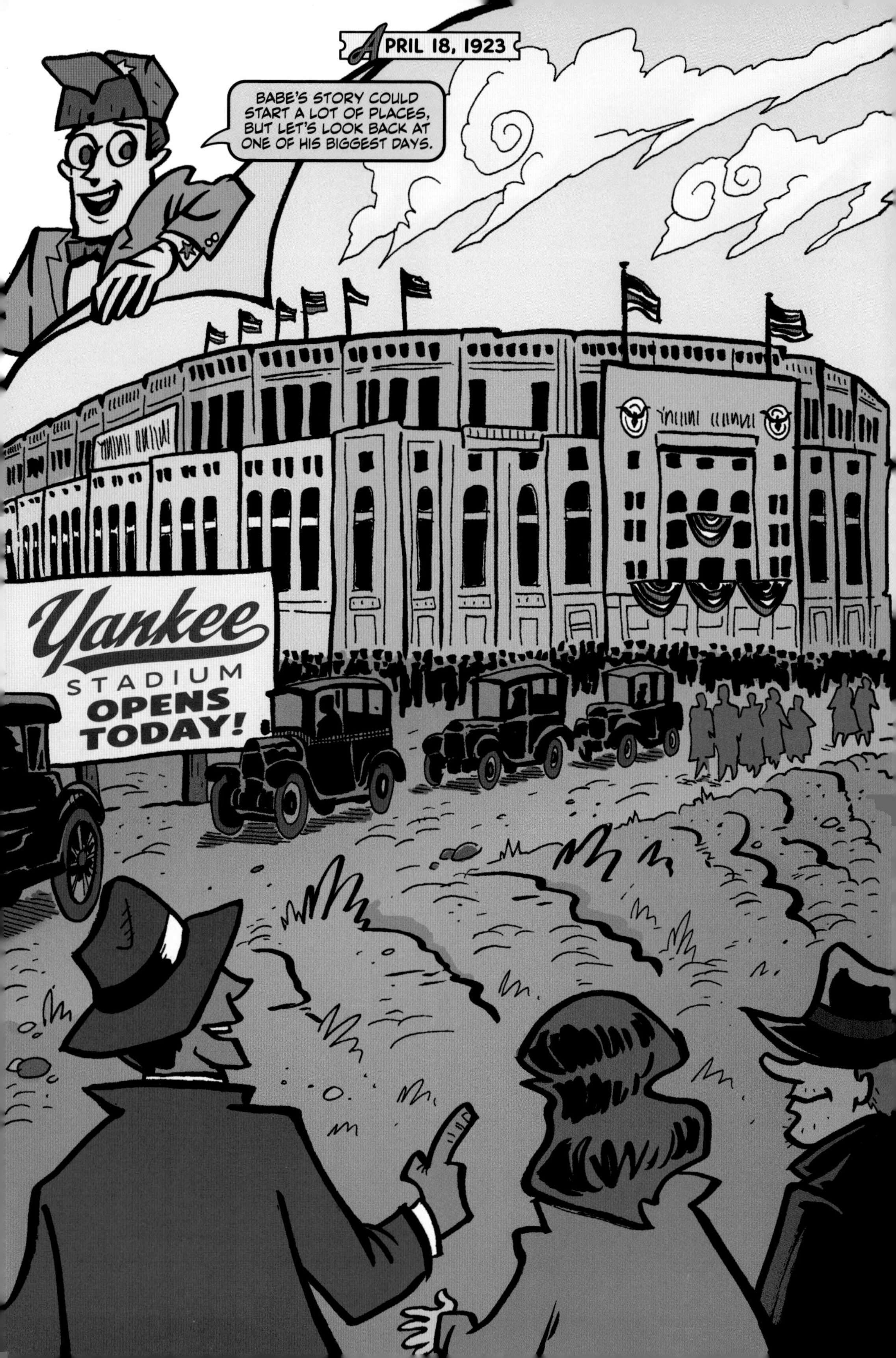
APRIL 18, 1923
BABE'S STORY COULD START A LOT OF PLACES, BUT LET'S LOOK BACK AT ONE OF HIS BIGGEST DAYS.
Yankee STADIUM OPENS TODAY!

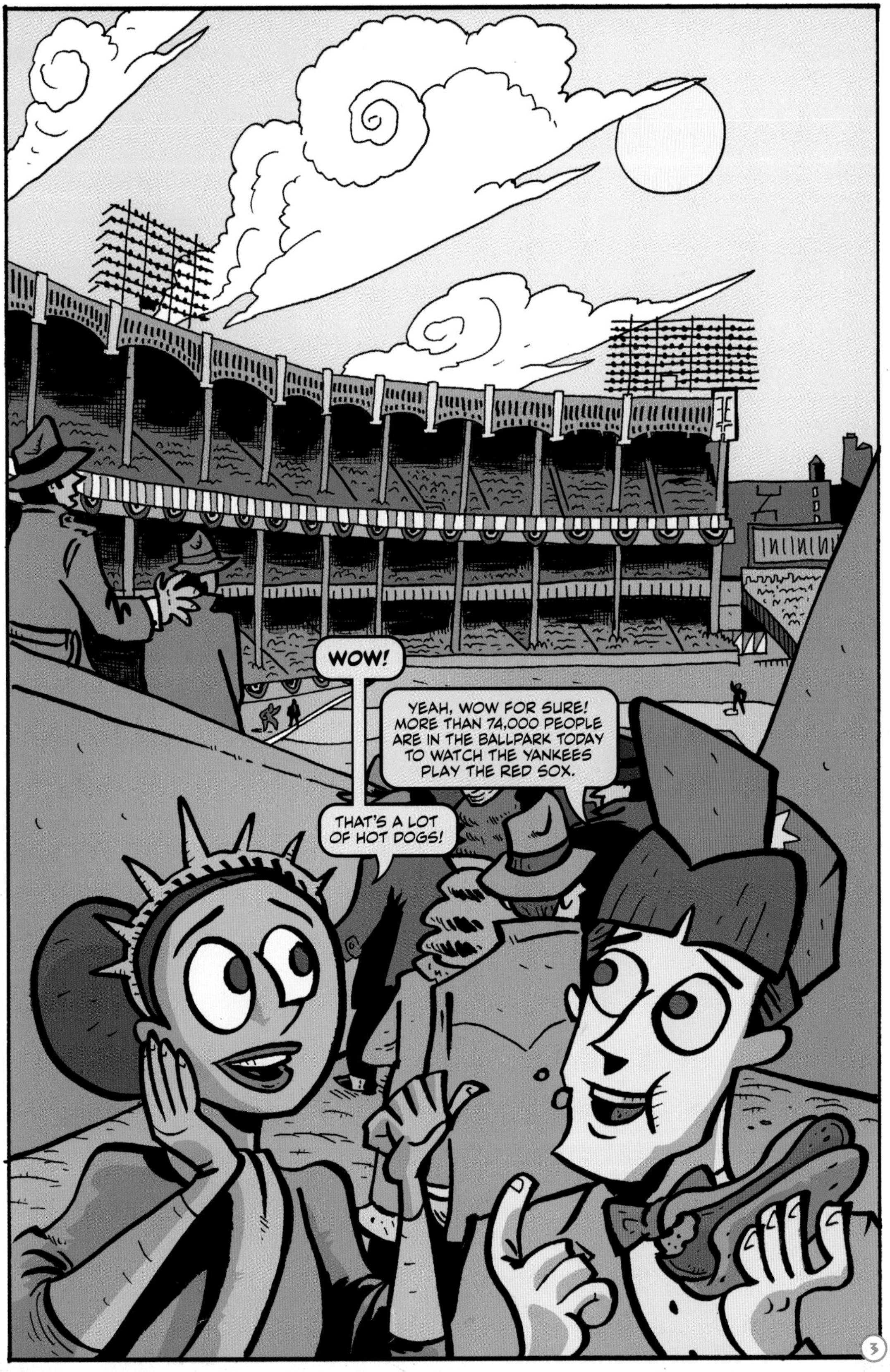
WOW!
YEAH, WOW FOR SURE! MORE THAN 74,000 PEOPLE ARE IN THE BALLPARK TODAY TO WATCH THE YANKEES PLAY THE RED SOX.
THAT'S A LOT OF HOT DOGS!

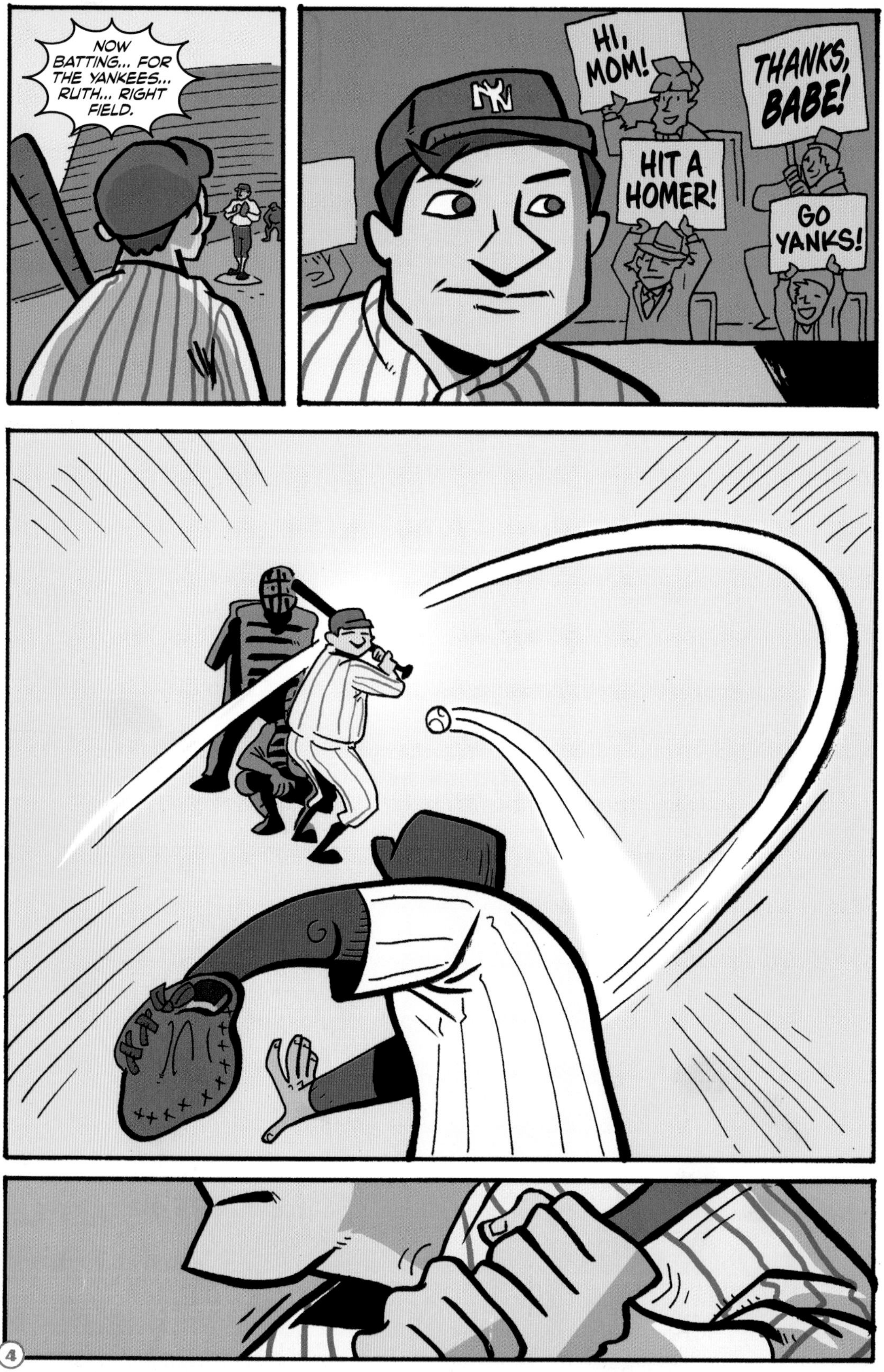
NOW BATTING... FOR THE YANKEES... RUTH... RIGHT FIELD.
HI, MOM!
THANKS, BABE!
HIT A HOMER!
GO YANKS!

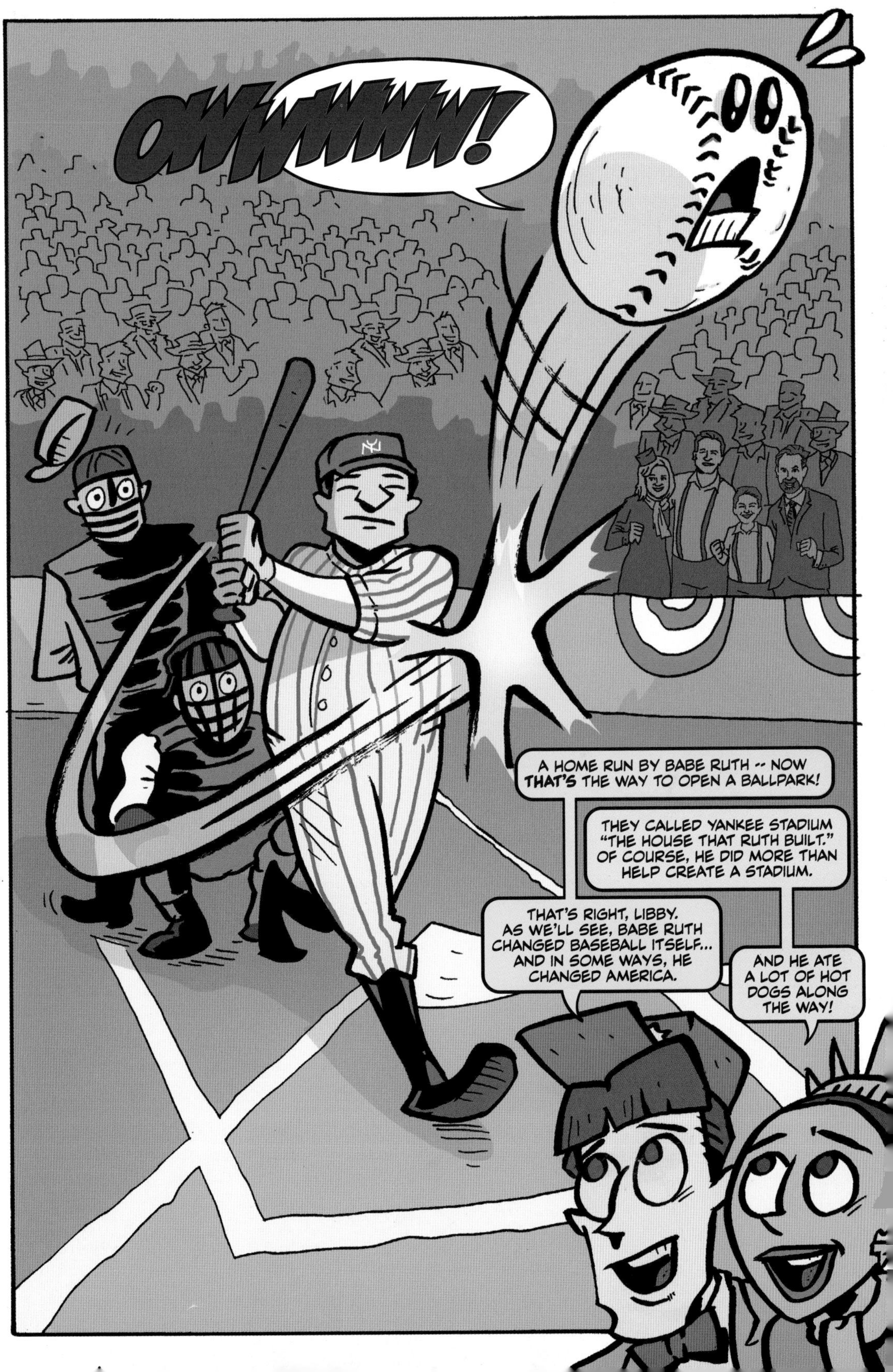
OWWWWW!
A HOME RUN BY BABE RUTH -- NOW THAT'S THE WAY TO OPEN A BALLPARK!
THEY CALLED YANKEE STADIUM "THE HOUSE THAT RUTH BUILT." OF COURSE, HE DID MORE THAN HELP CREATE A STADIUM.
THAT'S RIGHT, LIBBY. AS WE'LL SEE, BABE RUTH CHANGED BASEBALL ITSELF... AND IN SOME WAYS, HE CHANGED AMERICA.
AND HE ATE A LOT OF HOT DOGS ALONG THE WAY!

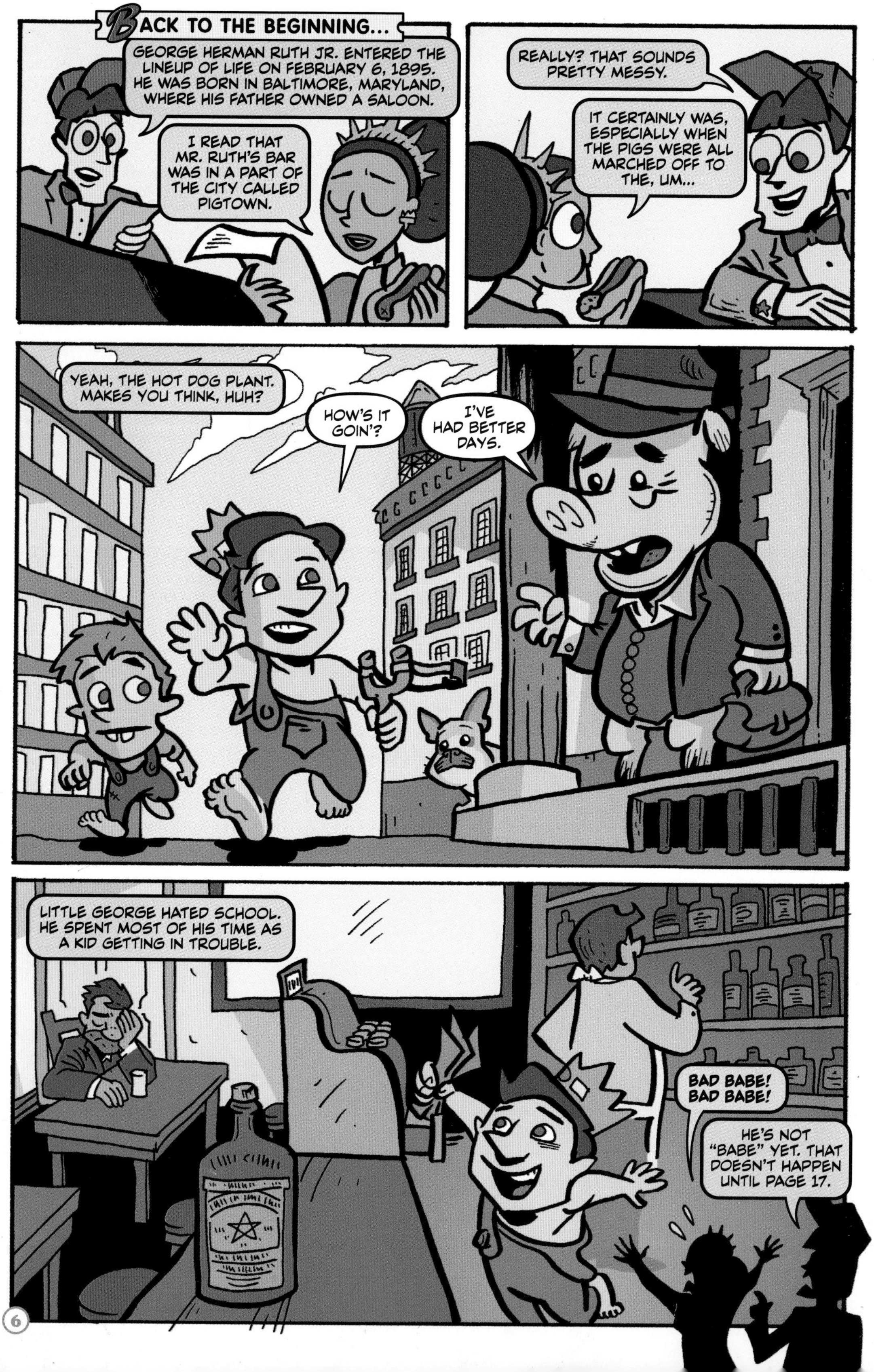
BACK TO THE BEGINNING...
GEORGE HERMAN RUTH JR. ENTERED THE LINEUP OF LIFE ON FEBRUARY 6, 1895. HE WAS BORN IN BALTIMORE, MARYLAND, WHERE HIS FATHER OWNED A SALOON.
I READ THAT MR. RUTH'S BAR WAS IN A PART OF THE CITY CALLED PIGTOWN.
REALLY? THAT SOUNDS PRETTY MESSY.
IT CERTAINLY WAS, ESPECIALLY WHEN THE PIGS WERE ALL MARCHED OFF TO THE, UM...
YEAH, THE HOT DOG PLANT. MAKES YOU THINK, HUH?
HOW'S IT GOIN'?
I'VE HAD BETTER DAYS.
LITTLE GEORGE HATED SCHOOL. HE SPENT MOST OF HIS TIME AS A KID GETTING IN TROUBLE.
BAD BABE! BAD BABE!
HE'S NOT "BABE" YET. THAT DOESN'T HAPPEN UNTIL PAGE 17.

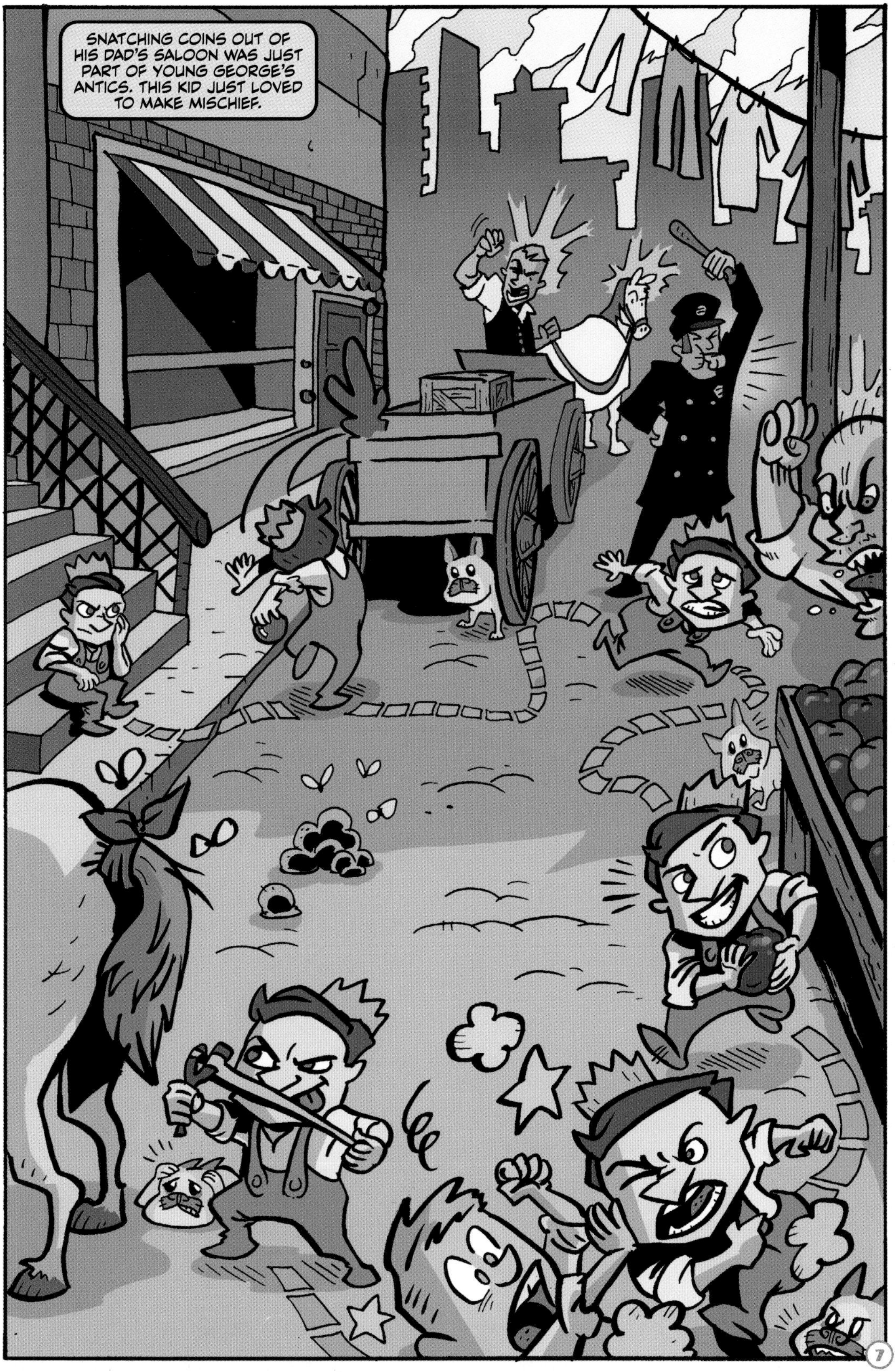
SNATCHING COINS OUT OF HIS DAD'S SALOON WAS JUST PART OF YOUNG GEORGE'S ANTICS. THIS KID JUST LOVED TO MAKE MISCHIEF.

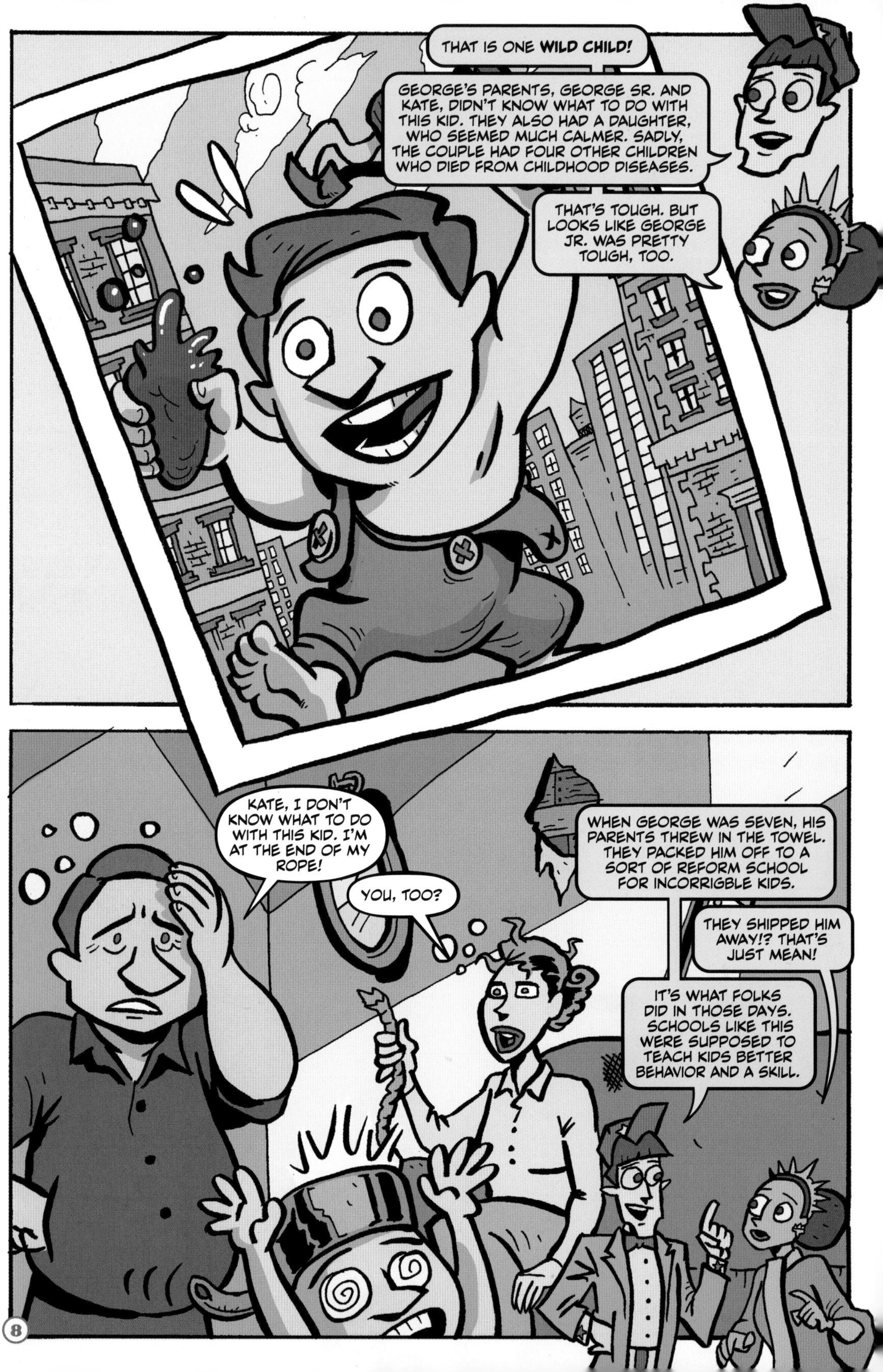
THAT IS ONE **WILD CHILD!**
GEORGE'S PARENTS, GEORGE SR. AND KATE, DIDN'T KNOW WHAT TO DO WITH THIS KID. THEY ALSO HAD A DAUGHTER, WHO SEEMED MUCH CALMER. SADLY, THE COUPLE HAD FOUR OTHER CHILDREN WHO DIED FROM CHILDHOOD DISEASES.
THAT'S TOUGH. BUT LOOKS LIKE GEORGE JR. WAS PRETTY TOUGH, TOO.
KATE, I DON'T KNOW WHAT TO DO WITH THIS KID. I'M AT THE END OF MY ROPE!
YOU, TOO?
WHEN GEORGE WAS SEVEN, HIS PARENTS THREW IN THE TOWEL. THEY PACKED HIM OFF TO A SORT OF REFORM SCHOOL FOR INCORRIGBLE KIDS.
THEY SHIPPED HIM AWAY!? THAT'S JUST MEAN!
IT'S WHAT FOLKS DID IN THOSE DAYS. SCHOOLS LIKE THIS WERE SUPPOSED TO TEACH KIDS BETTER BEHAVIOR AND A SKILL.

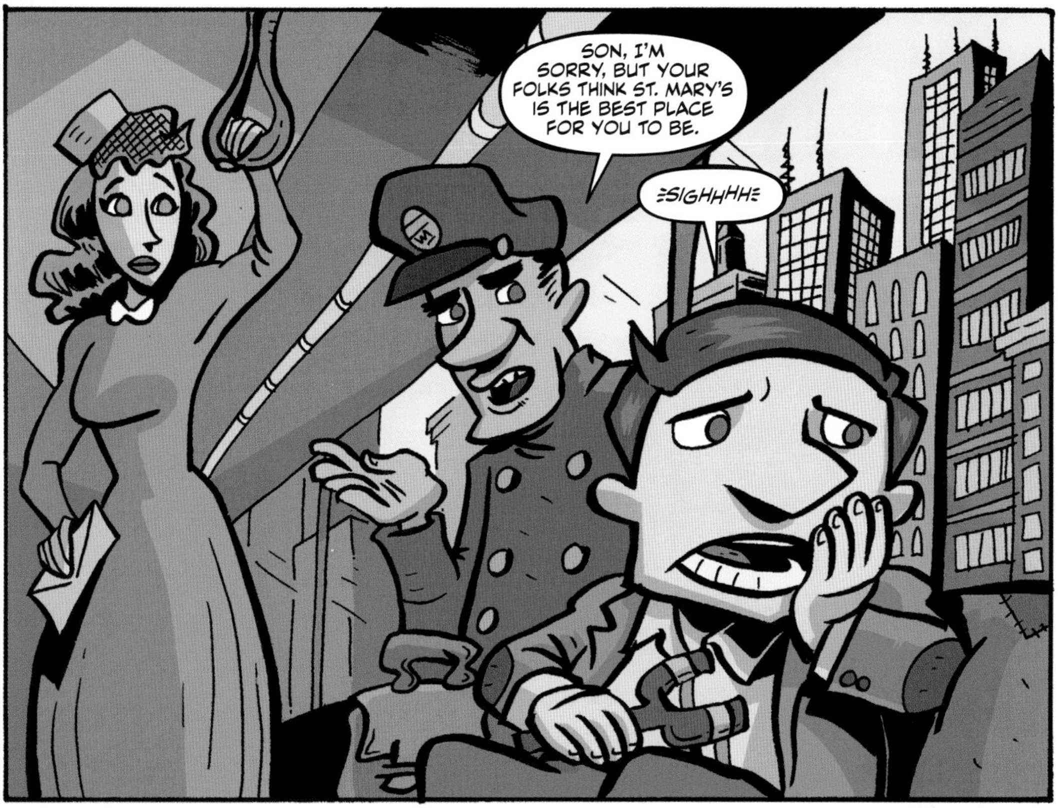
SON, I'M SORRY, BUT YOUR FOLKS THINK ST. MARY'S IS THE BEST PLACE FOR YOU TO BE.
SIGHHHH

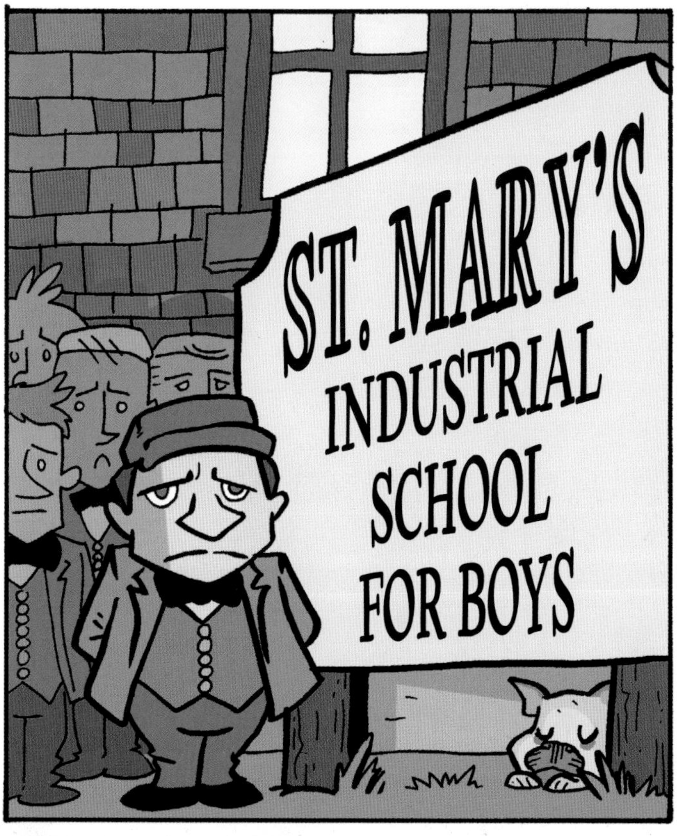
ST. MARY'S
INDUSTRIAL
SCHOOL
FOR BOYS

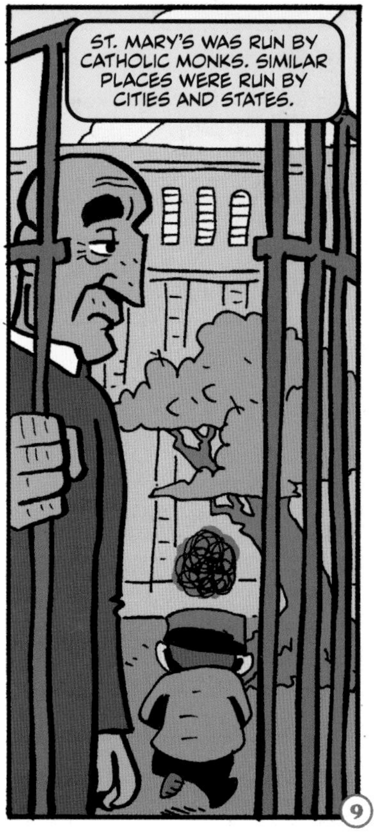
ST. MARY'S WAS RUN BY CATHOLIC MONKS. SIMILAR PLACES WERE RUN BY CITIES AND STATES.

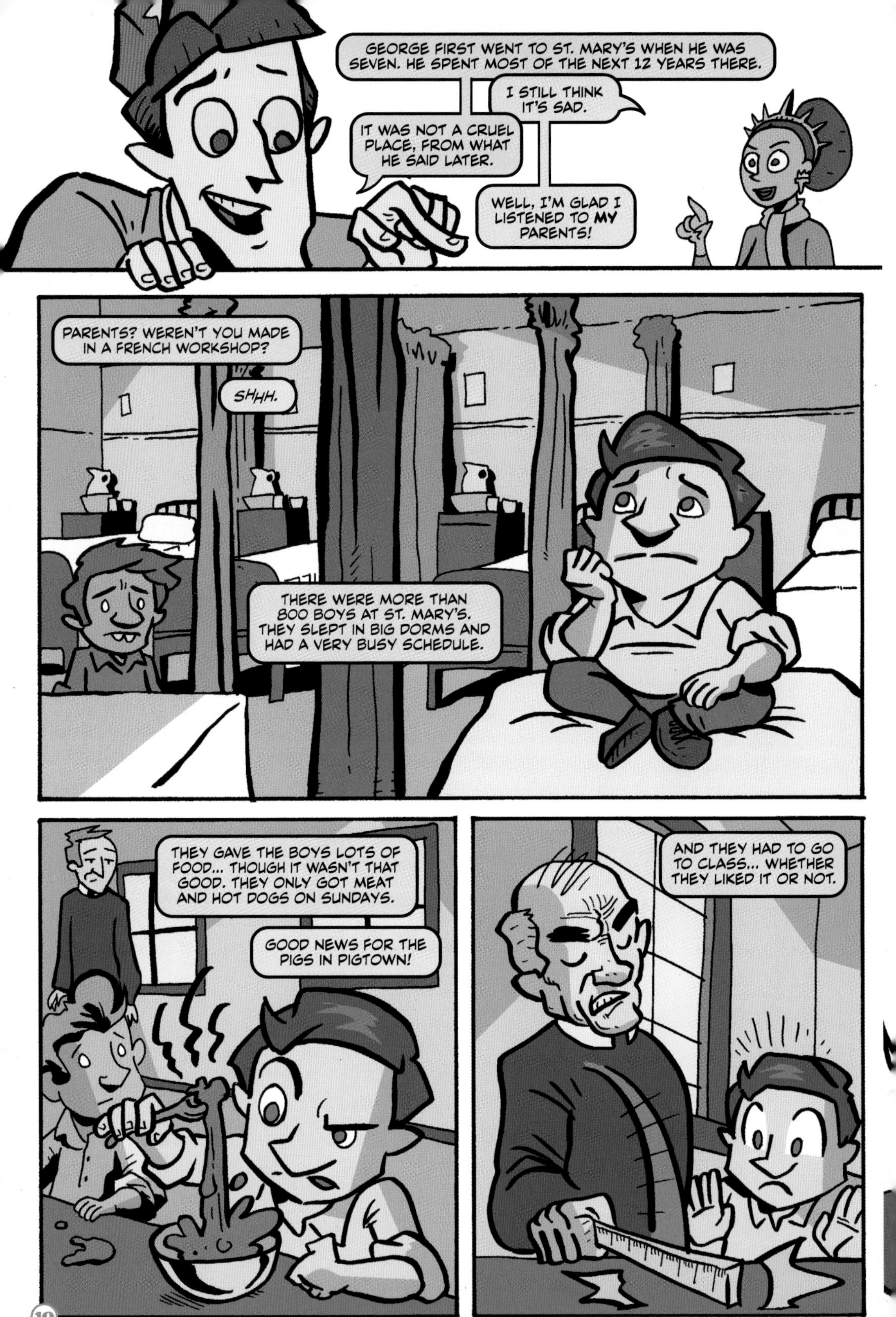
GEORGE FIRST WENT TO ST. MARY'S WHEN HE WAS SEVEN. HE SPENT MOST OF THE NEXT 12 YEARS THERE.
IT WAS NOT A CRUEL PLACE, FROM WHAT HE SAID LATER.
I STILL THINK IT'S SAD.
WELL, I'M GLAD I LISTENED TO **MY** PARENTS!
PARENTS? WEREN'T YOU MADE IN A FRENCH WORKSHOP?
SHHH.
THERE WERE MORE THAN 800 BOYS AT ST. MARY'S. THEY SLEPT IN BIG DORMS AND HAD A VERY BUSY SCHEDULE.
THEY GAVE THE BOYS LOTS OF FOOD... THOUGH IT WASN'T THAT GOOD. THEY ONLY GOT MEAT AND HOT DOGS ON SUNDAYS.
GOOD NEWS FOR THE PIGS IN PIGTOWN!
AND THEY HAD TO GO TO CLASS... WHETHER THEY LIKED IT OR NOT.

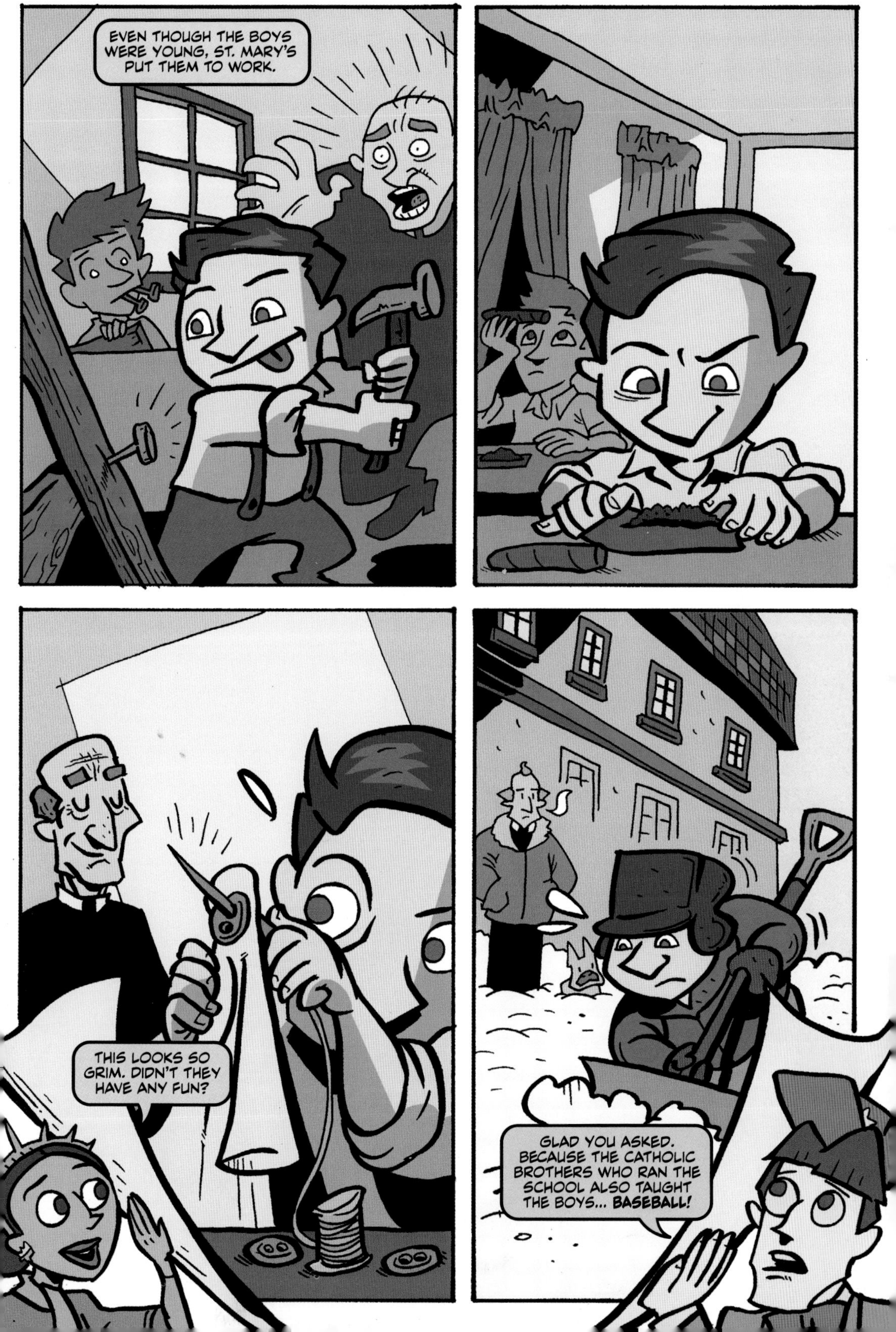
EVEN THOUGH THE BOYS WERE YOUNG, ST. MARY'S PUT THEM TO WORK.
THIS LOOKS SO GRIM. DIDN'T THEY HAVE ANY FUN?
GLAD YOU ASKED. BECAUSE THE CATHOLIC BROTHERS WHO RAN THE SCHOOL ALSO TAUGHT THE BOYS... **BASEBALL!**

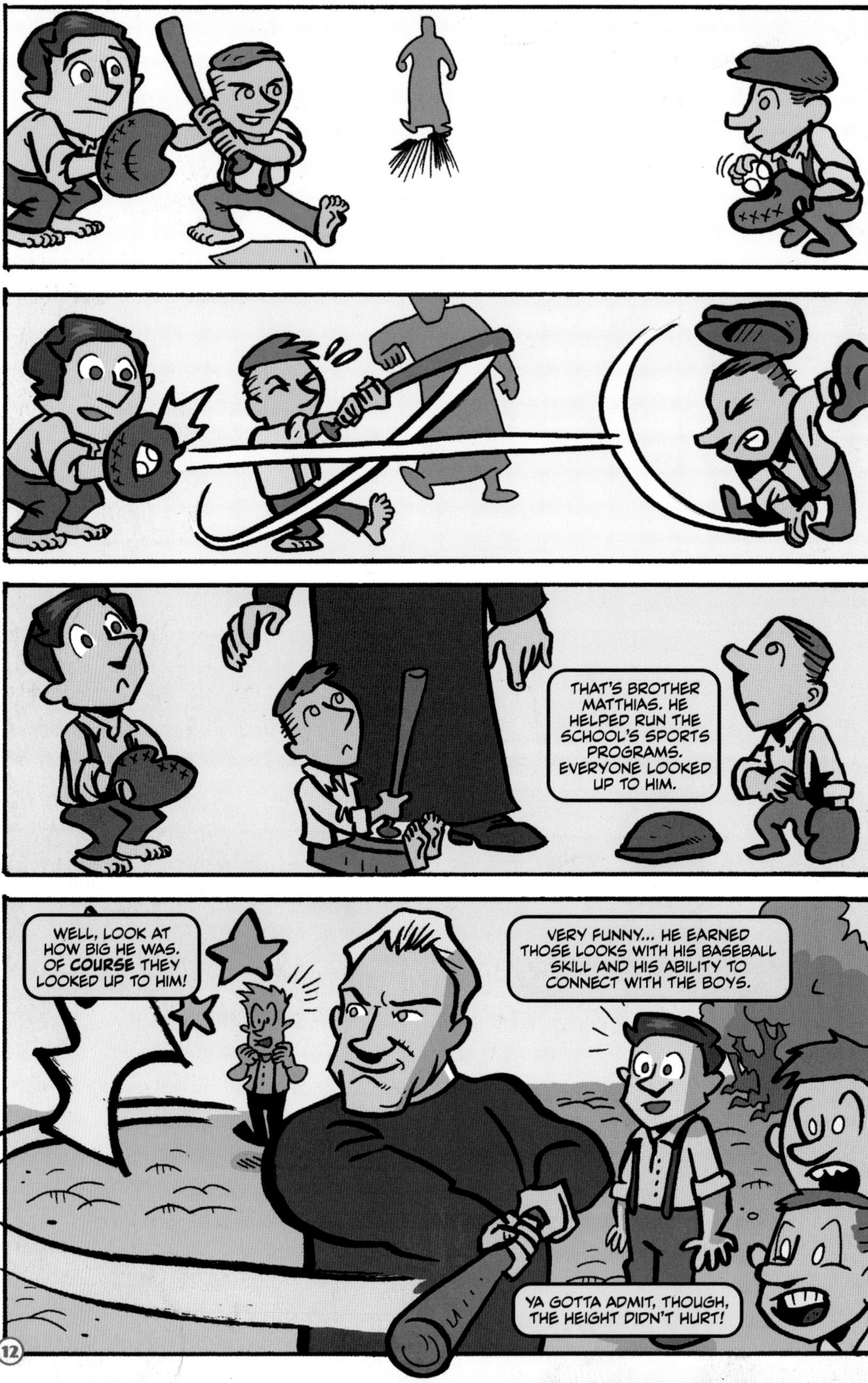
THAT'S BROTHER MATTHIAS. HE HELPED RUN THE SCHOOL'S SPORTS PROGRAMS. EVERYONE LOOKED UP TO HIM.
WELL, LOOK AT HOW BIG HE WAS. OF **COURSE** THEY LOOKED UP TO HIM!
VERY FUNNY... HE EARNED THOSE LOOKS WITH HIS BASEBALL SKILL AND HIS ABILITY TO CONNECT WITH THE BOYS.
YA GOTTA ADMIT, THOUGH, THE HEIGHT DIDN'T HURT!

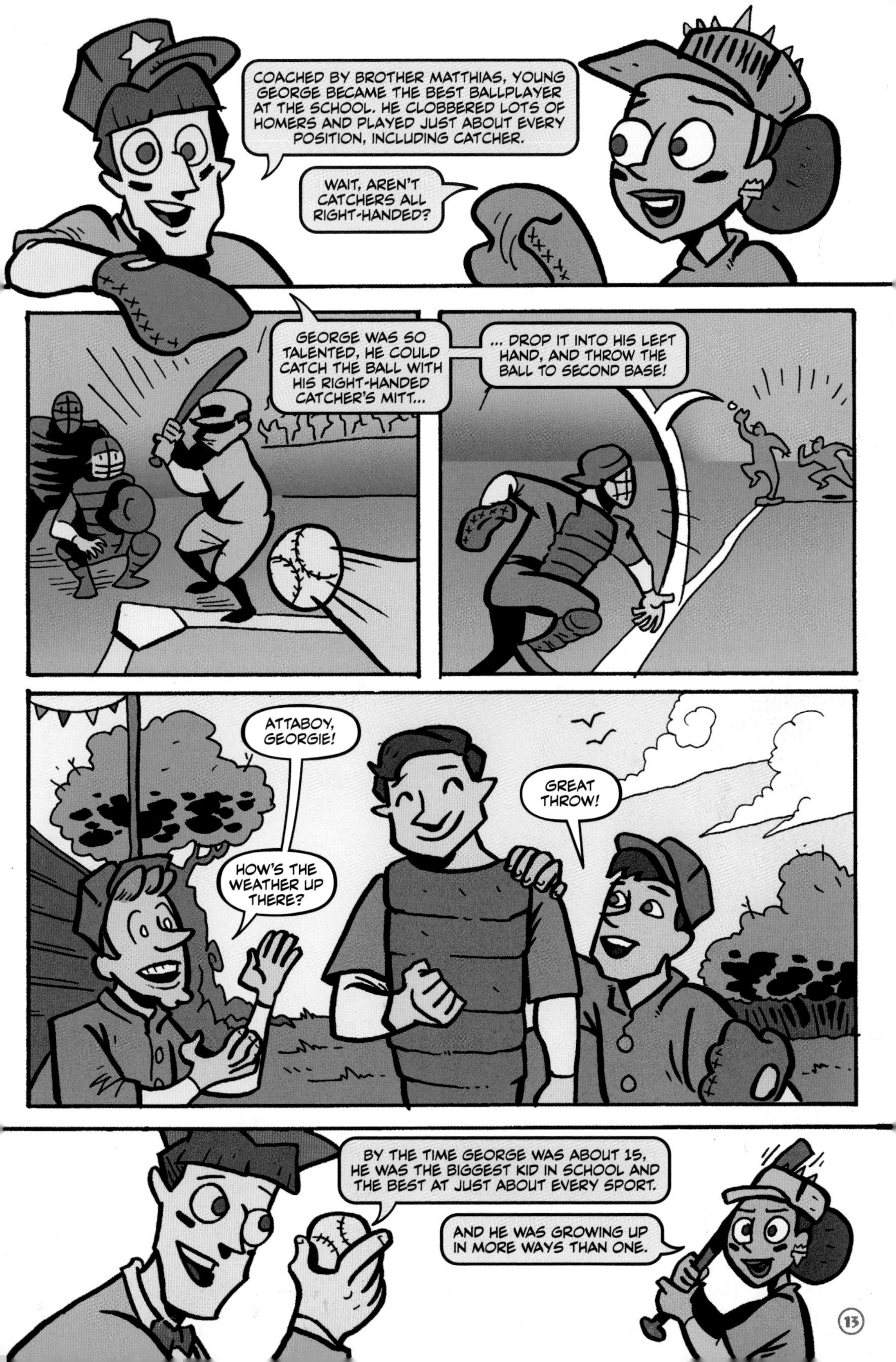
COACHED BY BROTHER MATTHIAS, YOUNG GEORGE BECAME THE BEST BALLPLAYER AT THE SCHOOL. HE CLOBBERED LOTS OF HOMERS AND PLAYED JUST ABOUT EVERY POSITION, INCLUDING CATCHER.
WAIT, AREN'T CATCHERS ALL RIGHT-HANDED?
GEORGE WAS SO TALENTED, HE COULD CATCH THE BALL WITH HIS RIGHT-HANDED CATCHER'S MITT...
... DROP IT INTO HIS LEFT HAND, AND THROW THE BALL TO SECOND BASE!
ATTABOY, GEORGIE!
HOW'S THE WEATHER UP THERE?
GREAT THROW!
BY THE TIME GEORGE WAS ABOUT 15, HE WAS THE BIGGEST KID IN SCHOOL AND THE BEST AT JUST ABOUT EVERY SPORT.
AND HE WAS GROWING UP IN MORE WAYS THAN ONE.

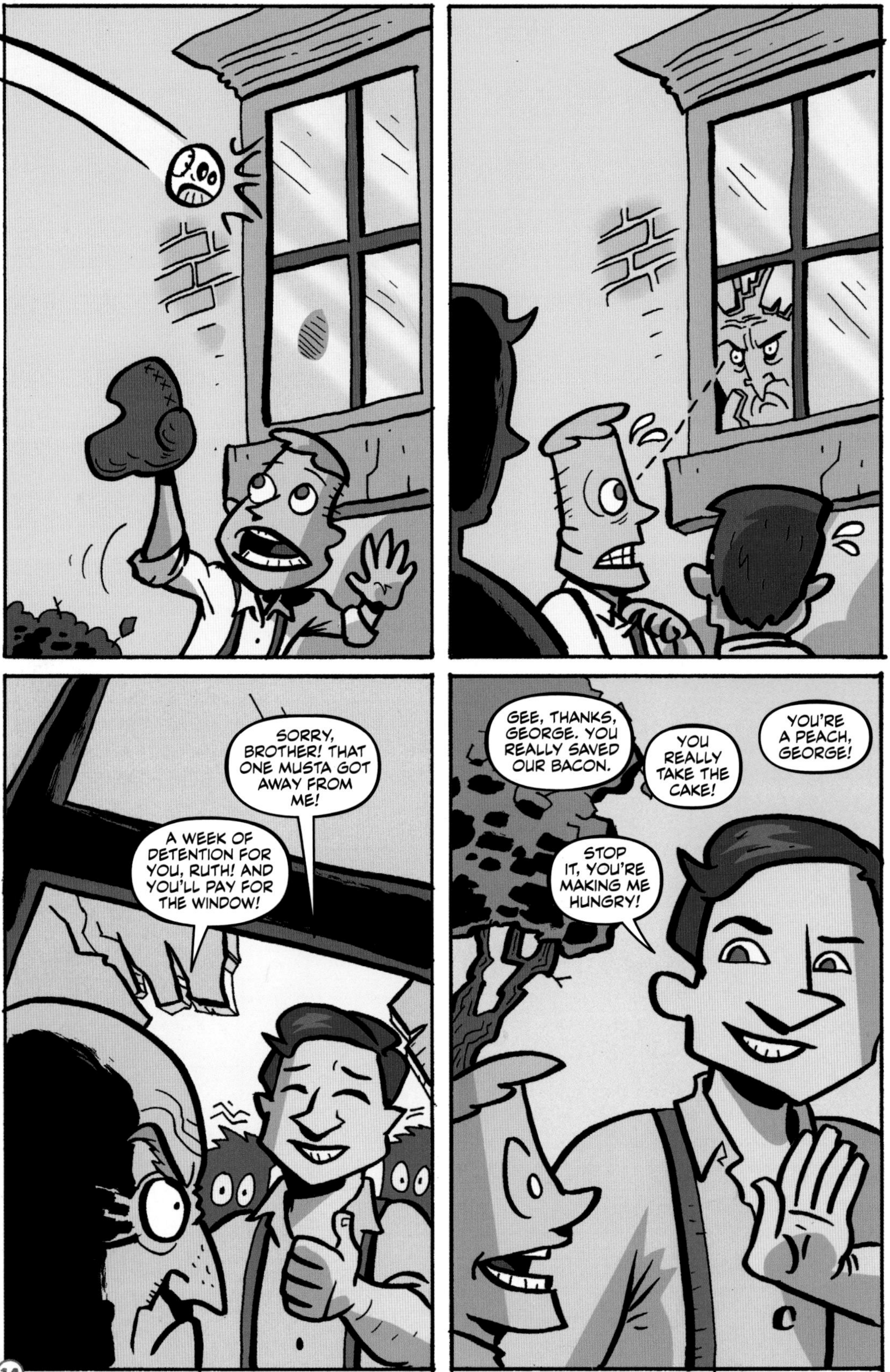
SORRY, BROTHER! THAT ONE MUSTA GOT AWAY FROM ME!
A WEEK OF DETENTION FOR YOU, RUTH! AND YOU'LL PAY FOR THE WINDOW!
GEE, THANKS, GEORGE. YOU REALLY SAVED OUR BACON.
YOU REALLY TAKE THE CAKE!
YOU'RE A PEACH, GEORGE!
STOP IT, YOU'RE MAKING ME HUNGRY!

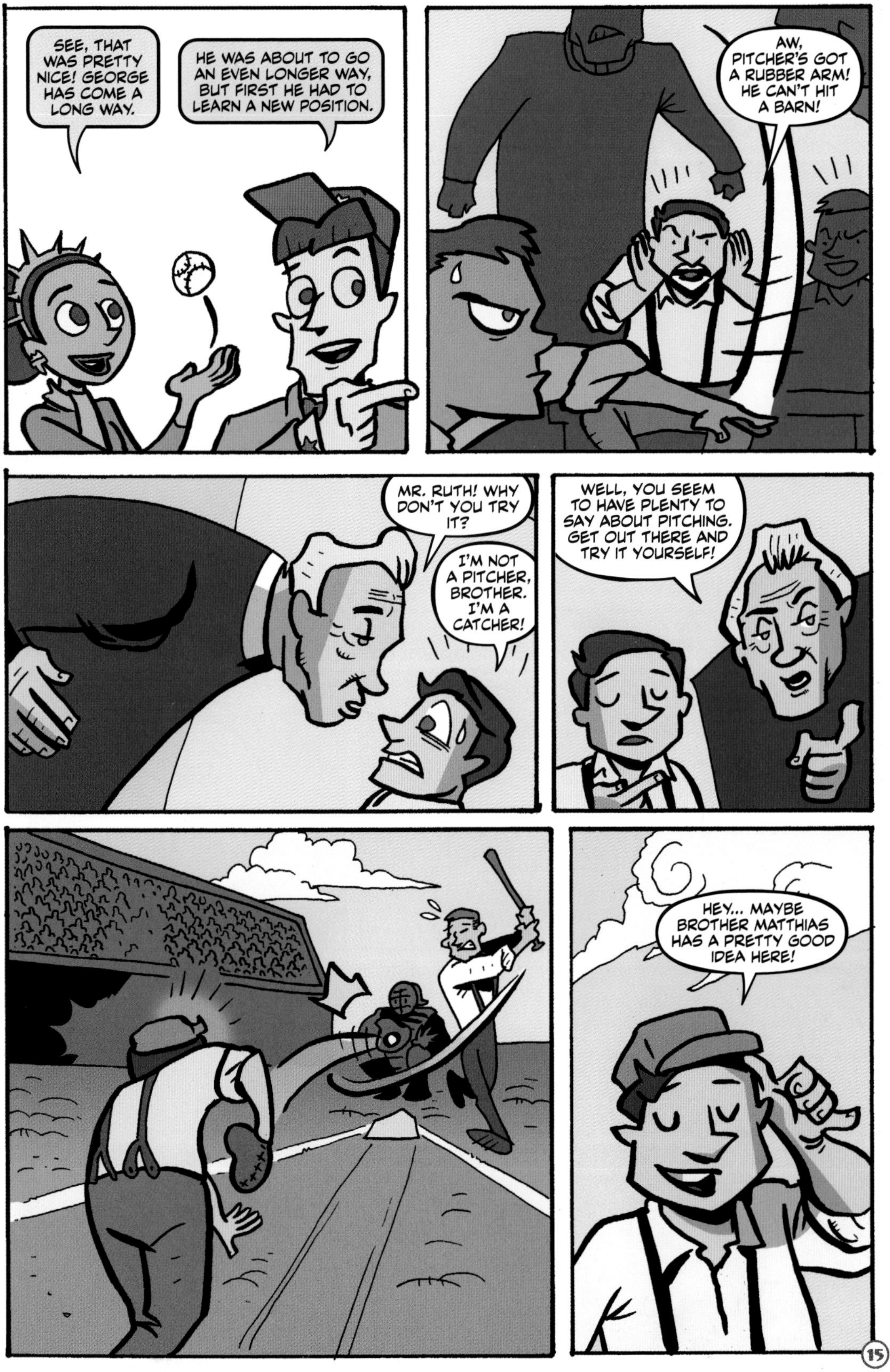

SEE, THAT WAS PRETTY NICE! GEORGE HAS COME A LONG WAY.
HE WAS ABOUT TO GO AN EVEN LONGER WAY, BUT FIRST HE HAD TO LEARN A NEW POSITION.
AW, PITCHER'S GOT A RUBBER ARM! HE CAN'T HIT A BARN!
MR. RUTH! WHY DON'T YOU TRY IT?
I'M NOT A PITCHER, BROTHER. I'M A CATCHER!
WELL, YOU SEEM TO HAVE PLENTY TO SAY ABOUT PITCHING. GET OUT THERE AND TRY IT YOURSELF!
HEY... MAYBE BROTHER MATTHIAS HAS A PRETTY GOOD IDEA HERE!

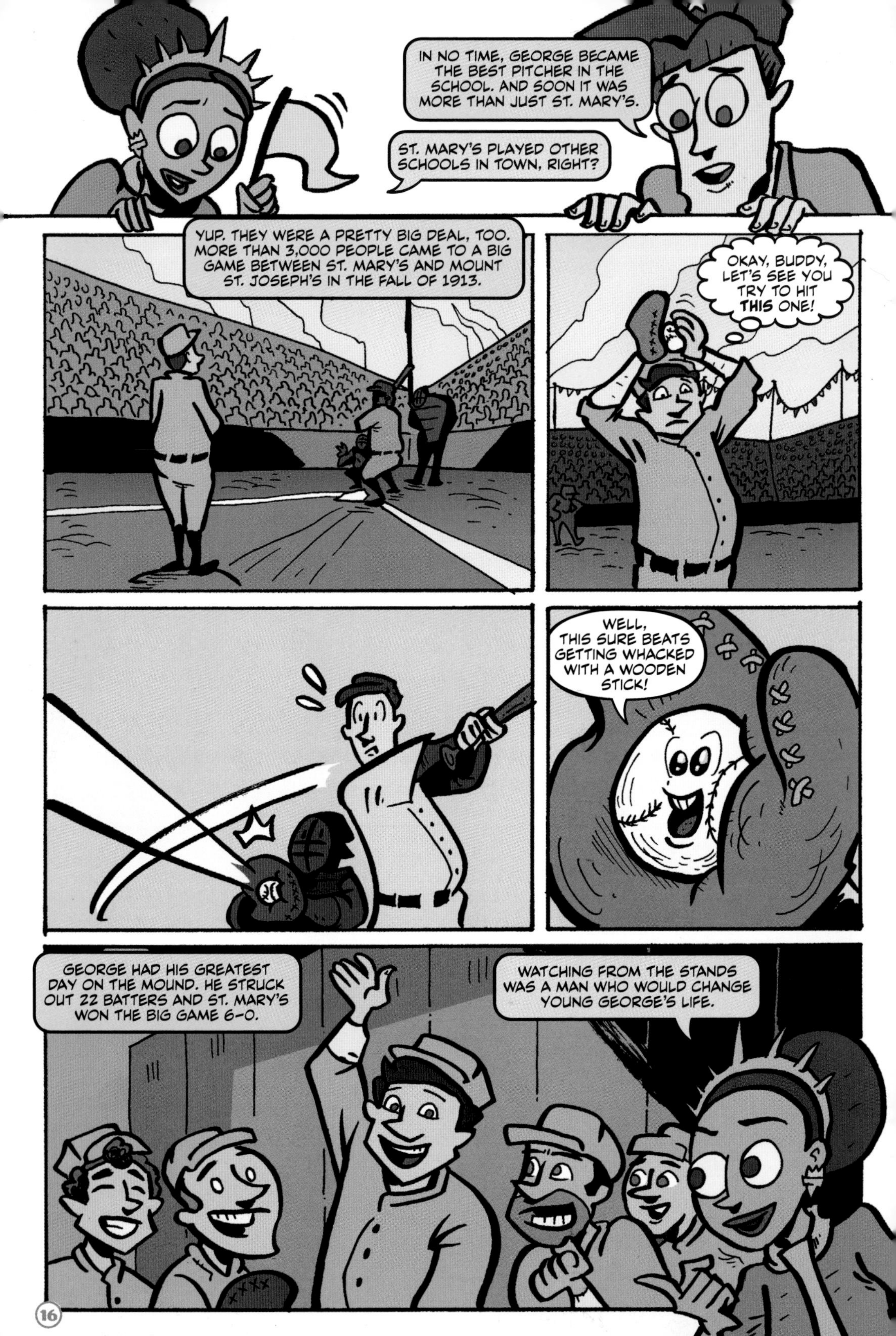
IN NO TIME, GEORGE BECAME THE BEST PITCHER IN THE SCHOOL. AND SOON IT WAS MORE THAN JUST ST. MARY'S.
ST. MARY'S PLAYED OTHER SCHOOLS IN TOWN, RIGHT?
YUP. THEY WERE A PRETTY BIG DEAL, TOO. MORE THAN 3,000 PEOPLE CAME TO A BIG GAME BETWEEN ST. MARY'S AND MOUNT ST. JOSEPH'S IN THE FALL OF 1913.
OKAY, BUDDY, LET'S SEE YOU TRY TO HIT **THIS** ONE!
WELL, THIS SURE BEATS GETTING WHACKED WITH A WOODEN STICK!
GEORGE HAD HIS GREATEST DAY ON THE MOUND. HE STRUCK OUT 22 BATTERS AND ST. MARY'S WON THE BIG GAME 6–0.
WATCHING FROM THE STANDS WAS A MAN WHO WOULD CHANGE YOUNG GEORGE'S LIFE.

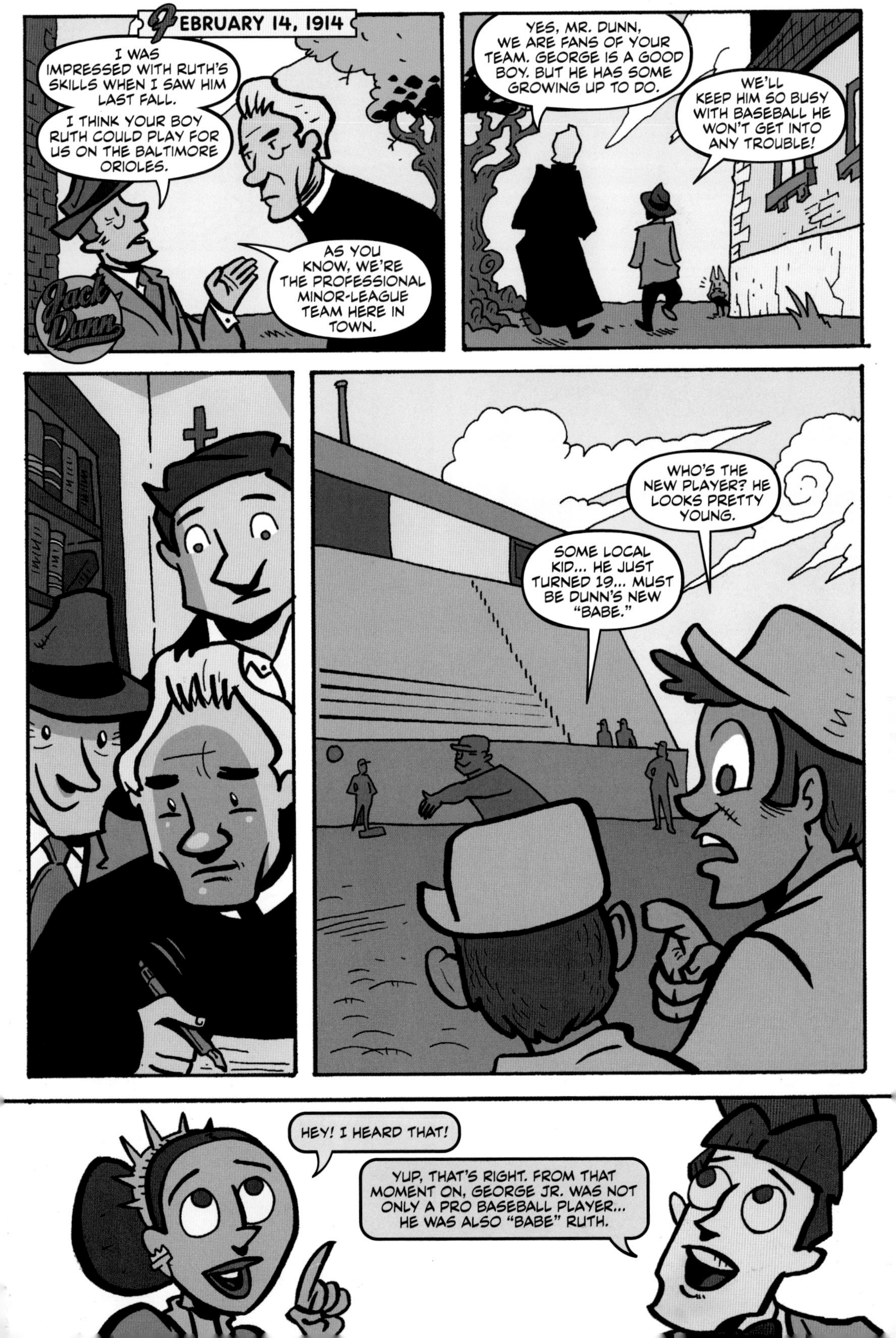
FEBRUARY 14, 1914
I WAS IMPRESSED WITH RUTH'S SKILLS WHEN I SAW HIM LAST FALL.
I THINK YOUR BOY RUTH COULD PLAY FOR US ON THE BALTIMORE ORIOLES.
Jack Dunn
AS YOU KNOW, WE'RE THE PROFESSIONAL MINOR-LEAGUE TEAM HERE IN TOWN.
YES, MR. DUNN, WE ARE FANS OF YOUR TEAM. GEORGE IS A GOOD BOY. BUT HE HAS SOME GROWING UP TO DO.
WE'LL KEEP HIM SO BUSY WITH BASEBALL HE WON'T GET INTO ANY TROUBLE!
WHO'S THE NEW PLAYER? HE LOOKS PRETTY YOUNG.
SOME LOCAL KID... HE JUST TURNED 19... MUST BE DUNN'S NEW "BABE."
HEY! I HEARD THAT!
YUP, THAT'S RIGHT. FROM THAT MOMENT ON, GEORGE JR. WAS NOT ONLY A PRO BASEBALL PLAYER... HE WAS ALSO "BABE" RUTH.

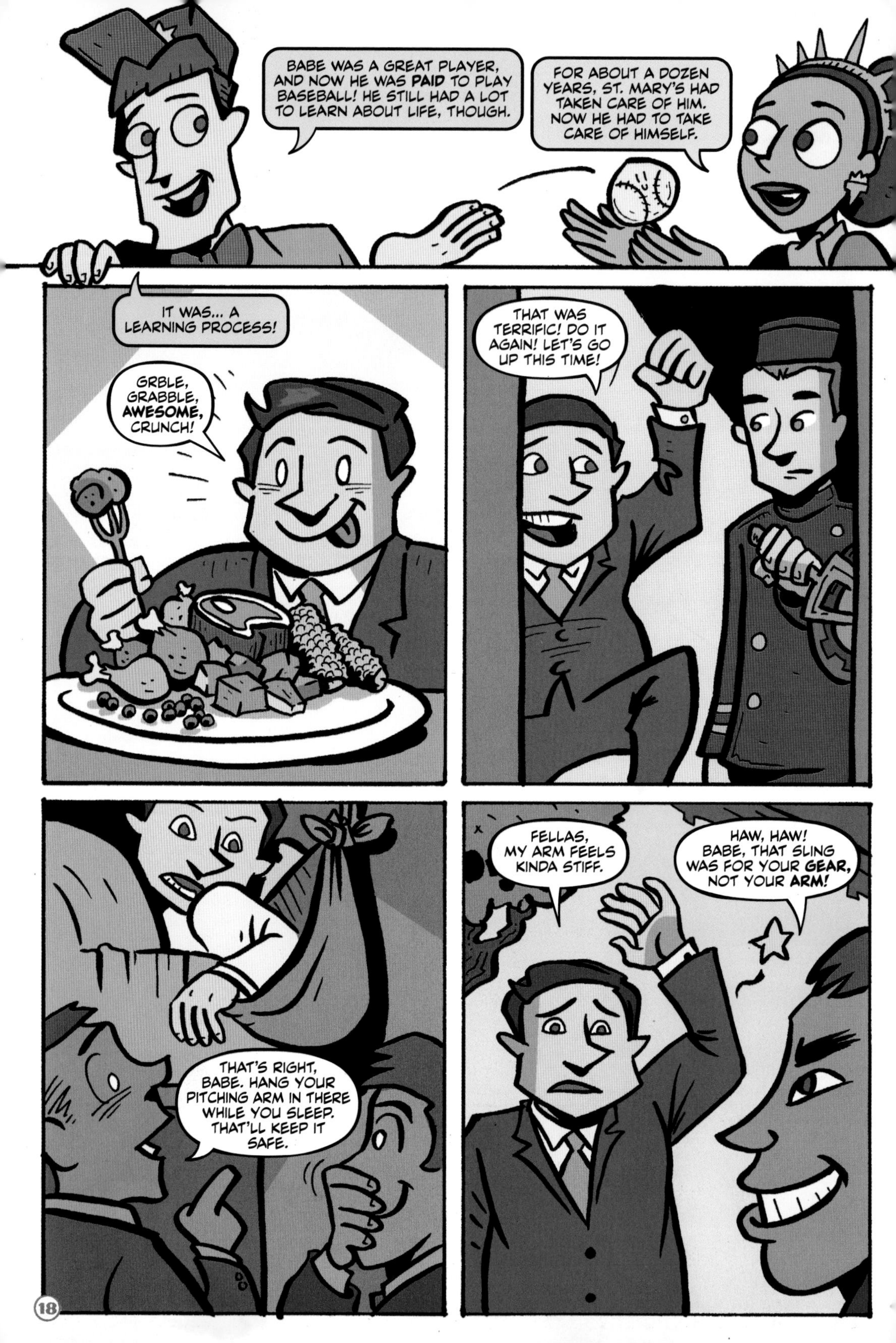
BABE WAS A GREAT PLAYER, AND NOW HE WAS **PAID** TO PLAY BASEBALL! HE STILL HAD A LOT TO LEARN ABOUT LIFE, THOUGH.
FOR ABOUT A DOZEN YEARS, ST. MARY'S HAD TAKEN CARE OF HIM. NOW HE HAD TO TAKE CARE OF HIMSELF.
IT WAS... A LEARNING PROCESS!
GRBLE, GRABBLE, **AWESOME,** CRUNCH!
THAT WAS TERRIFIC! DO IT AGAIN! LET'S GO UP THIS TIME!
THAT'S RIGHT, BABE. HANG YOUR PITCHING ARM IN THERE WHILE YOU SLEEP. THAT'LL KEEP IT SAFE.
FELLAS, MY ARM FEELS KINDA STIFF.
HAW, HAW! BABE, THAT SLING WAS FOR YOUR **GEAR,** NOT YOUR **ARM!**

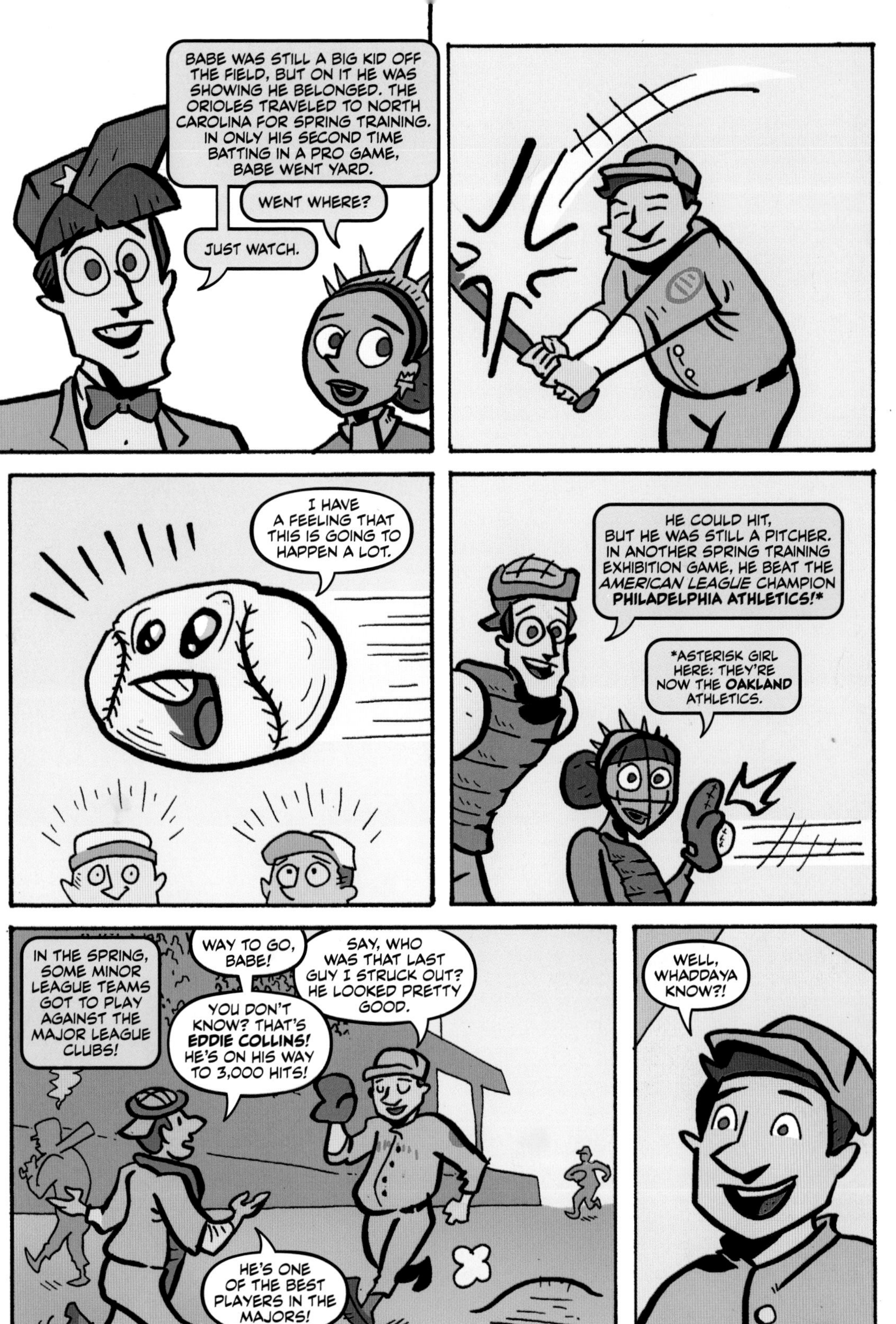

BABE WAS STILL A BIG KID OFF THE FIELD, BUT ON IT HE WAS SHOWING HE BELONGED. THE ORIOLES TRAVELED TO NORTH CAROLINA FOR SPRING TRAINING. IN ONLY HIS SECOND TIME BATTING IN A PRO GAME, BABE WENT YARD.
WENT WHERE?
JUST WATCH.
I HAVE A FEELING THAT THIS IS GOING TO HAPPEN A LOT.
HE COULD HIT, BUT HE WAS STILL A PITCHER. IN ANOTHER SPRING TRAINING EXHIBITION GAME, HE BEAT THE *AMERICAN LEAGUE* CHAMPION **PHILADELPHIA ATHLETICS!***
*ASTERISK GIRL HERE: THEY'RE NOW THE **OAKLAND** ATHLETICS.
IN THE SPRING, SOME MINOR LEAGUE TEAMS GOT TO PLAY AGAINST THE MAJOR LEAGUE CLUBS!
WAY TO GO, BABE!
SAY, WHO WAS THAT LAST GUY I STRUCK OUT? HE LOOKED PRETTY GOOD.
YOU DON'T KNOW? THAT'S **EDDIE COLLINS!** HE'S ON HIS WAY TO 3,000 HITS!
HE'S ONE OF THE BEST PLAYERS IN THE MAJORS!
WELL, WHADDAYA KNOW?!

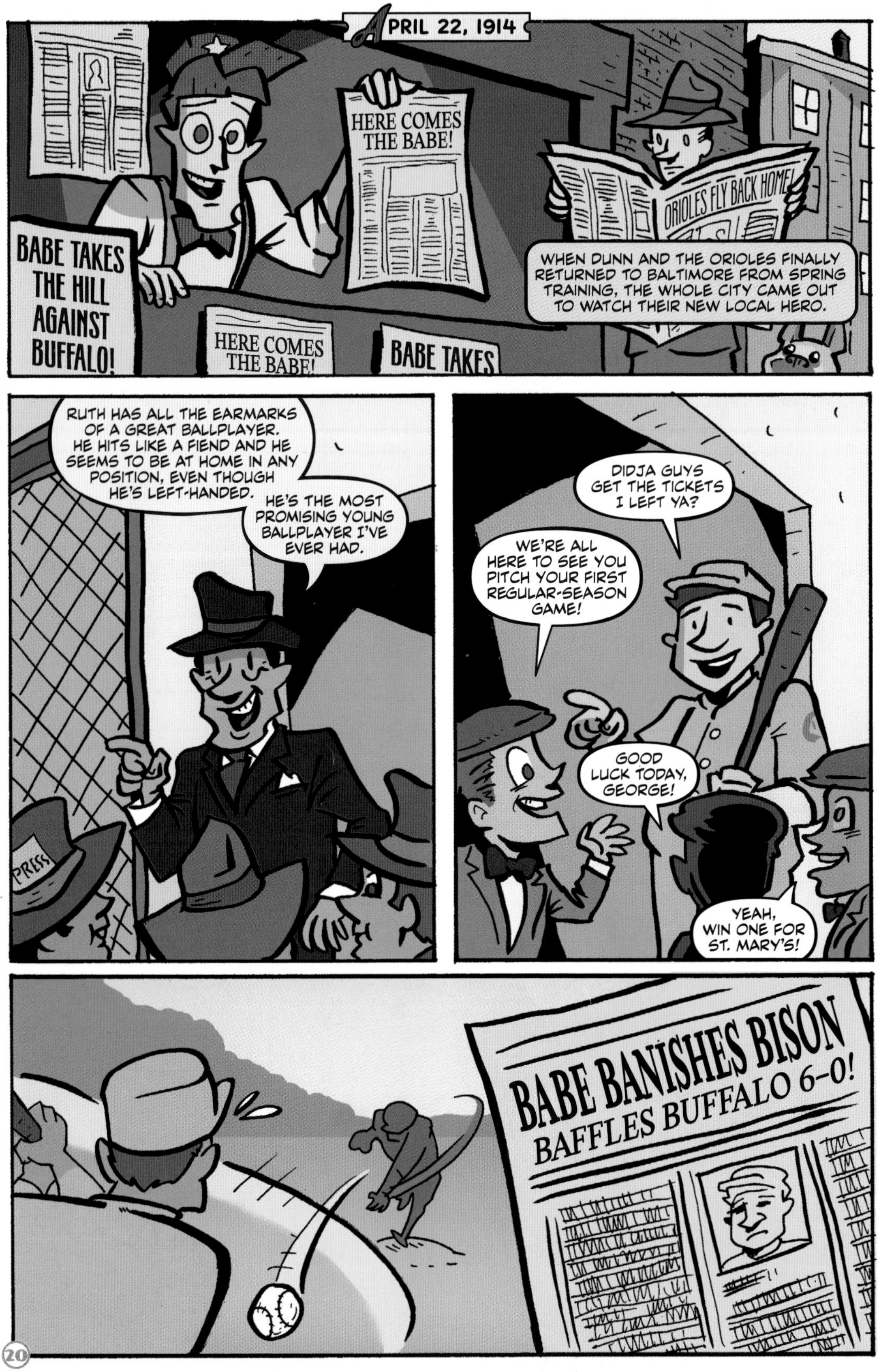
APRIL 22, 1914
HERE COMES THE BABE!
ORIOLES FLY BACK HOME!
BABE TAKES THE HILL AGAINST BUFFALO!
HERE COMES THE BABE!
BABE TAKES
WHEN DUNN AND THE ORIOLES FINALLY RETURNED TO BALTIMORE FROM SPRING TRAINING, THE WHOLE CITY CAME OUT TO WATCH THEIR NEW LOCAL HERO.
RUTH HAS ALL THE EARMARKS OF A GREAT BALLPLAYER. HE HITS LIKE A FIEND AND HE SEEMS TO BE AT HOME IN ANY POSITION, EVEN THOUGH HE'S LEFT-HANDED.
HE'S THE MOST PROMISING YOUNG BALLPLAYER I'VE EVER HAD.
PRESS
DIDJA GUYS GET THE TICKETS I LEFT YA?
WE'RE ALL HERE TO SEE YOU PITCH YOUR FIRST REGULAR-SEASON GAME!
GOOD LUCK TODAY, GEORGE!
YEAH, WIN ONE FOR ST. MARY'S!
BABE BANISHES BISON
BAFFLES BUFFALO 6-0!

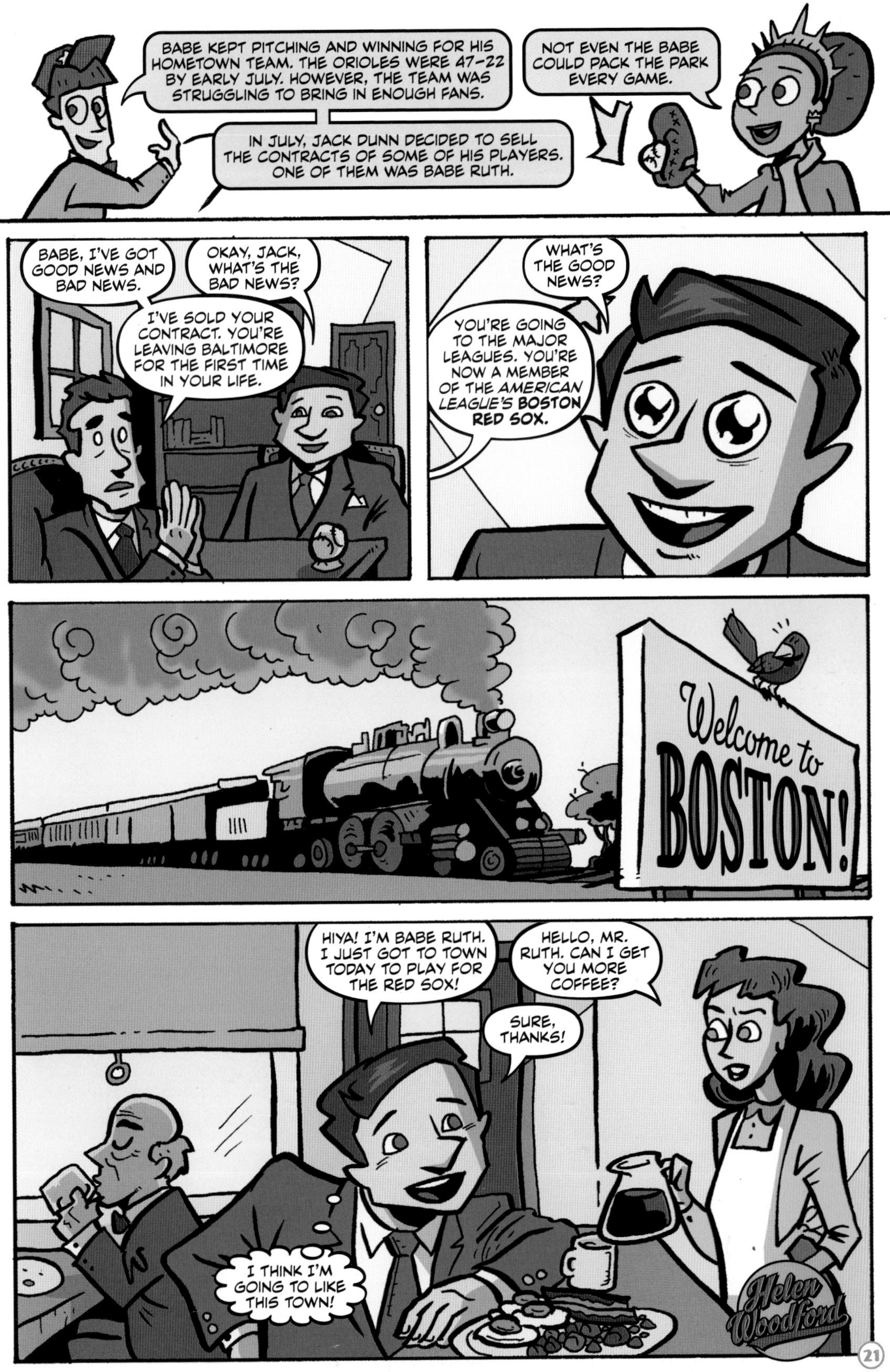
BABE KEPT PITCHING AND WINNING FOR HIS HOMETOWN TEAM. THE ORIOLES WERE 47–22 BY EARLY JULY. HOWEVER, THE TEAM WAS STRUGGLING TO BRING IN ENOUGH FANS.
NOT EVEN THE BABE COULD PACK THE PARK EVERY GAME.
IN JULY, JACK DUNN DECIDED TO SELL THE CONTRACTS OF SOME OF HIS PLAYERS. ONE OF THEM WAS BABE RUTH.
BABE, I'VE GOT GOOD NEWS AND BAD NEWS.
OKAY, JACK, WHAT'S THE BAD NEWS?
I'VE SOLD YOUR CONTRACT. YOU'RE LEAVING BALTIMORE FOR THE FIRST TIME IN YOUR LIFE.
WHAT'S THE GOOD NEWS?
YOU'RE GOING TO THE MAJOR LEAGUES. YOU'RE NOW A MEMBER OF THE *AMERICAN LEAGUE'S* **BOSTON RED SOX.**
Welcome to BOSTON!
HIYA! I'M BABE RUTH. I JUST GOT TO TOWN TODAY TO PLAY FOR THE RED SOX!
HELLO, MR. RUTH. CAN I GET YOU MORE COFFEE?
SURE, THANKS!
I THINK I'M GOING TO LIKE THIS TOWN!
Helen Woodford

BABE WAS THE STARTING PITCHER ON HIS FIRST DAY IN A BOSTON UNIFORM.

HE PROBABLY DIDN'T EVEN HAVE TIME TO UNPACK!

"Shoeless" Joe Jackson

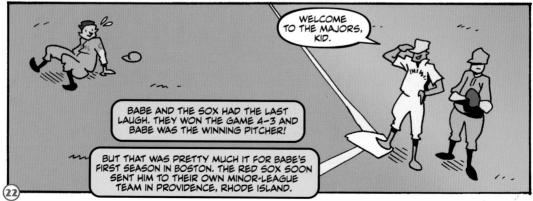

WELCOME TO THE MAJORS, KID.

BABE AND THE SOX HAD THE LAST LAUGH. THEY WON THE GAME 4-3 AND BABE WAS THE WINNING PITCHER!

BUT THAT WAS PRETTY MUCH IT FOR BABE'S FIRST SEASON IN BOSTON. THE RED SOX SOON SENT HIM TO THEIR OWN MINOR-LEAGUE TEAM IN PROVIDENCE, RHODE ISLAND.

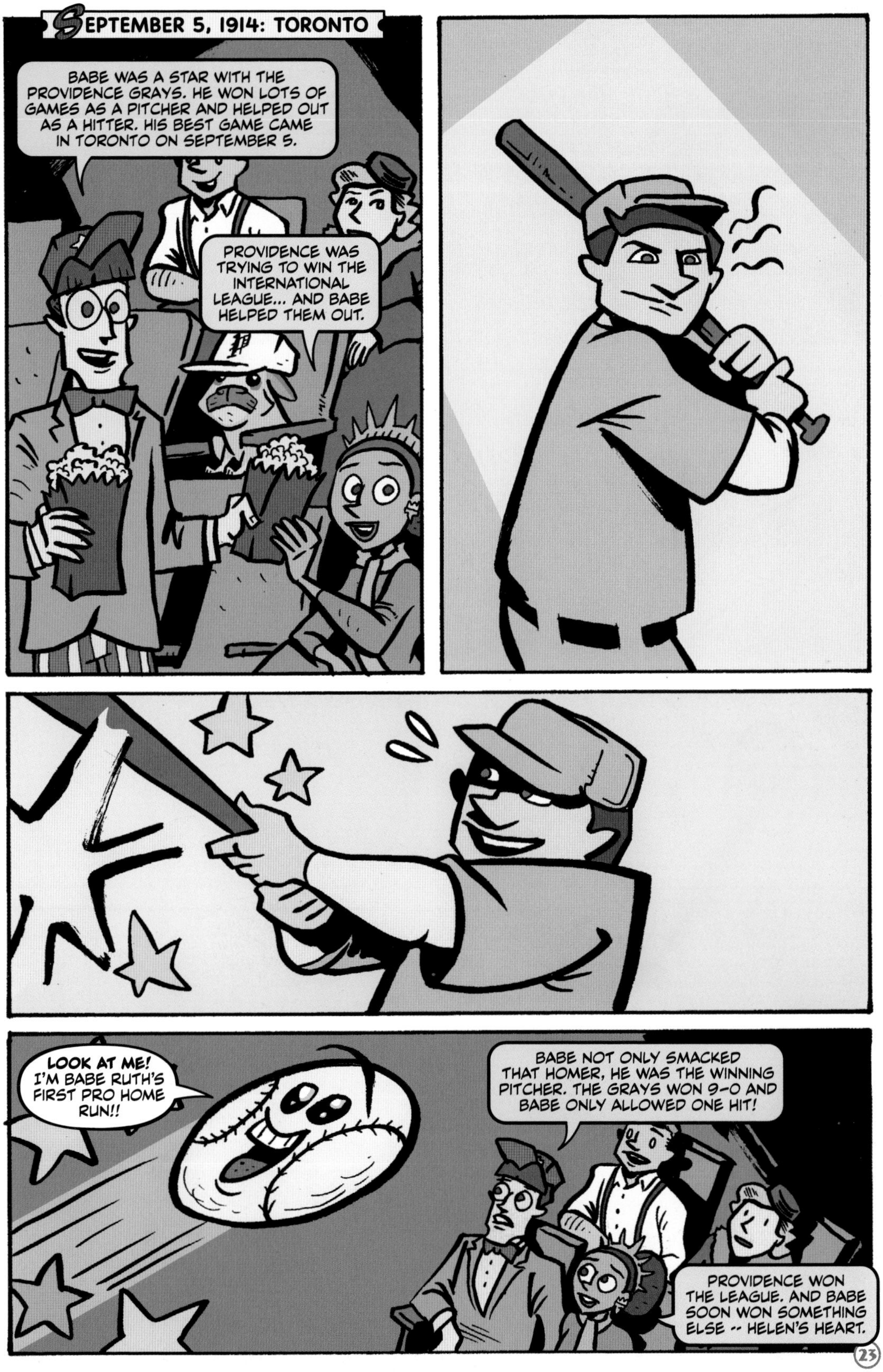
SEPTEMBER 5, 1914: TORONTO
BABE WAS A STAR WITH THE PROVIDENCE GRAYS. HE WON LOTS OF GAMES AS A PITCHER AND HELPED OUT AS A HITTER. HIS BEST GAME CAME IN TORONTO ON SEPTEMBER 5.
PROVIDENCE WAS TRYING TO WIN THE INTERNATIONAL LEAGUE... AND BABE HELPED THEM OUT.
LOOK AT ME! I'M BABE RUTH'S FIRST PRO HOME RUN!!
BABE NOT ONLY SMACKED THAT HOMER, HE WAS THE WINNING PITCHER. THE GRAYS WON 9-0 AND BABE ONLY ALLOWED ONE HIT!
PROVIDENCE WON THE LEAGUE. AND BABE SOON WON SOMETHING ELSE -- HELEN'S HEART.

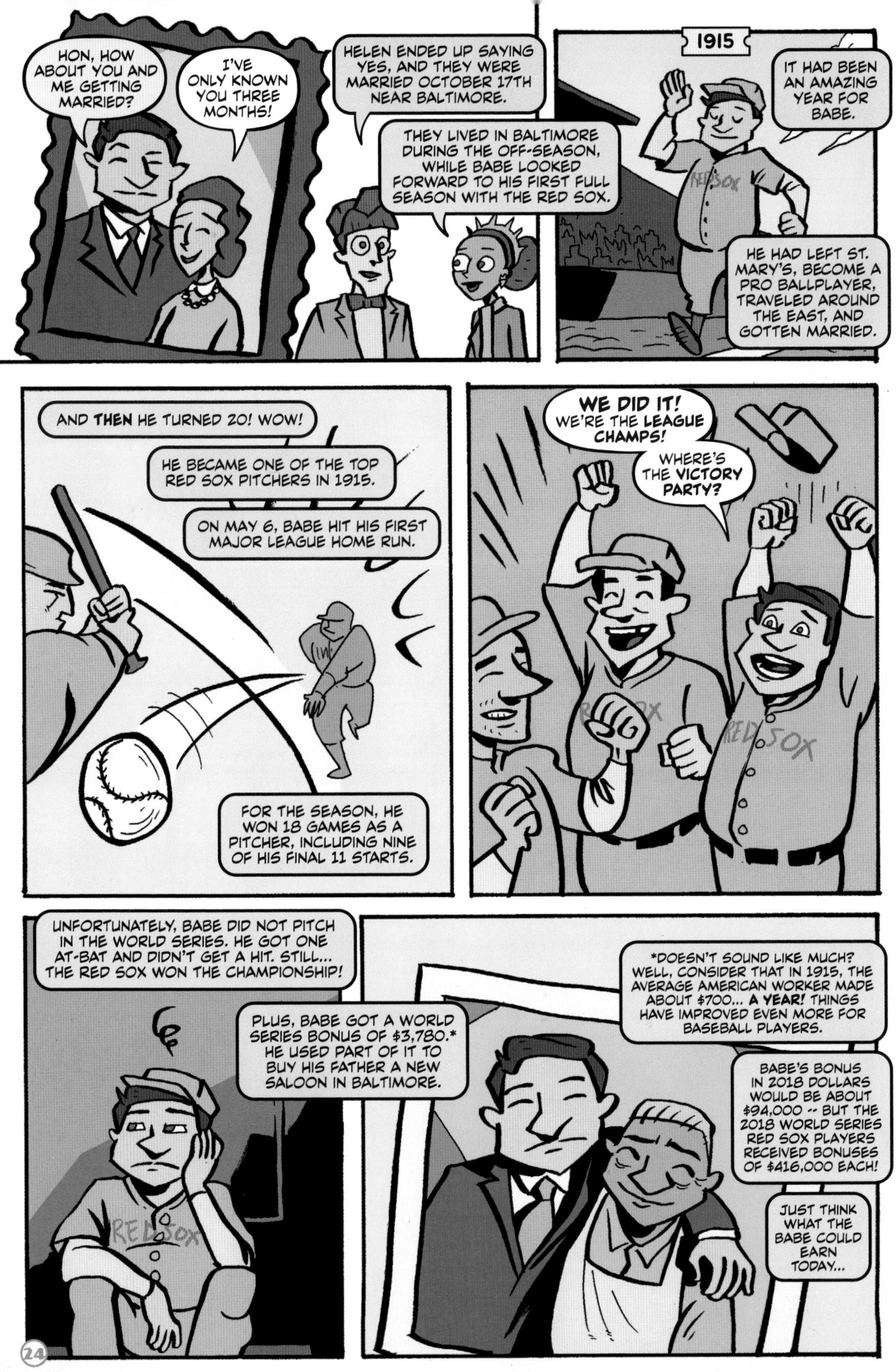
HON, HOW ABOUT YOU AND ME GETTING MARRIED?
I'VE ONLY KNOWN YOU THREE MONTHS!
HELEN ENDED UP SAYING YES, AND THEY WERE MARRIED OCTOBER 17TH NEAR BALTIMORE.
THEY LIVED IN BALTIMORE DURING THE OFF-SEASON, WHILE BABE LOOKED FORWARD TO HIS FIRST FULL SEASON WITH THE RED SOX.
1915
IT HAD BEEN AN AMAZING YEAR FOR BABE.
HE HAD LEFT ST. MARY'S, BECOME A PRO BALLPLAYER, TRAVELED AROUND THE EAST, AND GOTTEN MARRIED.
AND **THEN** HE TURNED 20! WOW!
HE BECAME ONE OF THE TOP RED SOX PITCHERS IN 1915.
ON MAY 6, BABE HIT HIS FIRST MAJOR LEAGUE HOME RUN.
FOR THE SEASON, HE WON 18 GAMES AS A PITCHER, INCLUDING NINE OF HIS FINAL 11 STARTS.
WE DID IT! WE'RE THE **LEAGUE CHAMPS!**
WHERE'S THE **VICTORY PARTY?**
UNFORTUNATELY, BABE DID NOT PITCH IN THE WORLD SERIES. HE GOT ONE AT-BAT AND DIDN'T GET A HIT. STILL... THE RED SOX WON THE CHAMPIONSHIP!
PLUS, BABE GOT A WORLD SERIES BONUS OF $3,780.* HE USED PART OF IT TO BUY HIS FATHER A NEW SALOON IN BALTIMORE.
*DOESN'T SOUND LIKE MUCH? WELL, CONSIDER THAT IN 1915, THE AVERAGE AMERICAN WORKER MADE ABOUT $700... **A YEAR!** THINGS HAVE IMPROVED EVEN MORE FOR BASEBALL PLAYERS.
BABE'S BONUS IN 2018 DOLLARS WOULD BE ABOUT $94,000 -- BUT THE 2018 WORLD SERIES RED SOX PLAYERS RECEIVED BONUSES OF $416,000 EACH!
JUST THINK WHAT THE BABE COULD EARN TODAY...

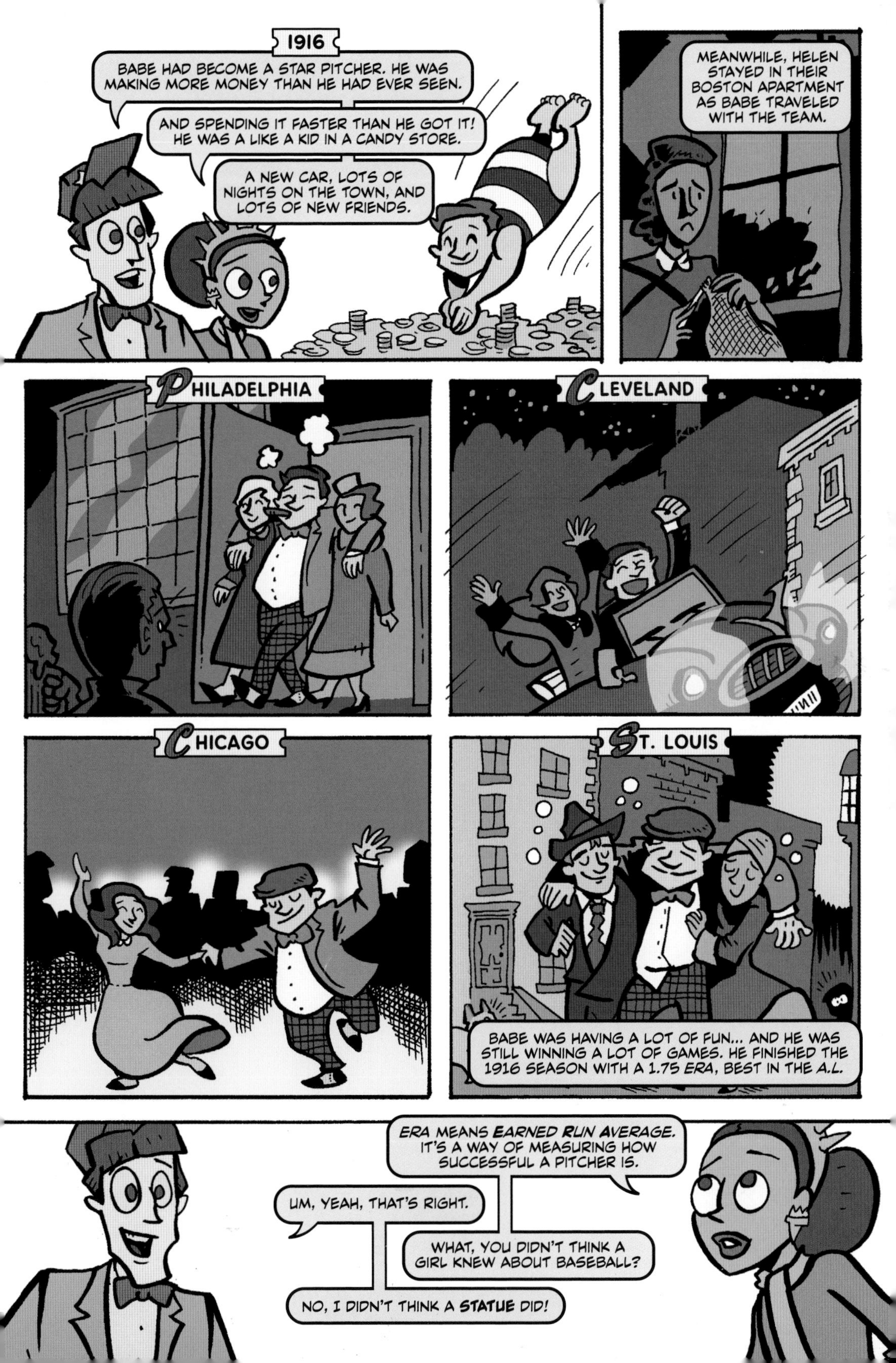
1916
BABE HAD BECOME A STAR PITCHER. HE WAS MAKING MORE MONEY THAN HE HAD EVER SEEN.
AND SPENDING IT FASTER THAN HE GOT IT! HE WAS A LIKE A KID IN A CANDY STORE.
A NEW CAR, LOTS OF NIGHTS ON THE TOWN, AND LOTS OF NEW FRIENDS.
MEANWHILE, HELEN STAYED IN THEIR BOSTON APARTMENT AS BABE TRAVELED WITH THE TEAM.
PHILADELPHIA
CLEVELAND
CHICAGO
ST. LOUIS
BABE WAS HAVING A LOT OF FUN... AND HE WAS STILL WINNING A LOT OF GAMES. HE FINISHED THE 1916 SEASON WITH A 1.75 ERA, BEST IN THE A.L.
ERA MEANS EARNED RUN AVERAGE. IT'S A WAY OF MEASURING HOW SUCCESSFUL A PITCHER IS.
UM, YEAH, THAT'S RIGHT.
WHAT, YOU DIDN'T THINK A GIRL KNEW ABOUT BASEBALL?
NO, I DIDN'T THINK A STATUE DID!

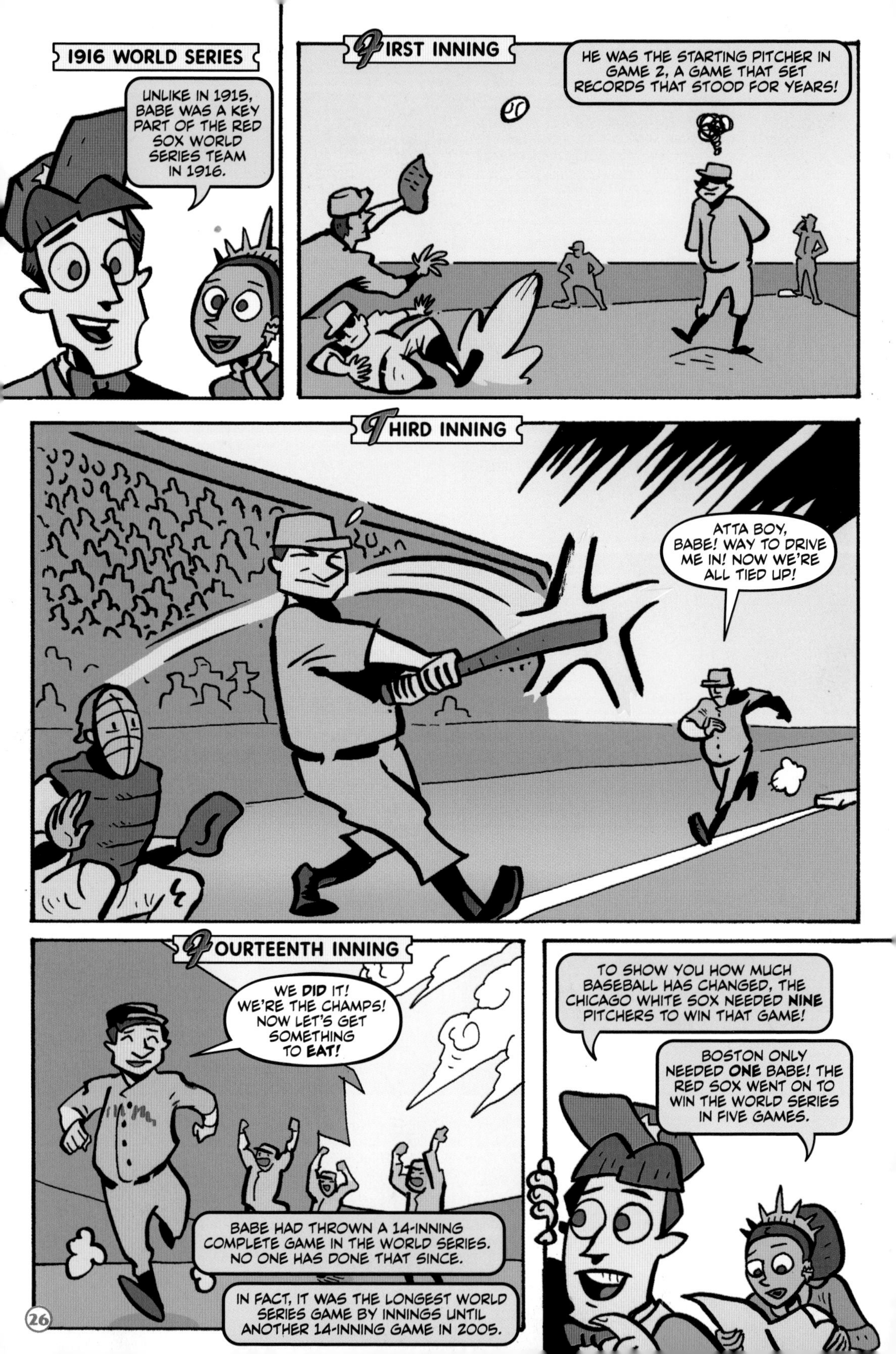

1916 WORLD SERIES
UNLIKE IN 1915, BABE WAS A KEY PART OF THE RED SOX WORLD SERIES TEAM IN 1916.
FIRST INNING
HE WAS THE STARTING PITCHER IN GAME 2, A GAME THAT SET RECORDS THAT STOOD FOR YEARS!
THIRD INNING
ATTA BOY, BABE! WAY TO DRIVE ME IN! NOW WE'RE ALL TIED UP!
FOURTEENTH INNING
WE DID IT! WE'RE THE CHAMPS! NOW LET'S GET SOMETHING TO EAT!
BABE HAD THROWN A 14-INNING COMPLETE GAME IN THE WORLD SERIES. NO ONE HAS DONE THAT SINCE.
IN FACT, IT WAS THE LONGEST WORLD SERIES GAME BY INNINGS UNTIL ANOTHER 14-INNING GAME IN 2005.
TO SHOW YOU HOW MUCH BASEBALL HAS CHANGED, THE CHICAGO WHITE SOX NEEDED NINE PITCHERS TO WIN THAT GAME!
BOSTON ONLY NEEDED ONE BABE! THE RED SOX WENT ON TO WIN THE WORLD SERIES IN FIVE GAMES.

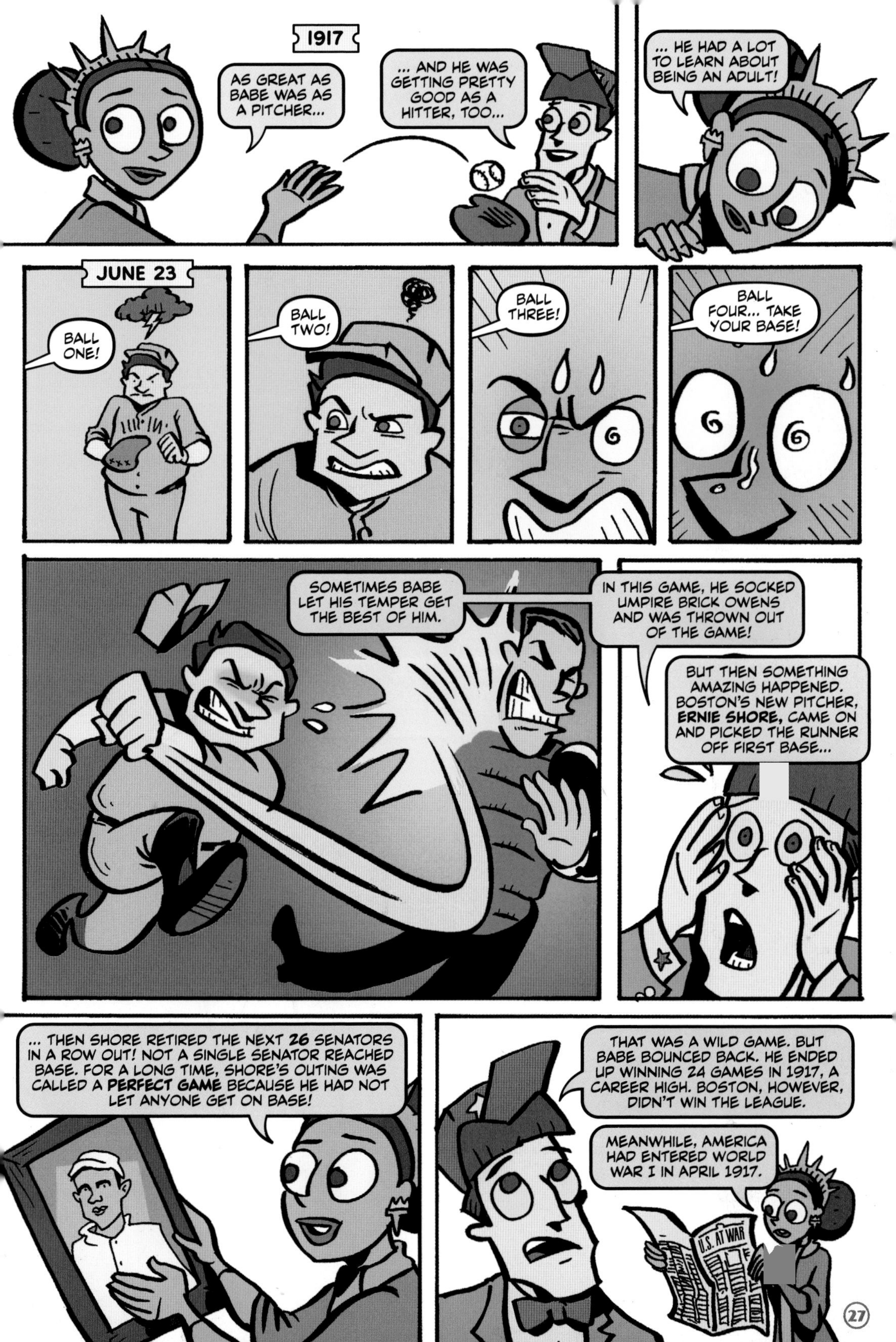

1917
AS GREAT AS BABE WAS AS A PITCHER...
... AND HE WAS GETTING PRETTY GOOD AS A HITTER, TOO...
... HE HAD A LOT TO LEARN ABOUT BEING AN ADULT!
JUNE 23
BALL ONE!
BALL TWO!
BALL THREE!
BALL FOUR... TAKE YOUR BASE!
SOMETIMES BABE LET HIS TEMPER GET THE BEST OF HIM.
IN THIS GAME, HE SOCKED UMPIRE BRICK OWENS AND WAS THROWN OUT OF THE GAME!
BUT THEN SOMETHING AMAZING HAPPENED. BOSTON'S NEW PITCHER, ERNIE SHORE, CAME ON AND PICKED THE RUNNER OFF FIRST BASE...
... THEN SHORE RETIRED THE NEXT 26 SENATORS IN A ROW OUT! NOT A SINGLE SENATOR REACHED BASE. FOR A LONG TIME, SHORE'S OUTING WAS CALLED A PERFECT GAME BECAUSE HE HAD NOT LET ANYONE GET ON BASE!
THAT WAS A WILD GAME. BUT BABE BOUNCED BACK. HE ENDED UP WINNING 24 GAMES IN 1917, A CAREER HIGH. BOSTON, HOWEVER, DIDN'T WIN THE LEAGUE.
MEANWHILE, AMERICA HAD ENTERED WORLD WAR I IN APRIL 1917.
U.S. AT WAR

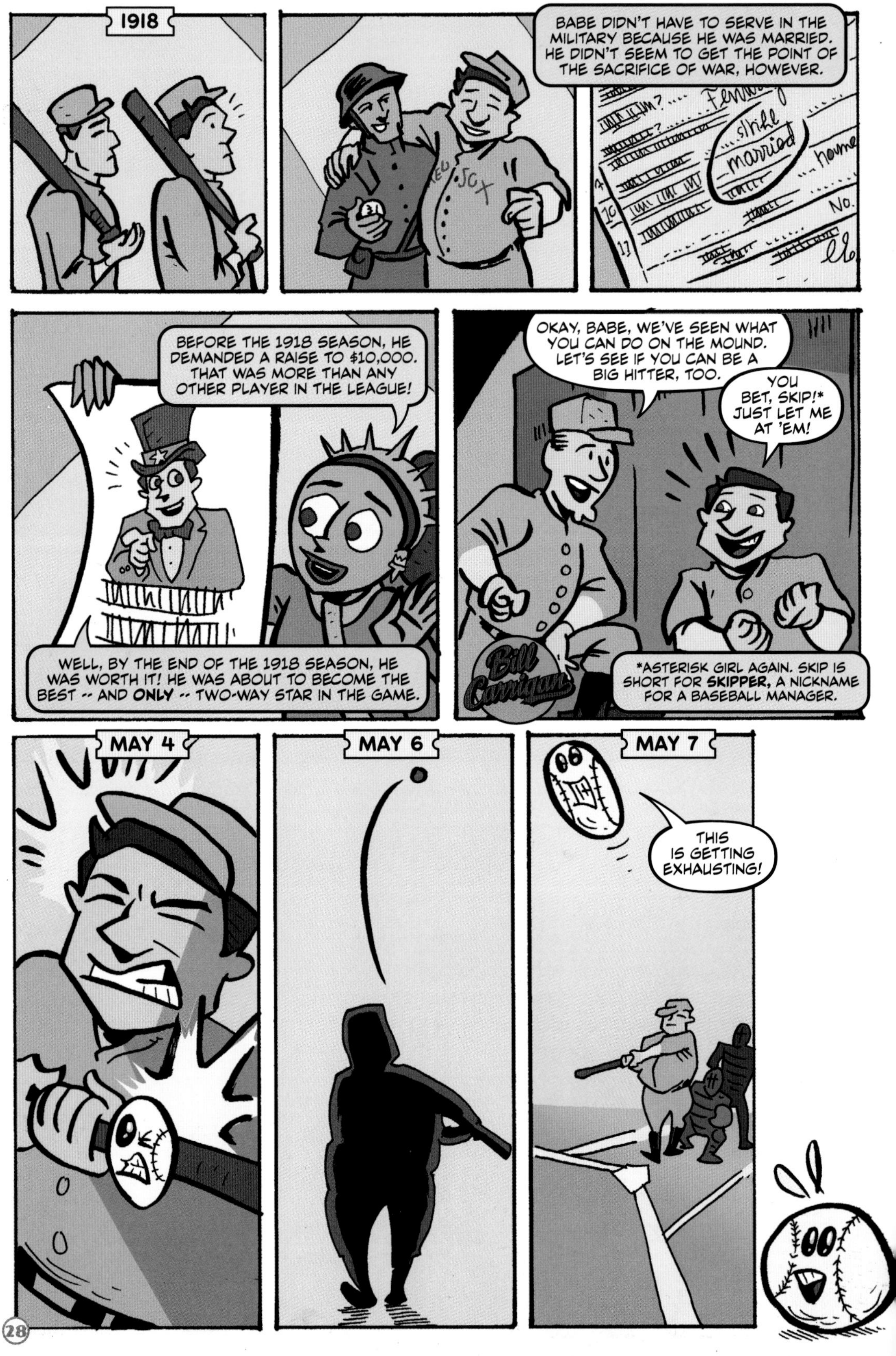
1918
BABE DIDN'T HAVE TO SERVE IN THE MILITARY BECAUSE HE WAS MARRIED. HE DIDN'T SEEM TO GET THE POINT OF THE SACRIFICE OF WAR, HOWEVER.
married
No.
BEFORE THE 1918 SEASON, HE DEMANDED A RAISE TO $10,000. THAT WAS MORE THAN ANY OTHER PLAYER IN THE LEAGUE!
WELL, BY THE END OF THE 1918 SEASON, HE WAS WORTH IT! HE WAS ABOUT TO BECOME THE BEST -- AND **ONLY** -- TWO-WAY STAR IN THE GAME.
OKAY, BABE, WE'VE SEEN WHAT YOU CAN DO ON THE MOUND. LET'S SEE IF YOU CAN BE A BIG HITTER, TOO.
YOU BET, SKIP!* JUST LET ME AT 'EM!
Bill Carrigan
*ASTERISK GIRL AGAIN. SKIP IS SHORT FOR **SKIPPER,** A NICKNAME FOR A BASEBALL MANAGER.
MAY 4
MAY 6
MAY 7
THIS IS GETTING EXHAUSTING!

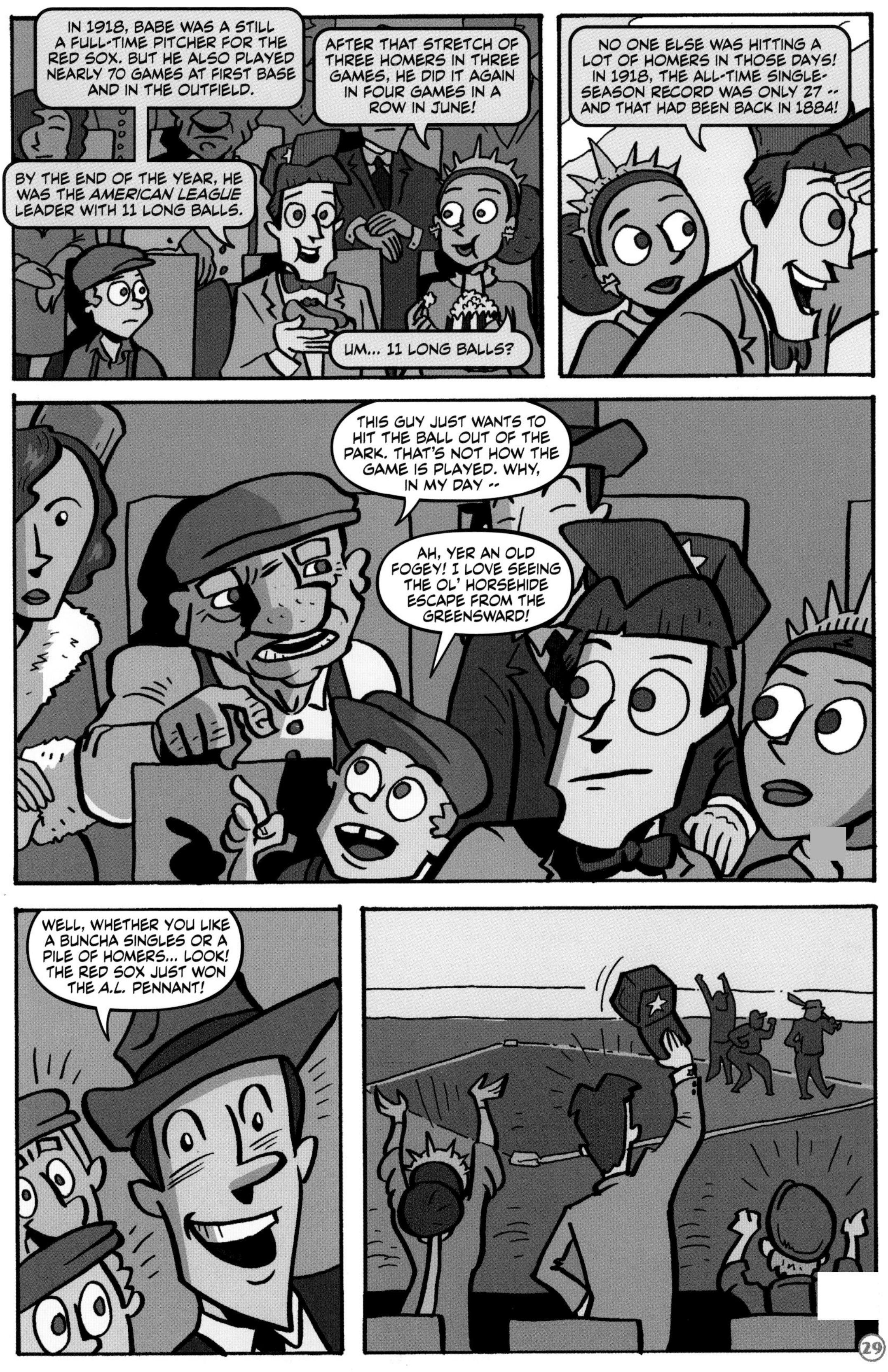
IN 1918, BABE WAS A STILL A FULL-TIME PITCHER FOR THE RED SOX. BUT HE ALSO PLAYED NEARLY 70 GAMES AT FIRST BASE AND IN THE OUTFIELD.
BY THE END OF THE YEAR, HE WAS THE *AMERICAN LEAGUE* LEADER WITH 11 LONG BALLS.
AFTER THAT STRETCH OF THREE HOMERS IN THREE GAMES, HE DID IT AGAIN IN FOUR GAMES IN A ROW IN JUNE!
UM... 11 LONG BALLS?
NO ONE ELSE WAS HITTING A LOT OF HOMERS IN THOSE DAYS! IN 1918, THE ALL-TIME SINGLE-SEASON RECORD WAS ONLY 27 -- AND THAT HAD BEEN BACK IN 1884!
THIS GUY JUST WANTS TO HIT THE BALL OUT OF THE PARK. THAT'S NOT HOW THE GAME IS PLAYED. WHY, IN MY DAY --
AH, YER AN OLD FOGEY! I LOVE SEEING THE OL' HORSEHIDE ESCAPE FROM THE GREENSWARD!
WELL, WHETHER YOU LIKE A BUNCHA SINGLES OR A PILE OF HOMERS... LOOK! THE RED SOX JUST WON THE *A.L.* PENNANT!

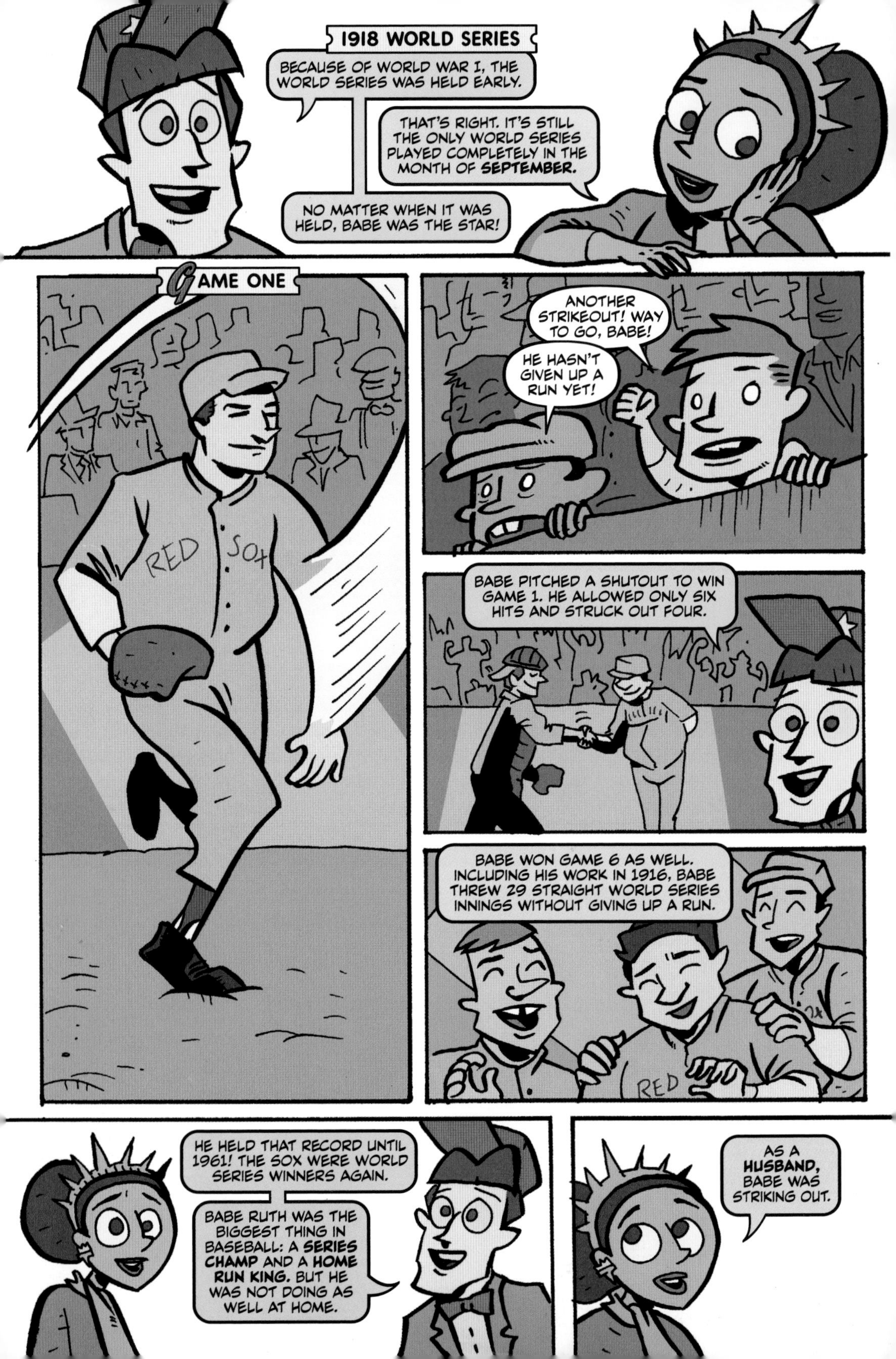
1918 WORLD SERIES
BECAUSE OF WORLD WAR I, THE WORLD SERIES WAS HELD EARLY.
THAT'S RIGHT. IT'S STILL THE ONLY WORLD SERIES PLAYED COMPLETELY IN THE MONTH OF SEPTEMBER.
NO MATTER WHEN IT WAS HELD, BABE WAS THE STAR!
GAME ONE
RED SOX
ANOTHER STRIKEOUT! WAY TO GO, BABE!
HE HASN'T GIVEN UP A RUN YET!
BABE PITCHED A SHUTOUT TO WIN GAME 1. HE ALLOWED ONLY SIX HITS AND STRUCK OUT FOUR.
BABE WON GAME 6 AS WELL. INCLUDING HIS WORK IN 1916, BABE THREW 29 STRAIGHT WORLD SERIES INNINGS WITHOUT GIVING UP A RUN.
RED
HE HELD THAT RECORD UNTIL 1961! THE SOX WERE WORLD SERIES WINNERS AGAIN.
BABE RUTH WAS THE BIGGEST THING IN BASEBALL: A SERIES CHAMP AND A HOME RUN KING. BUT HE WAS NOT DOING AS WELL AT HOME.
AS A HUSBAND, BABE WAS STRIKING OUT.

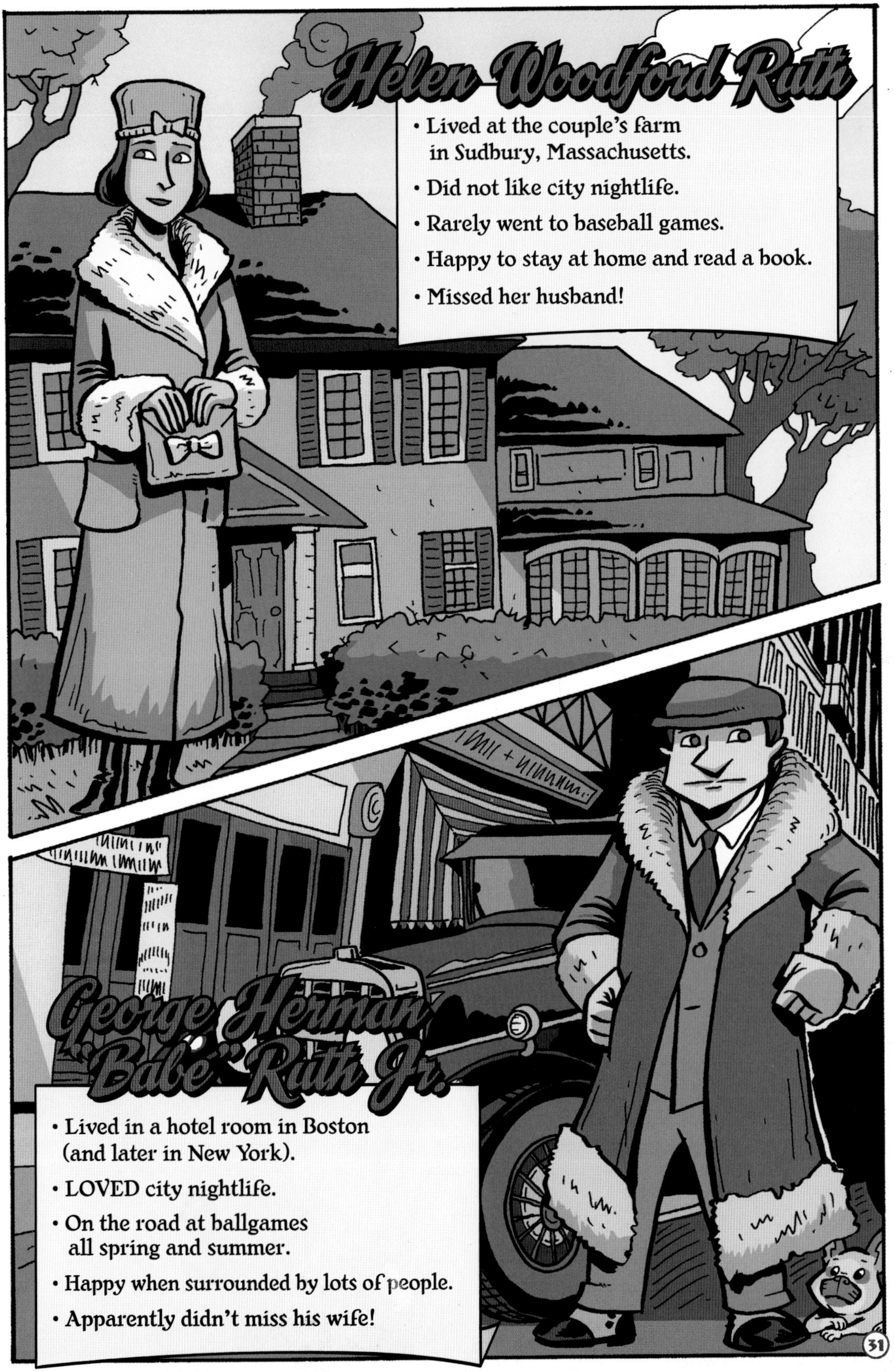
Helen Woodford Ruth
• Lived at the couple's farm in Sudbury, Massachusetts.
• Did not like city nightlife.
• Rarely went to baseball games.
• Happy to stay at home and read a book.
• Missed her husband!
George Herman "Babe" Ruth Jr.
• Lived in a hotel room in Boston (and later in New York).
• LOVED city nightlife.
• On the road at ballgames all spring and summer.
• Happy when surrounded by lots of people.
• Apparently didn't miss his wife!

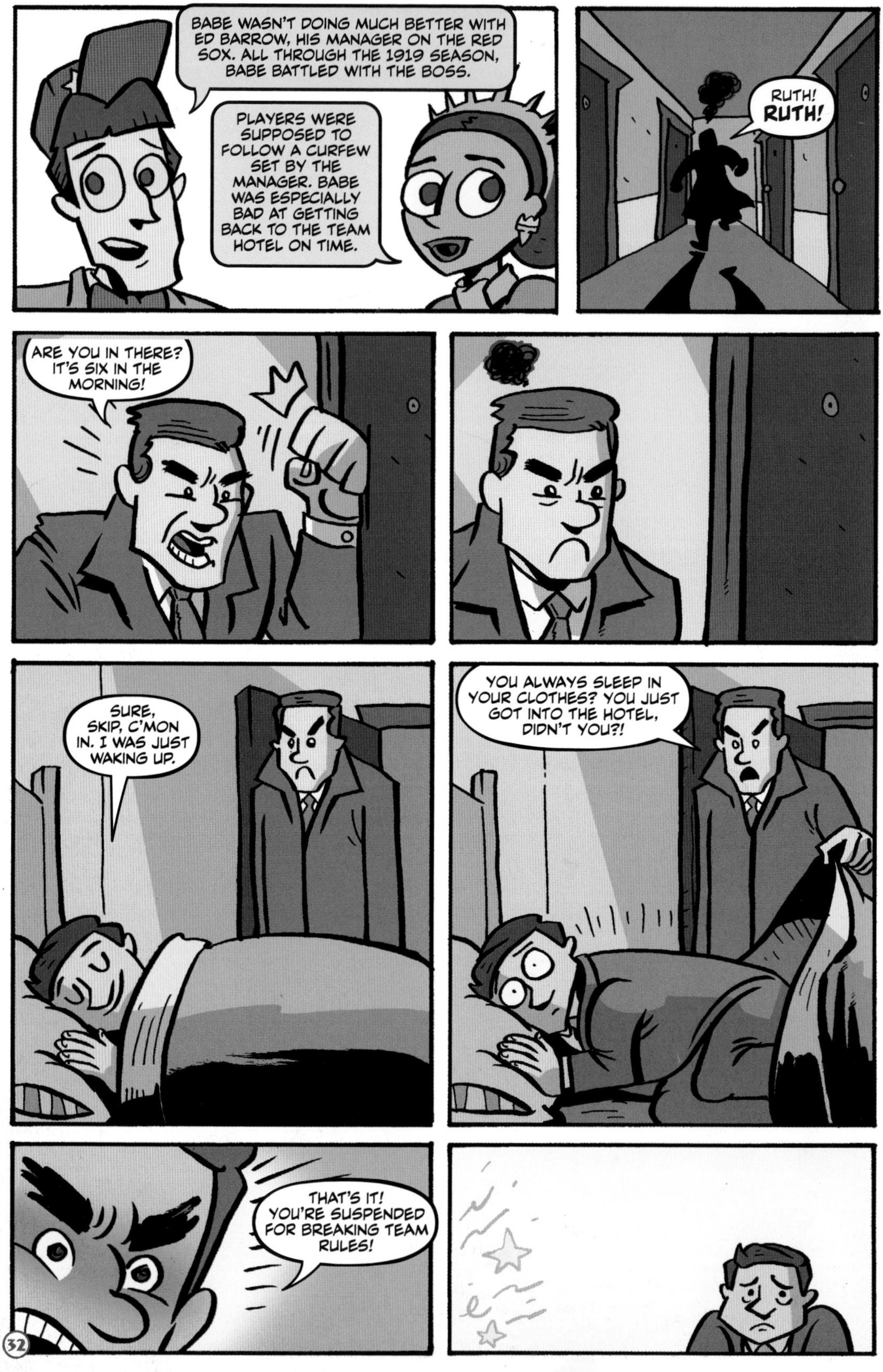
BABE WASN'T DOING MUCH BETTER WITH ED BARROW, HIS MANAGER ON THE RED SOX. ALL THROUGH THE 1919 SEASON, BABE BATTLED WITH THE BOSS.
PLAYERS WERE SUPPOSED TO FOLLOW A CURFEW SET BY THE MANAGER. BABE WAS ESPECIALLY BAD AT GETTING BACK TO THE TEAM HOTEL ON TIME.
RUTH! RUTH!
ARE YOU IN THERE? IT'S SIX IN THE MORNING!
SURE, SKIP, C'MON IN. I WAS JUST WAKING UP.
YOU ALWAYS SLEEP IN YOUR CLOTHES? YOU JUST GOT INTO THE HOTEL, DIDN'T YOU?!
THAT'S IT! YOU'RE SUSPENDED FOR BREAKING TEAM RULES!

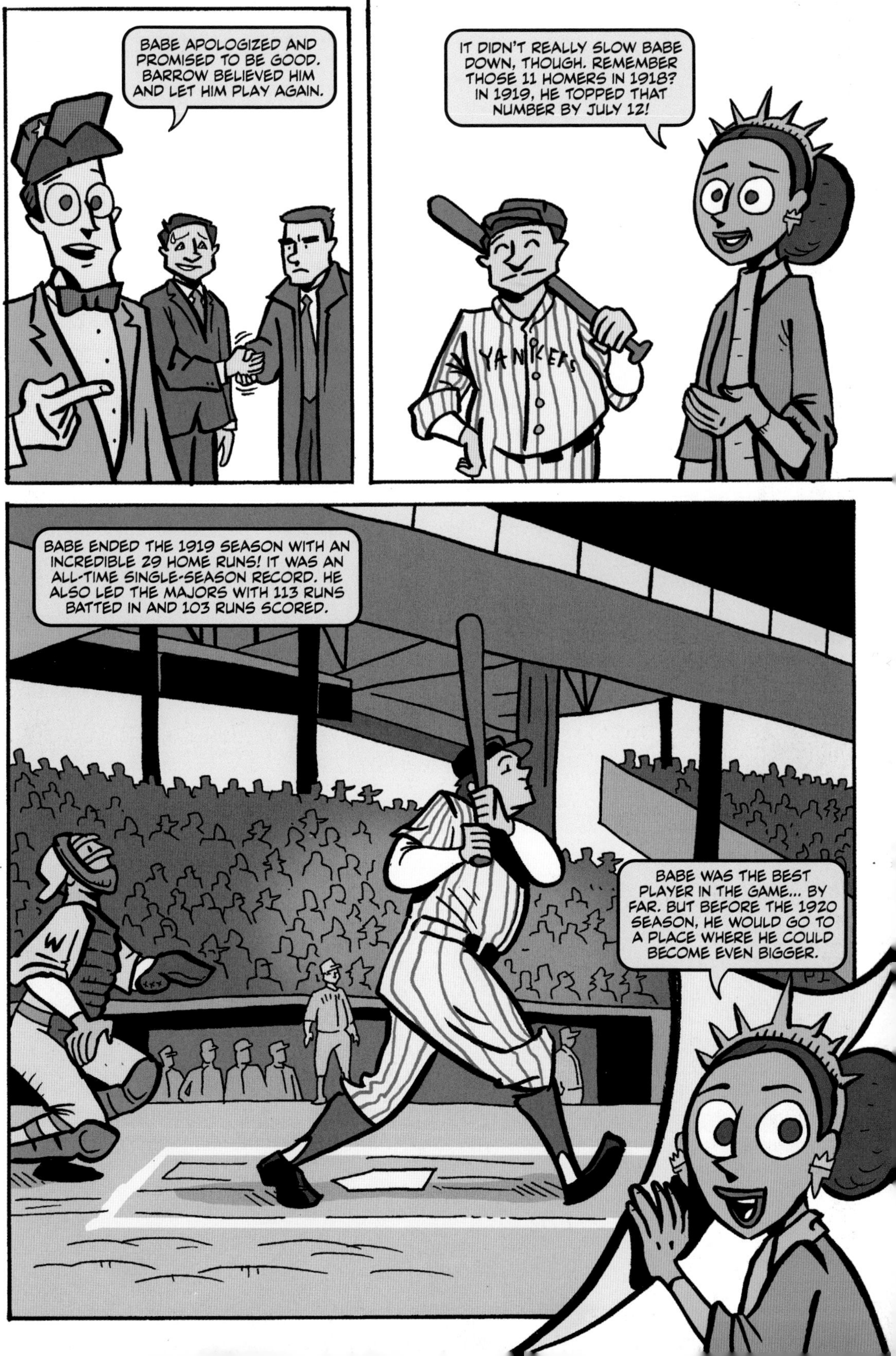
BABE APOLOGIZED AND PROMISED TO BE GOOD. BARROW BELIEVED HIM AND LET HIM PLAY AGAIN.
IT DIDN'T REALLY SLOW BABE DOWN, THOUGH. REMEMBER THOSE 11 HOMERS IN 1918? IN 1919, HE TOPPED THAT NUMBER BY JULY 12!
YANKEES
BABE ENDED THE 1919 SEASON WITH AN INCREDIBLE 29 HOME RUNS! IT WAS AN ALL-TIME SINGLE-SEASON RECORD. HE ALSO LED THE MAJORS WITH 113 RUNS BATTED IN AND 103 RUNS SCORED.
W
BABE WAS THE BEST PLAYER IN THE GAME... BY FAR. BUT BEFORE THE 1920 SEASON, HE WOULD GO TO A PLACE WHERE HE COULD BECOME EVEN BIGGER.

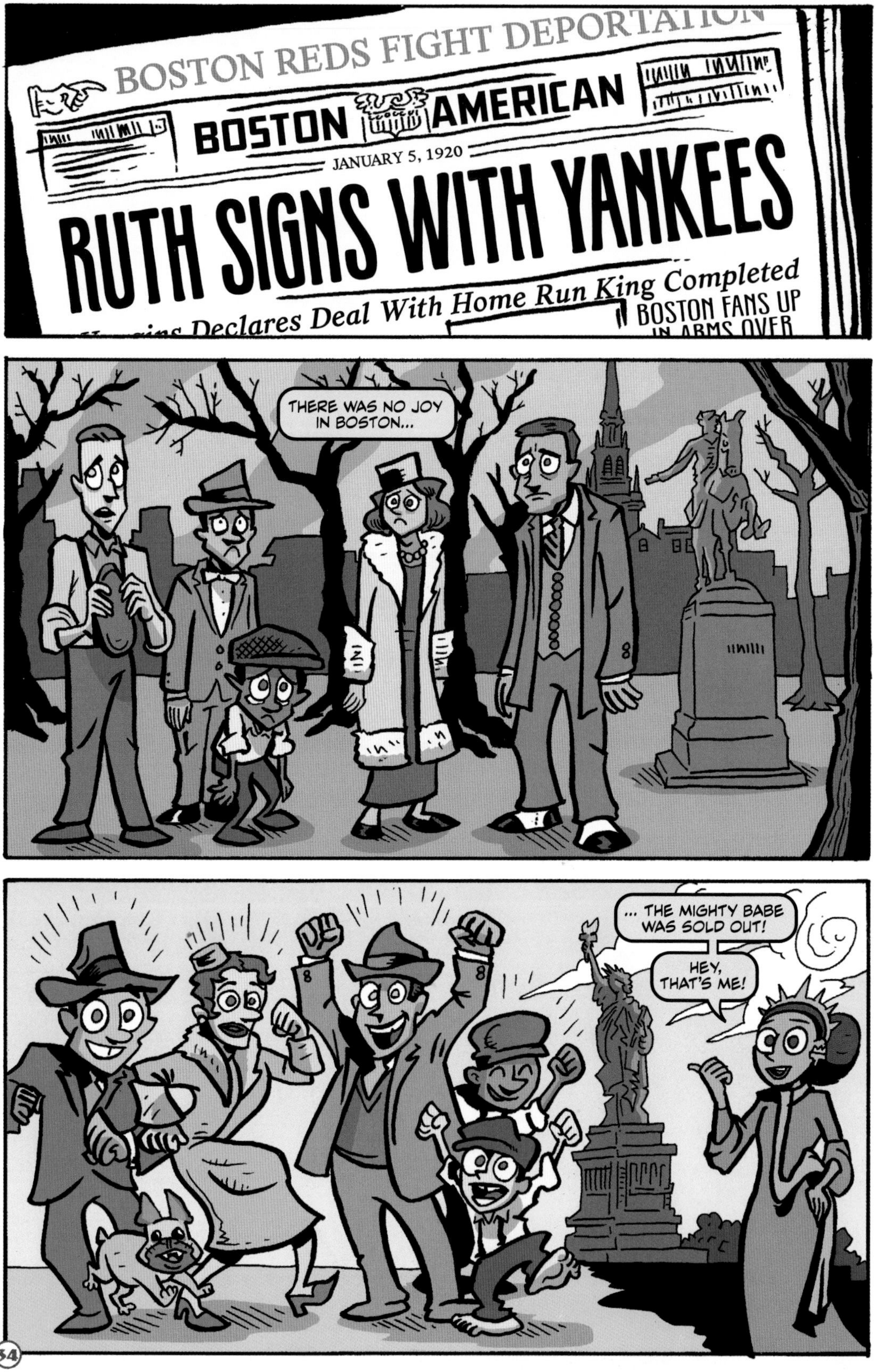
BOSTON REDS FIGHT DEPORTATION
BOSTON AMERICAN
JANUARY 5, 1920
RUTH SIGNS WITH YANKEES
Declares Deal With Home Run King Completed
BOSTON FANS UP
THERE WAS NO JOY IN BOSTON...
... THE MIGHTY BABE WAS SOLD OUT!
HEY, THAT'S ME!

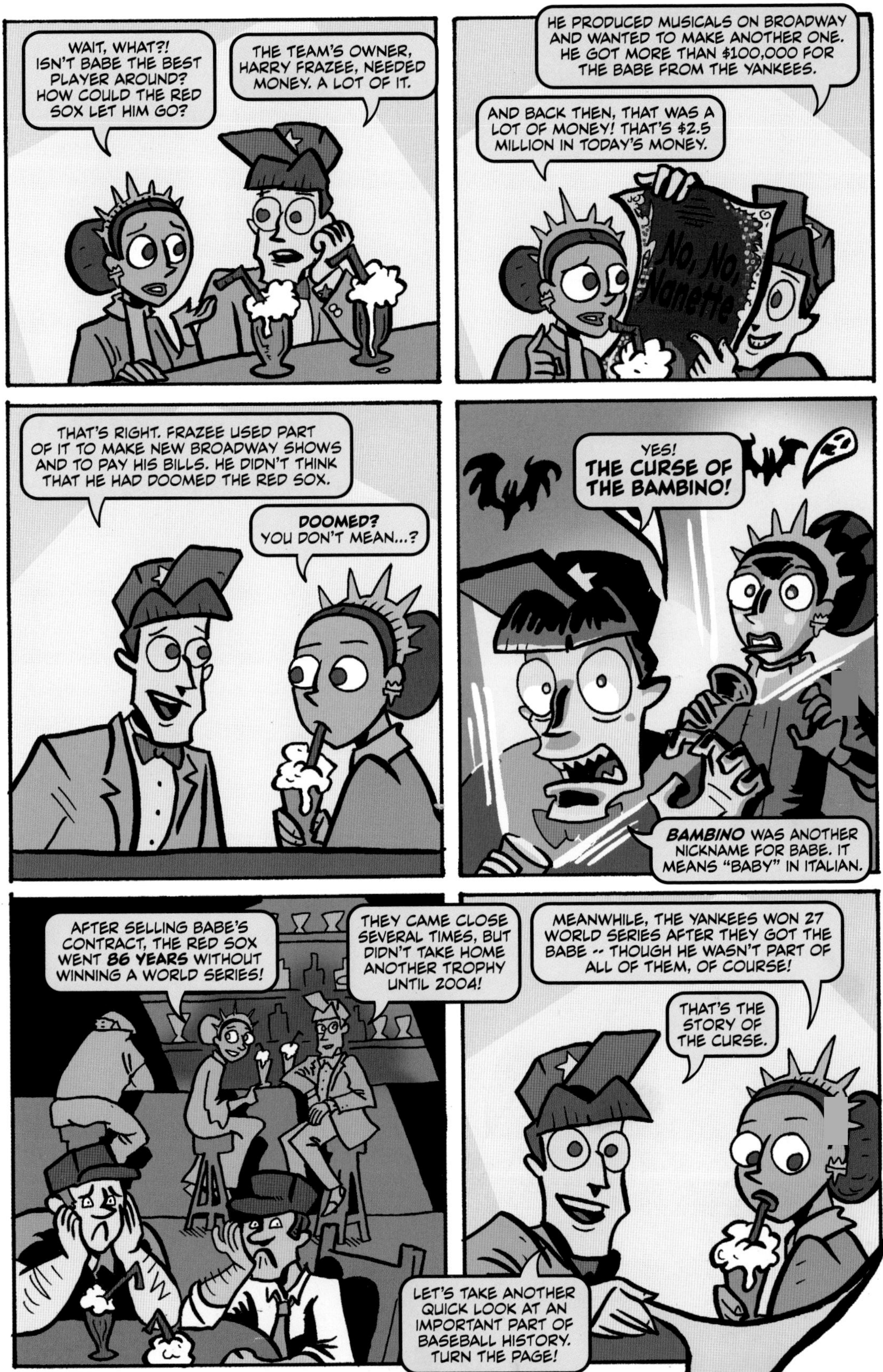
WAIT, WHAT?! ISN'T BABE THE BEST PLAYER AROUND? HOW COULD THE RED SOX LET HIM GO?
THE TEAM'S OWNER, HARRY FRAZEE, NEEDED MONEY. A LOT OF IT.
HE PRODUCED MUSICALS ON BROADWAY AND WANTED TO MAKE ANOTHER ONE. HE GOT MORE THAN $100,000 FOR THE BABE FROM THE YANKEES.
AND BACK THEN, THAT WAS A LOT OF MONEY! THAT'S $2.5 MILLION IN TODAY'S MONEY.
No, No, Nanette
THAT'S RIGHT. FRAZEE USED PART OF IT TO MAKE NEW BROADWAY SHOWS AND TO PAY HIS BILLS. HE DIDN'T THINK THAT HE HAD DOOMED THE RED SOX.
DOOMED? YOU DON'T MEAN...?
YES! THE CURSE OF THE BAMBINO!
BAMBINO WAS ANOTHER NICKNAME FOR BABE. IT MEANS "BABY" IN ITALIAN.
AFTER SELLING BABE'S CONTRACT, THE RED SOX WENT 86 YEARS WITHOUT WINNING A WORLD SERIES!
THEY CAME CLOSE SEVERAL TIMES, BUT DIDN'T TAKE HOME ANOTHER TROPHY UNTIL 2004!
MEANWHILE, THE YANKEES WON 27 WORLD SERIES AFTER THEY GOT THE BABE -- THOUGH HE WASN'T PART OF ALL OF THEM, OF COURSE!
THAT'S THE STORY OF THE CURSE.
LET'S TAKE ANOTHER QUICK LOOK AT AN IMPORTANT PART OF BASEBALL HISTORY. TURN THE PAGE!

BEFORE 1920, MOST TEAMS PLAYED "SMALL BALL." IT WAS THE WAY BASEBALL HAD BEEN PLAYED SINCE THE SPORT STARTED IN THE 1830s.

Small Ball

- Few home runs.

- Batters tried to hit singles.

- Famous saying: "Hit 'em where they ain't!"

- Lots of stolen bases.

- Lots of bunts.

- Average homers per season for all Major League teams combined 1903–1919: 354.

AFTER 1920, AND AFTER BABE RUTH CAME ALONG, BASEBALL CHANGED. A LOT! THE BABE SHOWED THAT HITTING HOMERS NOT ONLY WORKED, IT BROUGHT IN TONS OF FANS. PEOPLE LOVED WATCHING HOMERS!

Long Ball

- Lots of home runs.

- Batters tried to crush the ball.

- Famous saying: "Good-bye, Mr. Spalding!"

- Fewer stolen bases.

- Not as many bunts.

- Average homers per season for all Major League teams combined 1920–1929: 989.

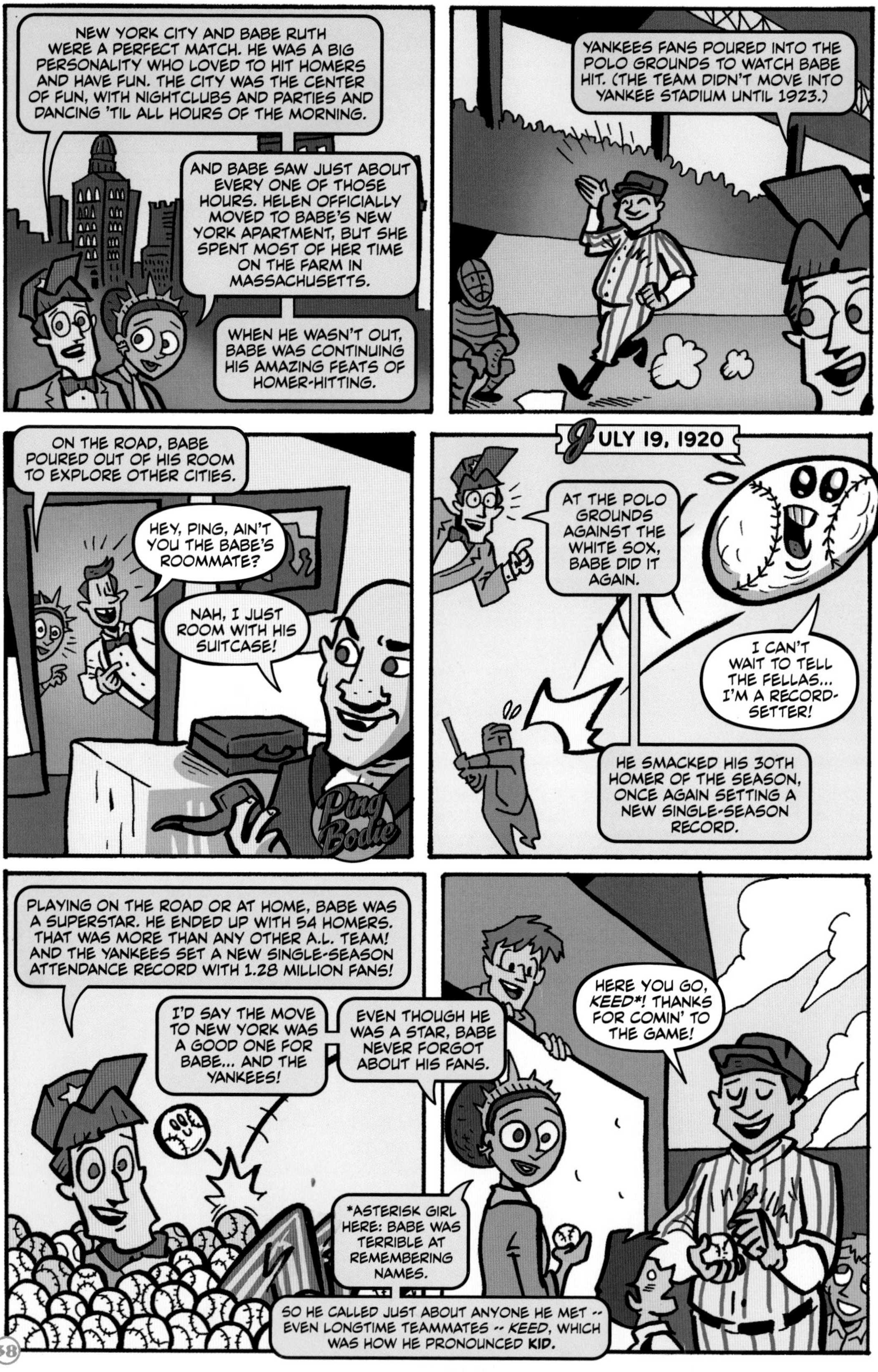
NEW YORK CITY AND BABE RUTH WERE A PERFECT MATCH. HE WAS A BIG PERSONALITY WHO LOVED TO HIT HOMERS AND HAVE FUN. THE CITY WAS THE CENTER OF FUN, WITH NIGHTCLUBS AND PARTIES AND DANCING 'TIL ALL HOURS OF THE MORNING.
AND BABE SAW JUST ABOUT EVERY ONE OF THOSE HOURS. HELEN OFFICIALLY MOVED TO BABE'S NEW YORK APARTMENT, BUT SHE SPENT MOST OF HER TIME ON THE FARM IN MASSACHUSETTS.
WHEN HE WASN'T OUT, BABE WAS CONTINUING HIS AMAZING FEATS OF HOMER-HITTING.
YANKEES FANS POURED INTO THE POLO GROUNDS TO WATCH BABE HIT. (THE TEAM DIDN'T MOVE INTO YANKEE STADIUM UNTIL 1923.)
ON THE ROAD, BABE POURED OUT OF HIS ROOM TO EXPLORE OTHER CITIES.
HEY, PING, AIN'T YOU THE BABE'S ROOMMATE?
NAH, I JUST ROOM WITH HIS SUITCASE!
Ping Bodie
JULY 19, 1920
AT THE POLO GROUNDS AGAINST THE WHITE SOX, BABE DID IT AGAIN.
I CAN'T WAIT TO TELL THE FELLAS... I'M A RECORD-SETTER!
HE SMACKED HIS 30TH HOMER OF THE SEASON, ONCE AGAIN SETTING A NEW SINGLE-SEASON RECORD.
PLAYING ON THE ROAD OR AT HOME, BABE WAS A SUPERSTAR. HE ENDED UP WITH 54 HOMERS. THAT WAS MORE THAN ANY OTHER A.L. TEAM! AND THE YANKEES SET A NEW SINGLE-SEASON ATTENDANCE RECORD WITH 1.28 MILLION FANS!
I'D SAY THE MOVE TO NEW YORK WAS A GOOD ONE FOR BABE... AND THE YANKEES!
EVEN THOUGH HE WAS A STAR, BABE NEVER FORGOT ABOUT HIS FANS.
HERE YOU GO, *KEED**! THANKS FOR COMIN' TO THE GAME!
*ASTERISK GIRL HERE: BABE WAS TERRIBLE AT REMEMBERING NAMES.
SO HE CALLED JUST ABOUT ANYONE HE MET -- EVEN LONGTIME TEAMMATES -- *KEED*, WHICH WAS HOW HE PRONOUNCED **KID**.

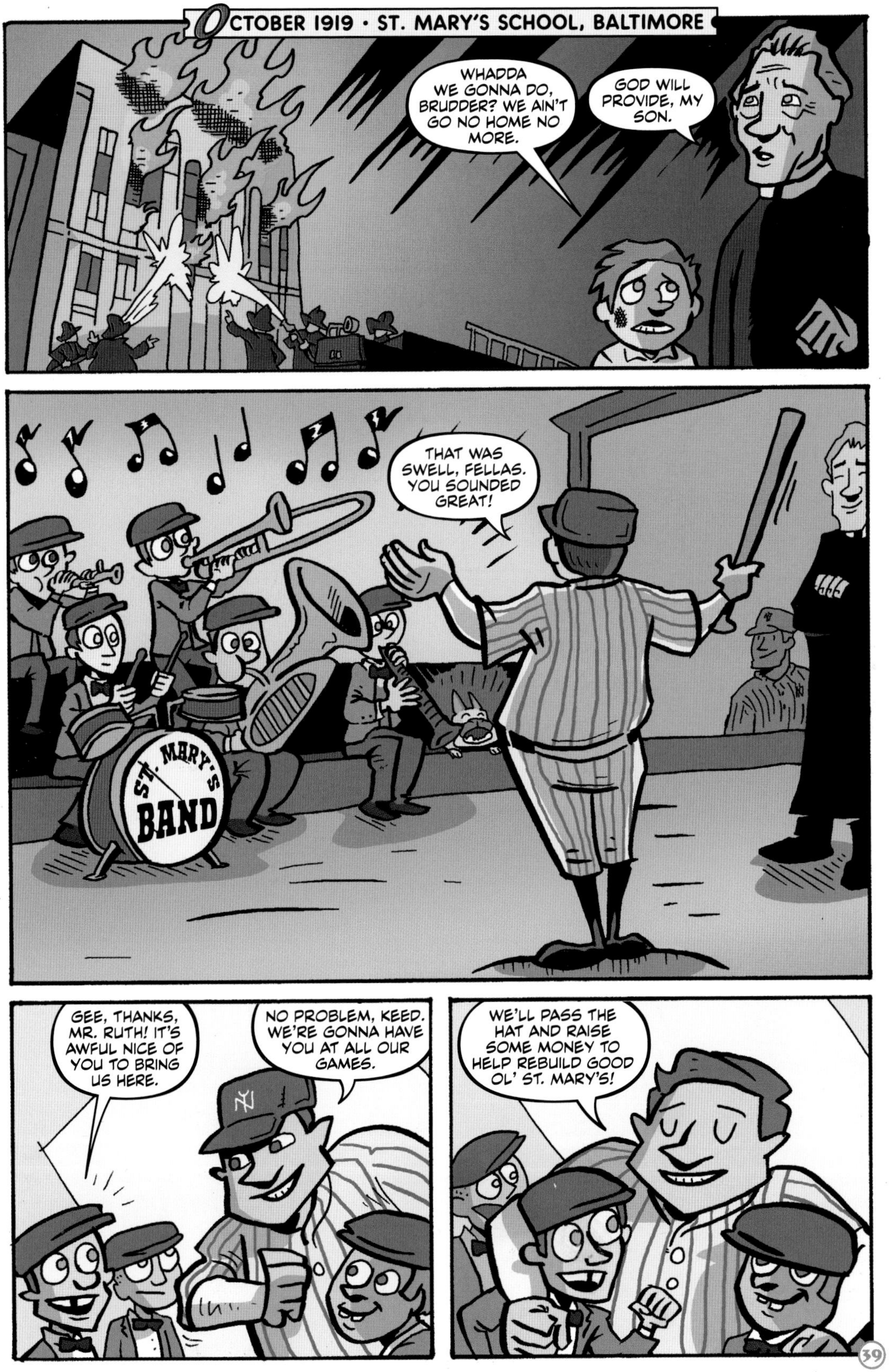

OCTOBER 1919 • ST. MARY'S SCHOOL, BALTIMORE
WHADDA WE GONNA DO, BRUDDER? WE AIN'T GO NO HOME NO MORE.
GOD WILL PROVIDE, MY SON.
THAT WAS SWELL, FELLAS. YOU SOUNDED GREAT!
ST. MARY'S BAND
GEE, THANKS, MR. RUTH! IT'S AWFUL NICE OF YOU TO BRING US HERE.
NO PROBLEM, KEED. WE'RE GONNA HAVE YOU AT ALL OUR GAMES.
WE'LL PASS THE HAT AND RAISE SOME MONEY TO HELP REBUILD GOOD OL' ST. MARY'S!

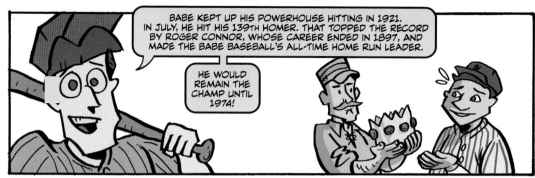

BABE KEPT UP HIS POWERHOUSE HITTING IN 1921. IN JULY, HE HIT HIS 139TH HOMER. THAT TOPPED THE RECORD BY ROGER CONNOR, WHOSE CAREER ENDED IN 1897, AND MADE THE BABE BASEBALL'S ALL-TIME HOME RUN LEADER.

HE WOULD REMAIN THE CHAMP UNTIL 1974!

HE ALSO KEPT GETTING IN TROUBLE.

BABE, I'M SORRY. YOU WERE JUST GOING TOO FAST. WE HAVE TO TAKE YOU IN THIS TIME.

C'MON, KEED, I GOT A GAME TODAY!

I DON'T CARE IF YOU HAVE A GAME. I'M A NEW YORK GIANTS' FAN! SIX HOURS IN JAIL!

BABE! WE GOTTA GO... NOW!

BABE GOT A POLICE ESCORT AND REACHED THE GAME IN THE FOURTH INNING. EVEN WHEN HE MADE TROUBLE, BABE SLIPPED OUT OF IT PRETTY QUICKLY!

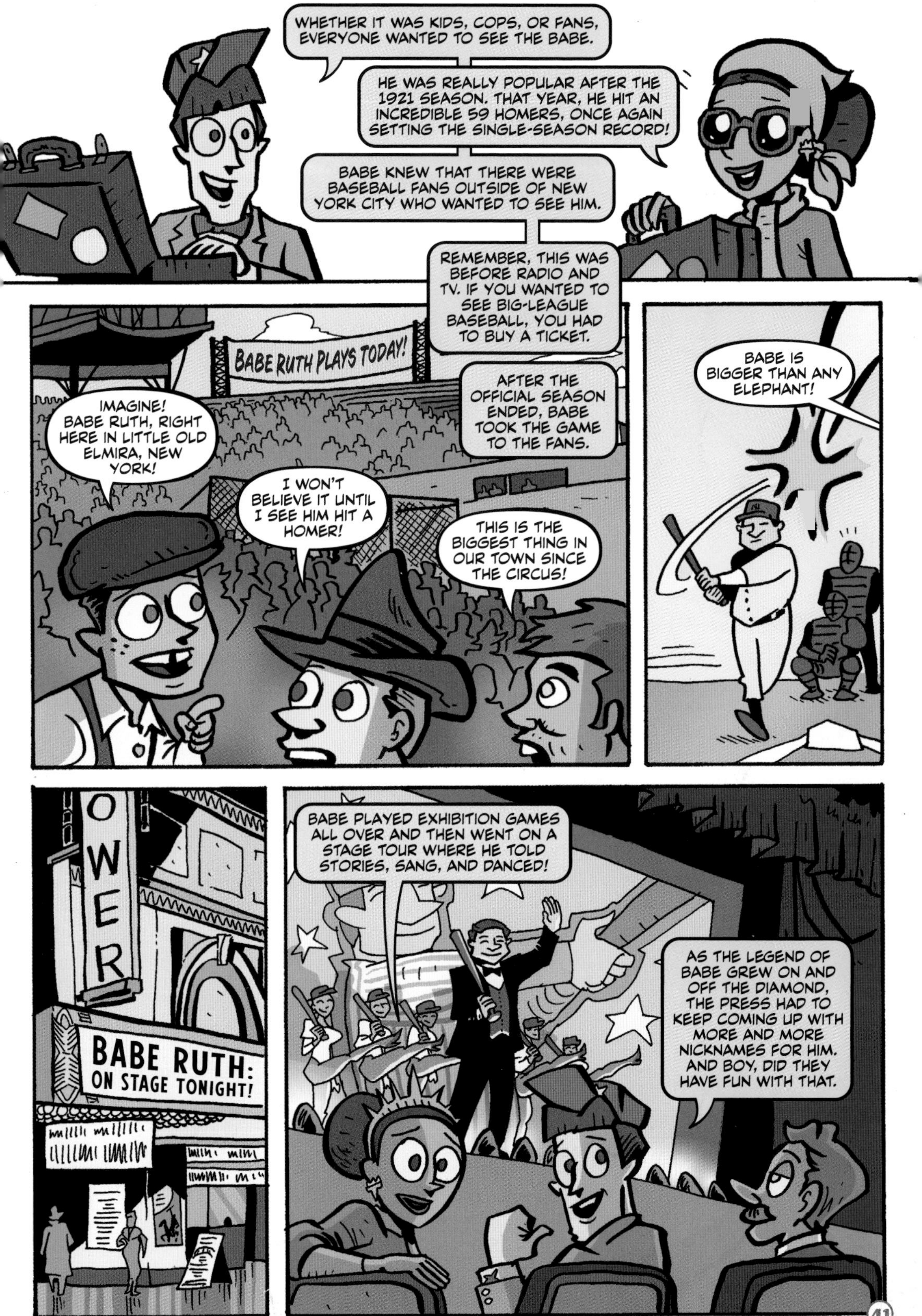
WHETHER IT WAS KIDS, COPS, OR FANS, EVERYONE WANTED TO SEE THE BABE.
HE WAS REALLY POPULAR AFTER THE 1921 SEASON. THAT YEAR, HE HIT AN INCREDIBLE 59 HOMERS, ONCE AGAIN SETTING THE SINGLE-SEASON RECORD!
BABE KNEW THAT THERE WERE BASEBALL FANS OUTSIDE OF NEW YORK CITY WHO WANTED TO SEE HIM.
REMEMBER, THIS WAS BEFORE RADIO AND TV. IF YOU WANTED TO SEE BIG-LEAGUE BASEBALL, YOU HAD TO BUY A TICKET.
BABE RUTH PLAYS TODAY!
AFTER THE OFFICIAL SEASON ENDED, BABE TOOK THE GAME TO THE FANS.
IMAGINE! BABE RUTH, RIGHT HERE IN LITTLE OLD ELMIRA, NEW YORK!
I WON'T BELIEVE IT UNTIL I SEE HIM HIT A HOMER!
THIS IS THE BIGGEST THING IN OUR TOWN SINCE THE CIRCUS!
BABE IS BIGGER THAN ANY ELEPHANT!
OWER
BABE RUTH: ON STAGE TONIGHT!
BABE PLAYED EXHIBITION GAMES ALL OVER AND THEN WENT ON A STAGE TOUR WHERE HE TOLD STORIES, SANG, AND DANCED!
AS THE LEGEND OF BABE GREW ON AND OFF THE DIAMOND, THE PRESS HAD TO KEEP COMING UP WITH MORE AND MORE NICKNAMES FOR HIM. AND BOY, DID THEY HAVE FUN WITH THAT.

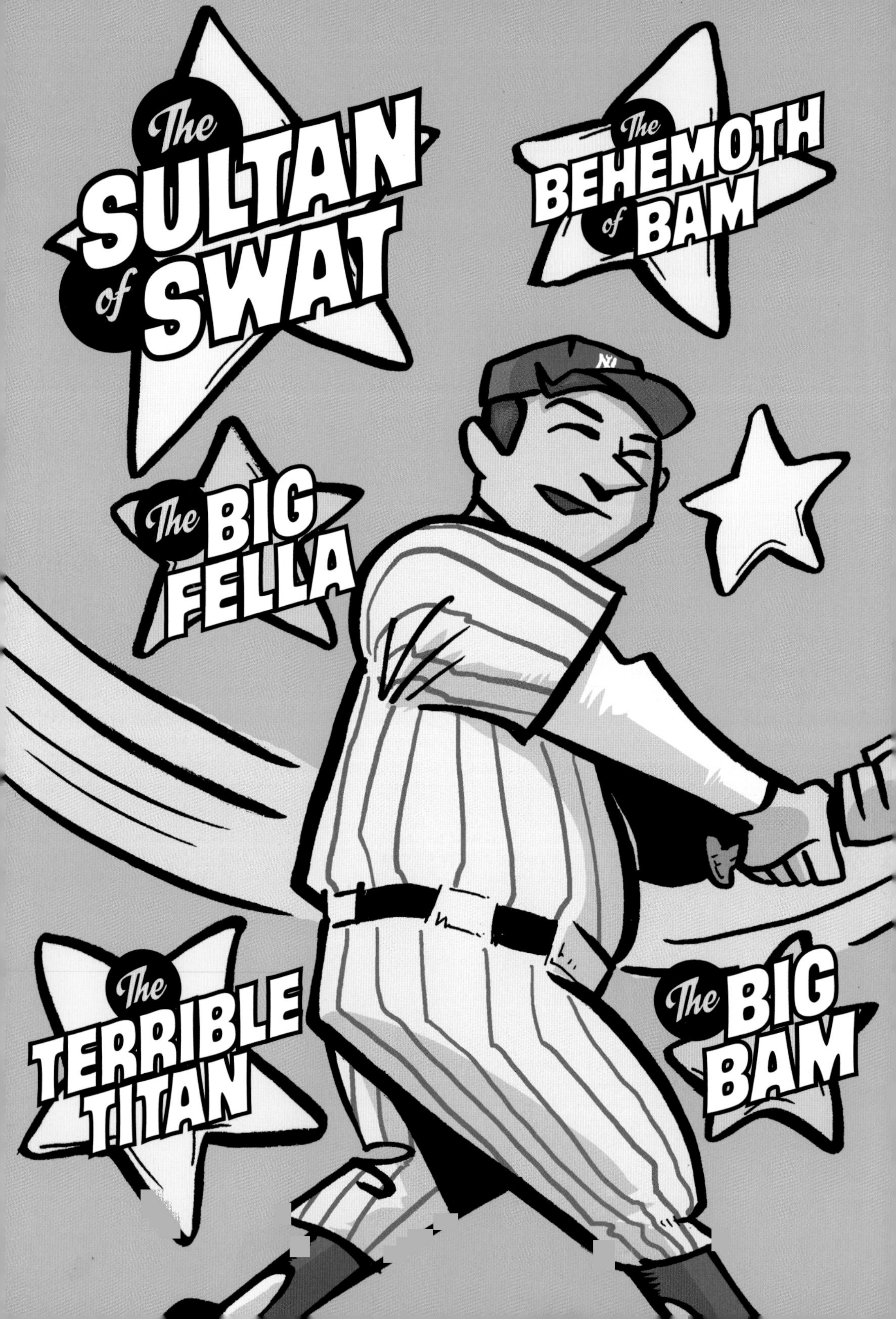
The SULTAN of SWAT
The BEHEMOTH of BAM
The BIG FELLA
The TERRIBLE TITAN
The BIG BAM

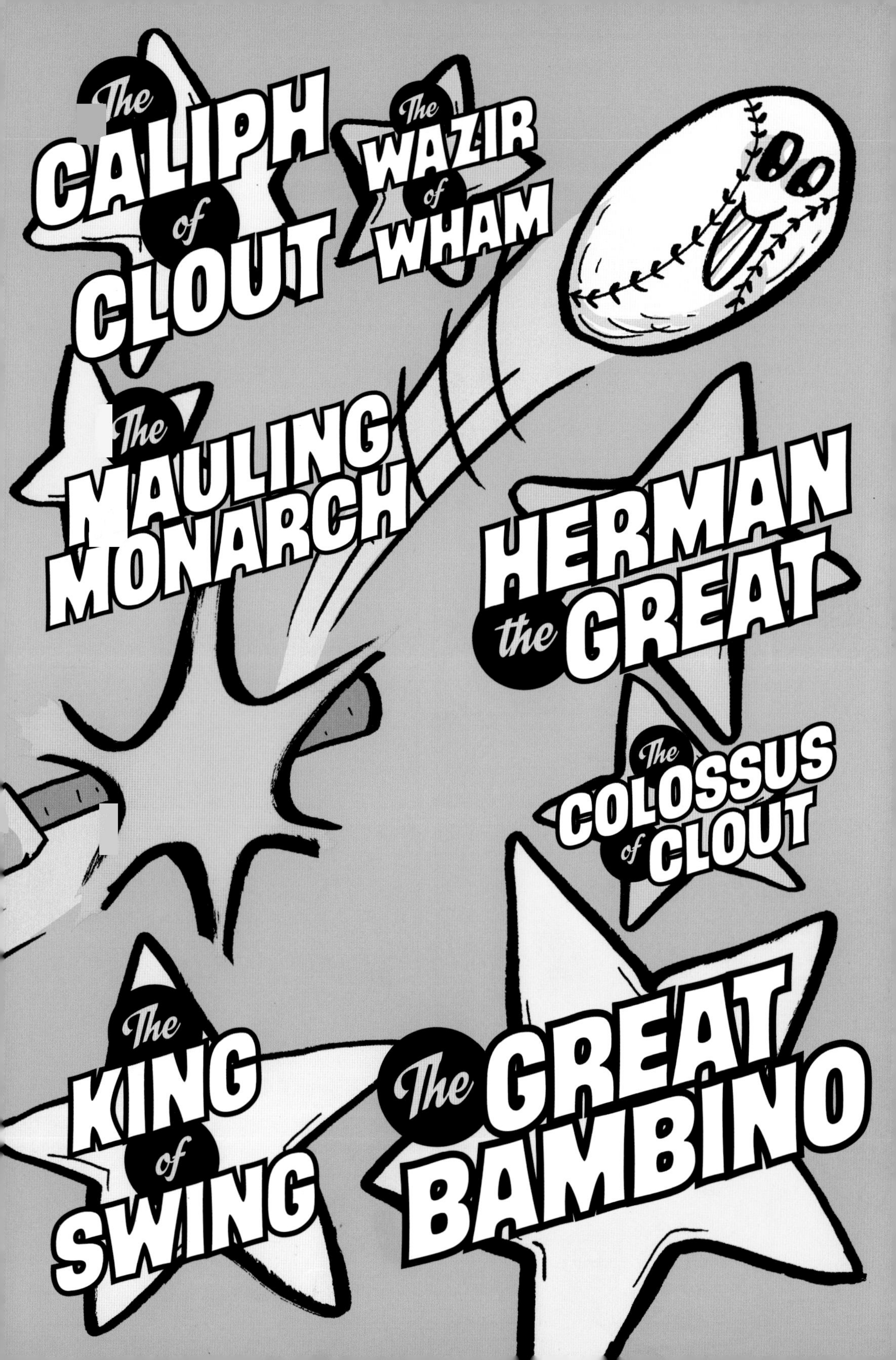
The Caliph of Clout
The Wazir of Wham
The Mauling Monarch
Herman the Great
The Colossus of Clout
The King of Swing
The Great Bambino

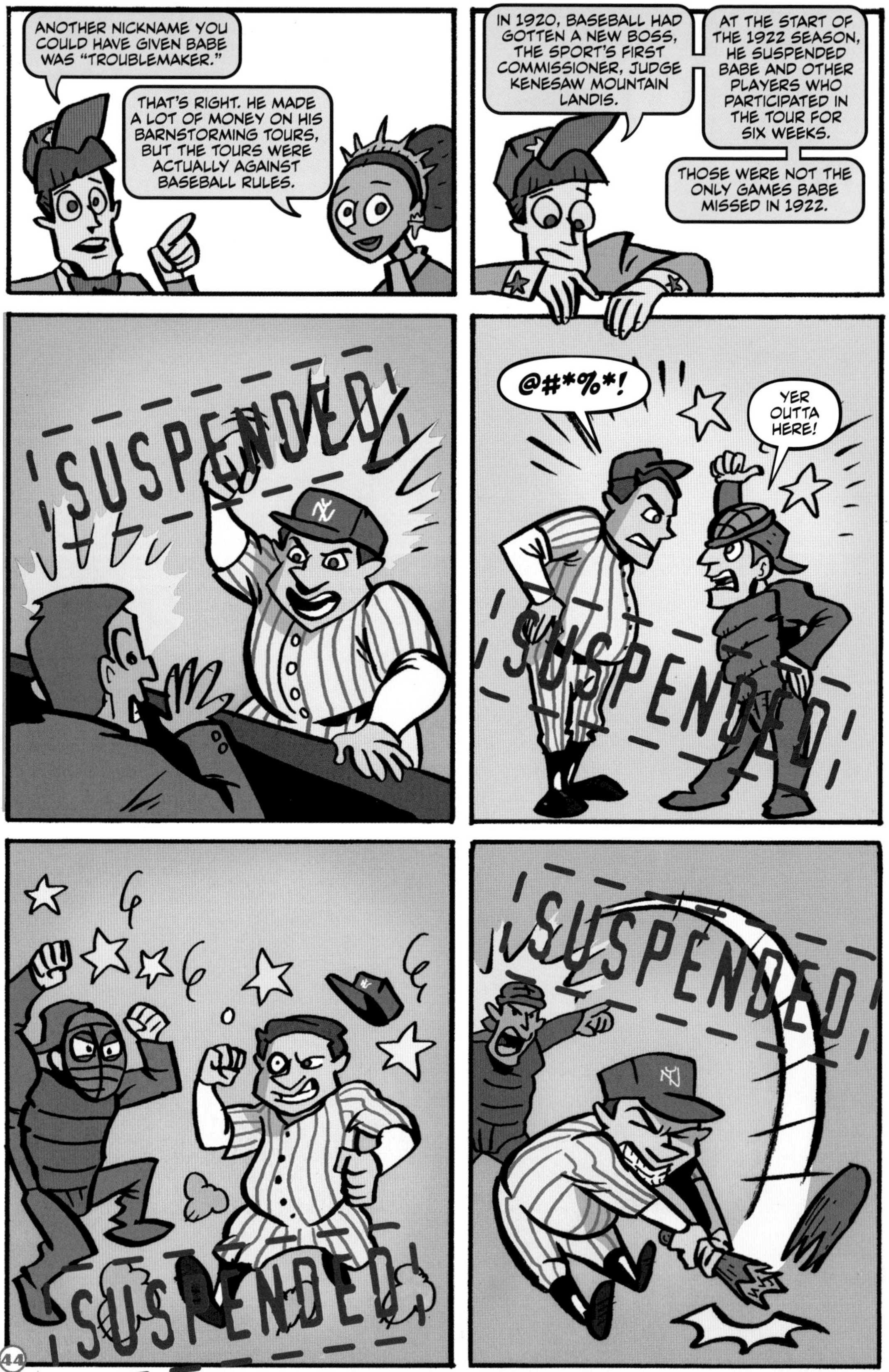
ANOTHER NICKNAME YOU COULD HAVE GIVEN BABE WAS "TROUBLEMAKER."
THAT'S RIGHT. HE MADE A LOT OF MONEY ON HIS BARNSTORMING TOURS, BUT THE TOURS WERE ACTUALLY AGAINST BASEBALL RULES.
IN 1920, BASEBALL HAD GOTTEN A NEW BOSS, THE SPORT'S FIRST COMMISSIONER, JUDGE KENESAW MOUNTAIN LANDIS.
AT THE START OF THE 1922 SEASON, HE SUSPENDED BABE AND OTHER PLAYERS WHO PARTICIPATED IN THE TOUR FOR SIX WEEKS.
THOSE WERE NOT THE ONLY GAMES BABE MISSED IN 1922.
SUSPENDED
@#*%*!
YER OUTTA HERE!
SUSPENDED
SUSPENDED
SUSPENDED

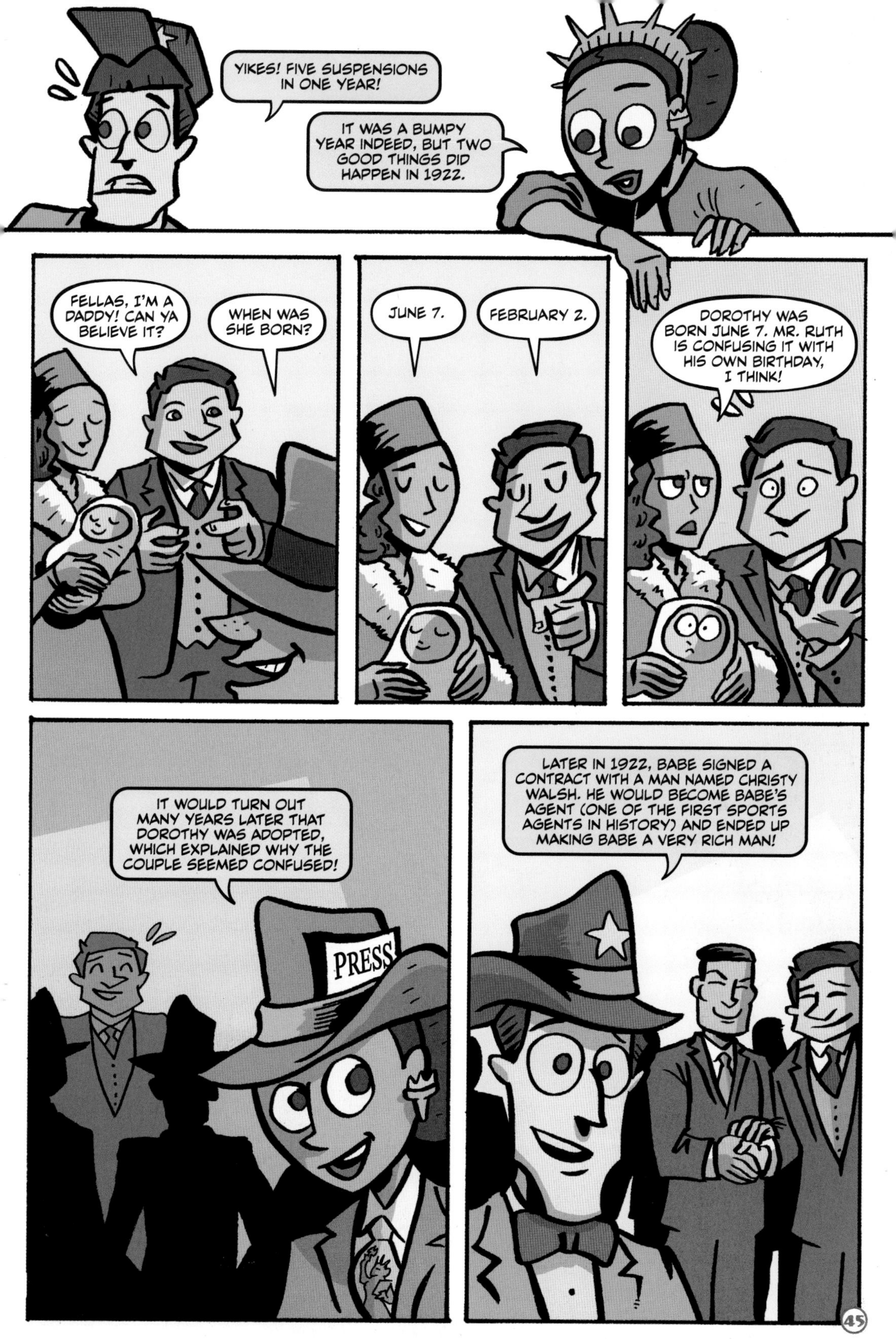

YIKES! FIVE SUSPENSIONS IN ONE YEAR!
IT WAS A BUMPY YEAR INDEED, BUT TWO GOOD THINGS DID HAPPEN IN 1922.
FELLAS, I'M A DADDY! CAN YA BELIEVE IT?
WHEN WAS SHE BORN?
JUNE 7.
FEBRUARY 2.
DOROTHY WAS BORN JUNE 7. MR. RUTH IS CONFUSING IT WITH HIS OWN BIRTHDAY, I THINK!
IT WOULD TURN OUT MANY YEARS LATER THAT DOROTHY WAS ADOPTED, WHICH EXPLAINED WHY THE COUPLE SEEMED CONFUSED!
PRESS
LATER IN 1922, BABE SIGNED A CONTRACT WITH A MAN NAMED CHRISTY WALSH. HE WOULD BECOME BABE'S AGENT (ONE OF THE FIRST SPORTS AGENTS IN HISTORY) AND ENDED UP MAKING BABE A VERY RICH MAN!

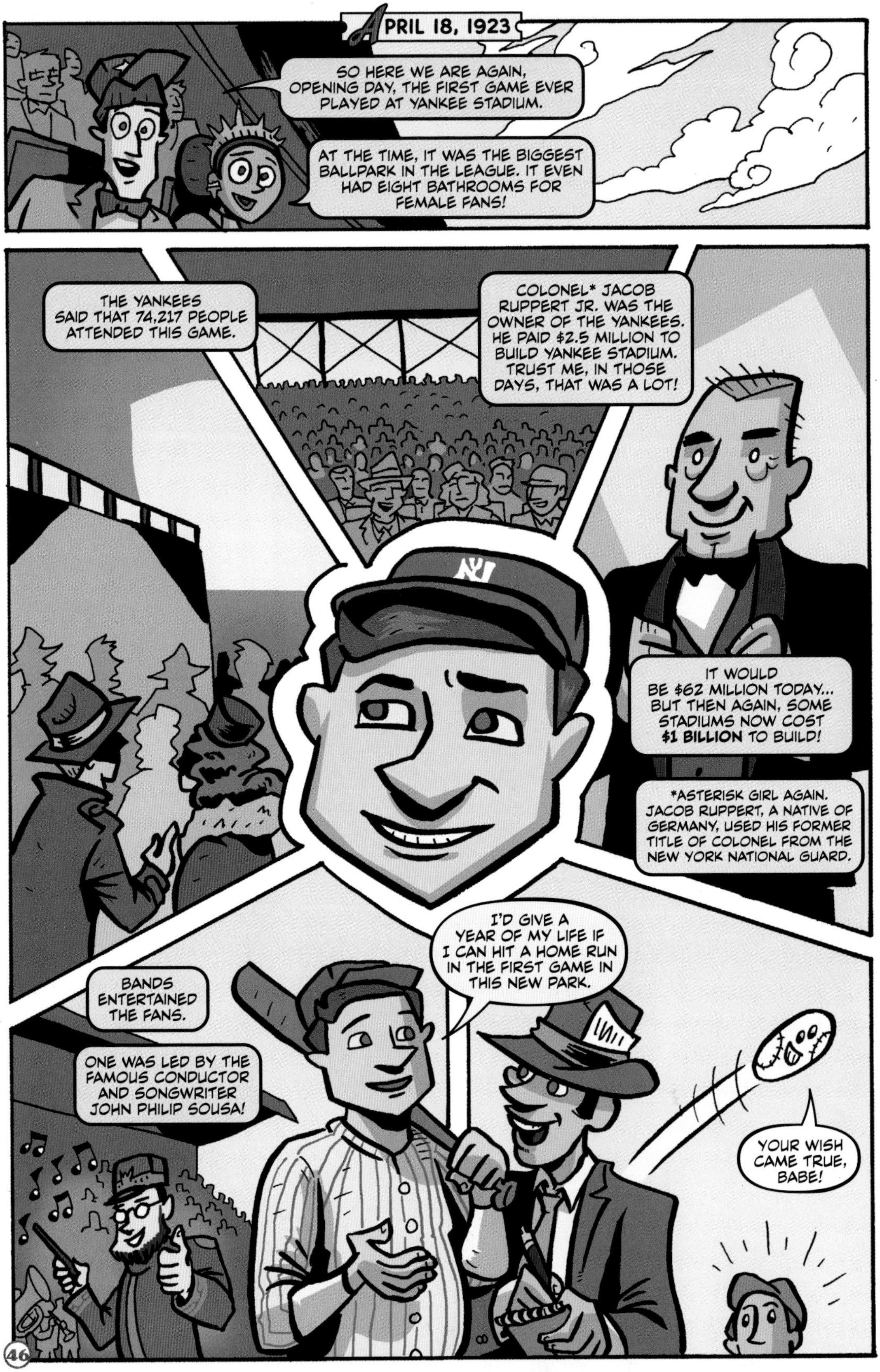
APRIL 18, 1923
SO HERE WE ARE AGAIN, OPENING DAY, THE FIRST GAME EVER PLAYED AT YANKEE STADIUM.
AT THE TIME, IT WAS THE BIGGEST BALLPARK IN THE LEAGUE. IT EVEN HAD EIGHT BATHROOMS FOR FEMALE FANS!
THE YANKEES SAID THAT 74,217 PEOPLE ATTENDED THIS GAME.
COLONEL* JACOB RUPPERT JR. WAS THE OWNER OF THE YANKEES. HE PAID $2.5 MILLION TO BUILD YANKEE STADIUM. TRUST ME, IN THOSE DAYS, THAT WAS A LOT!
IT WOULD BE $62 MILLION TODAY... BUT THEN AGAIN, SOME STADIUMS NOW COST **$1 BILLION** TO BUILD!
*ASTERISK GIRL AGAIN. JACOB RUPPERT, A NATIVE OF GERMANY, USED HIS FORMER TITLE OF COLONEL FROM THE NEW YORK NATIONAL GUARD.
BANDS ENTERTAINED THE FANS.
ONE WAS LED BY THE FAMOUS CONDUCTOR AND SONGWRITER JOHN PHILIP SOUSA!
I'D GIVE A YEAR OF MY LIFE IF I CAN HIT A HOME RUN IN THE FIRST GAME IN THIS NEW PARK.
YOUR WISH CAME TRUE, BABE!

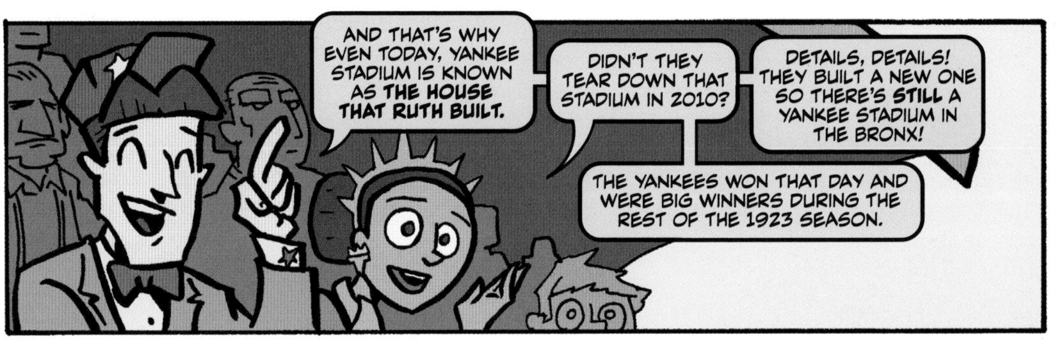
AND THAT'S WHY EVEN TODAY, YANKEE STADIUM IS KNOWN AS **THE HOUSE THAT RUTH BUILT.**
DIDN'T THEY TEAR DOWN THAT STADIUM IN 2010?
DETAILS, DETAILS! THEY BUILT A NEW ONE SO THERE'S **STILL** A YANKEE STADIUM IN THE BRONX!
THE YANKEES WON THAT DAY AND WERE BIG WINNERS DURING THE REST OF THE 1923 SEASON.

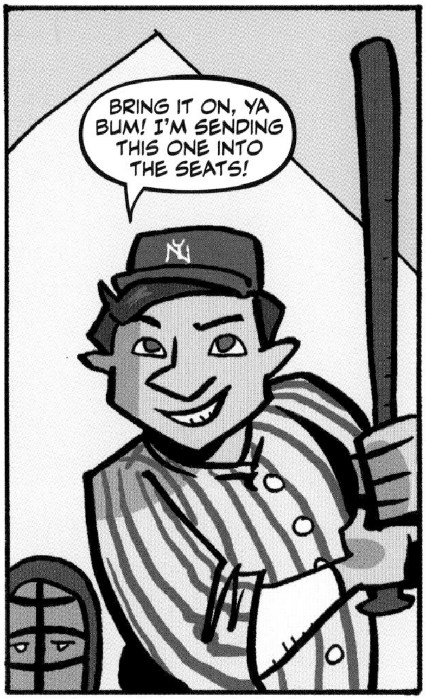
BRING IT ON, YA BUM! I'M SENDING THIS ONE INTO THE SEATS!

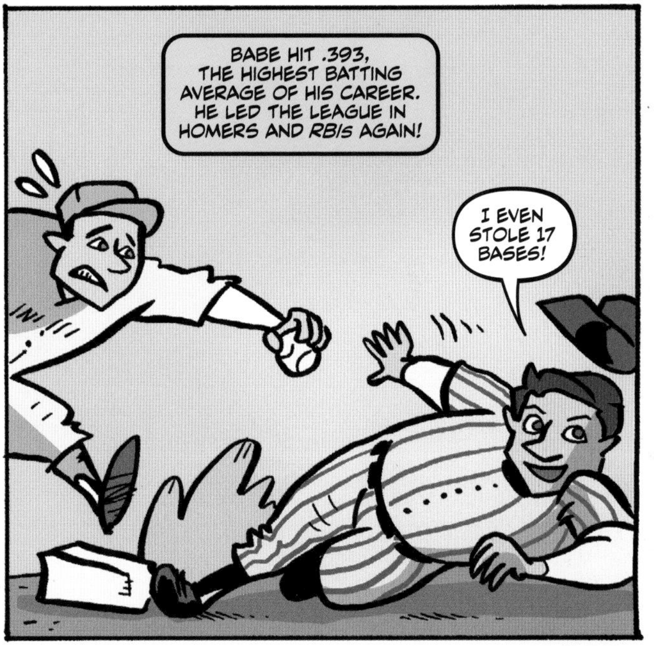
BABE HIT .393, THE HIGHEST BATTING AVERAGE OF HIS CAREER. HE LED THE LEAGUE IN HOMERS AND *RBIs* AGAIN!
I EVEN STOLE 17 BASES!

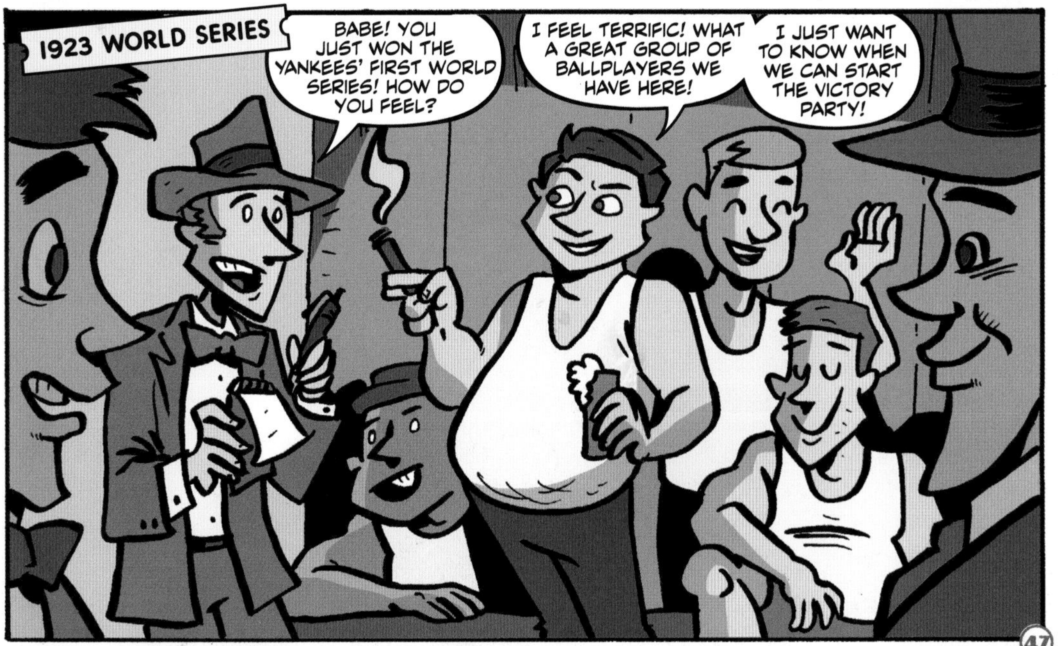
1923 WORLD SERIES
BABE! YOU JUST WON THE YANKEES' FIRST WORLD SERIES! HOW DO YOU FEEL?
I FEEL TERRIFIC! WHAT A GREAT GROUP OF BALLPLAYERS WE HAVE HERE!
I JUST WANT TO KNOW WHEN WE CAN START THE VICTORY PARTY!

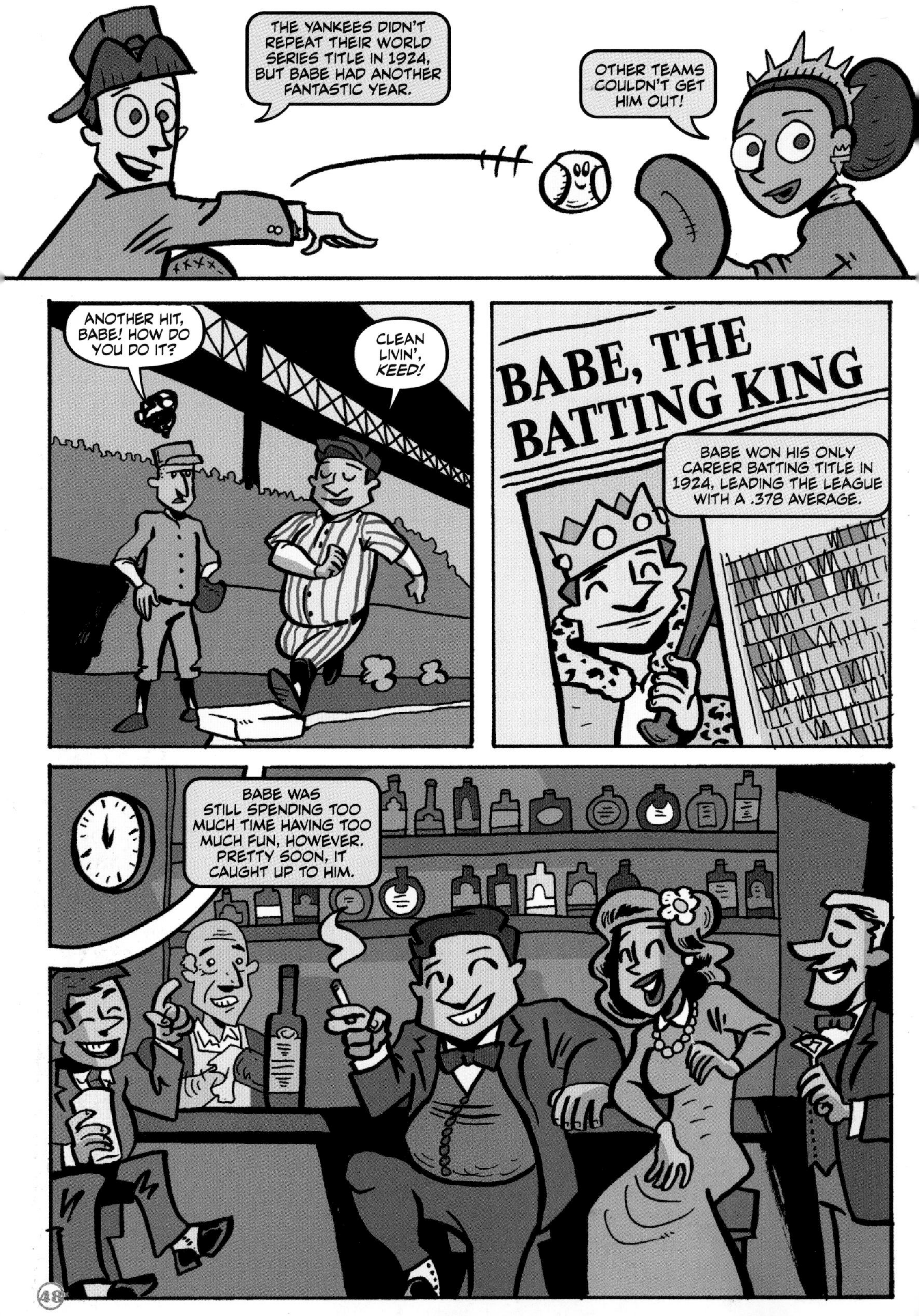
THE YANKEES DIDN'T REPEAT THEIR WORLD SERIES TITLE IN 1924, BUT BABE HAD ANOTHER FANTASTIC YEAR.
OTHER TEAMS COULDN'T GET HIM OUT!
ANOTHER HIT, BABE! HOW DO YOU DO IT?
CLEAN LIVIN', KEED!
BABE, THE BATTING KING
BABE WON HIS ONLY CAREER BATTING TITLE IN 1924, LEADING THE LEAGUE WITH A .378 AVERAGE.
BABE WAS STILL SPENDING TOO MUCH TIME HAVING TOO MUCH FUN, HOWEVER. PRETTY SOON, IT CAUGHT UP TO HIM.

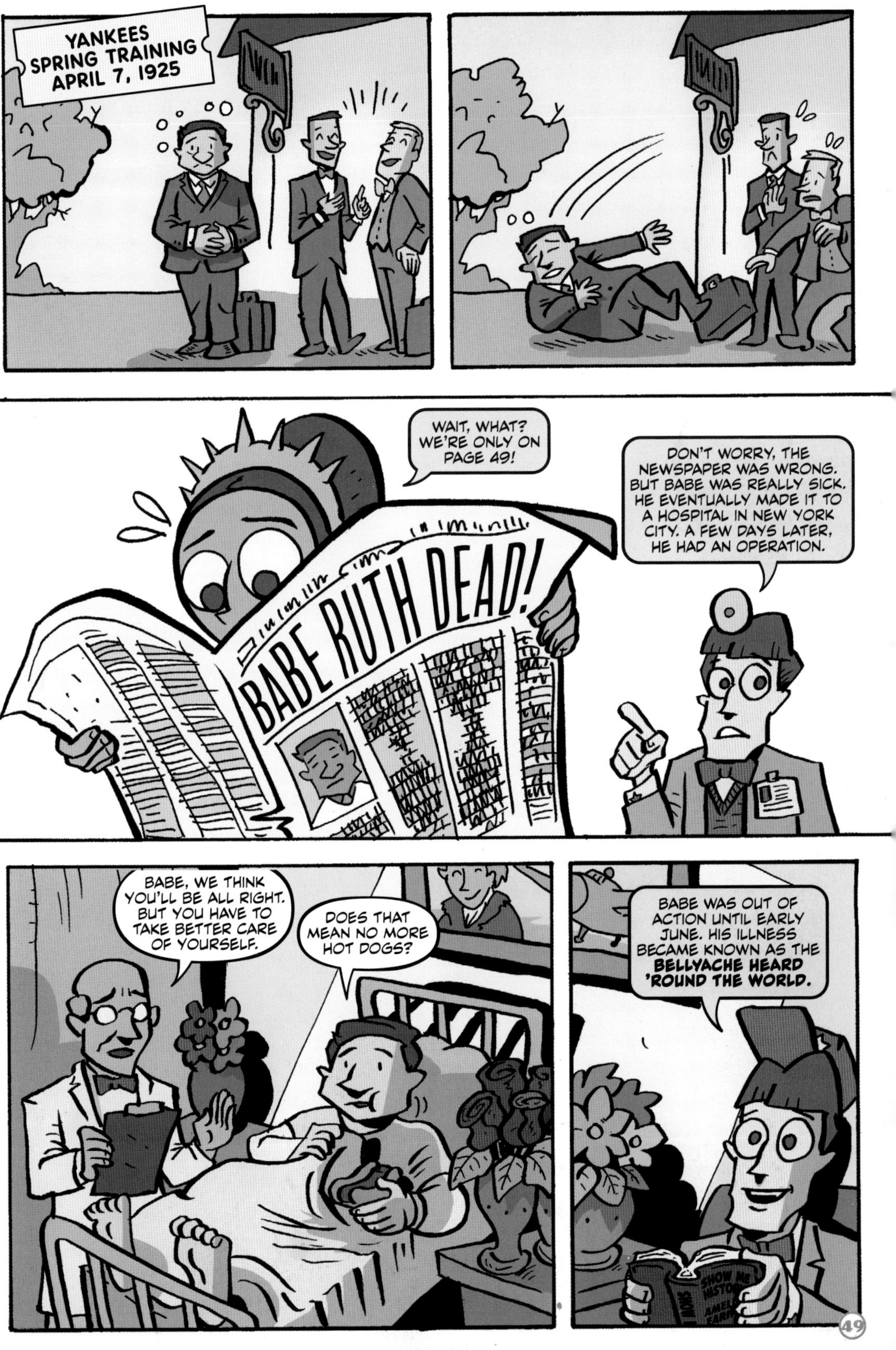
YANKEES SPRING TRAINING APRIL 7, 1925
WAIT, WHAT? WE'RE ONLY ON PAGE 49!
BABE RUTH DEAD!
DON'T WORRY, THE NEWSPAPER WAS WRONG. BUT BABE WAS REALLY SICK. HE EVENTUALLY MADE IT TO A HOSPITAL IN NEW YORK CITY. A FEW DAYS LATER, HE HAD AN OPERATION.
BABE, WE THINK YOU'LL BE ALL RIGHT. BUT YOU HAVE TO TAKE BETTER CARE OF YOURSELF.
DOES THAT MEAN NO MORE HOT DOGS?
BABE WAS OUT OF ACTION UNTIL EARLY JUNE. HIS ILLNESS BECAME KNOWN AS THE **BELLYACHE HEARD 'ROUND THE WORLD.**

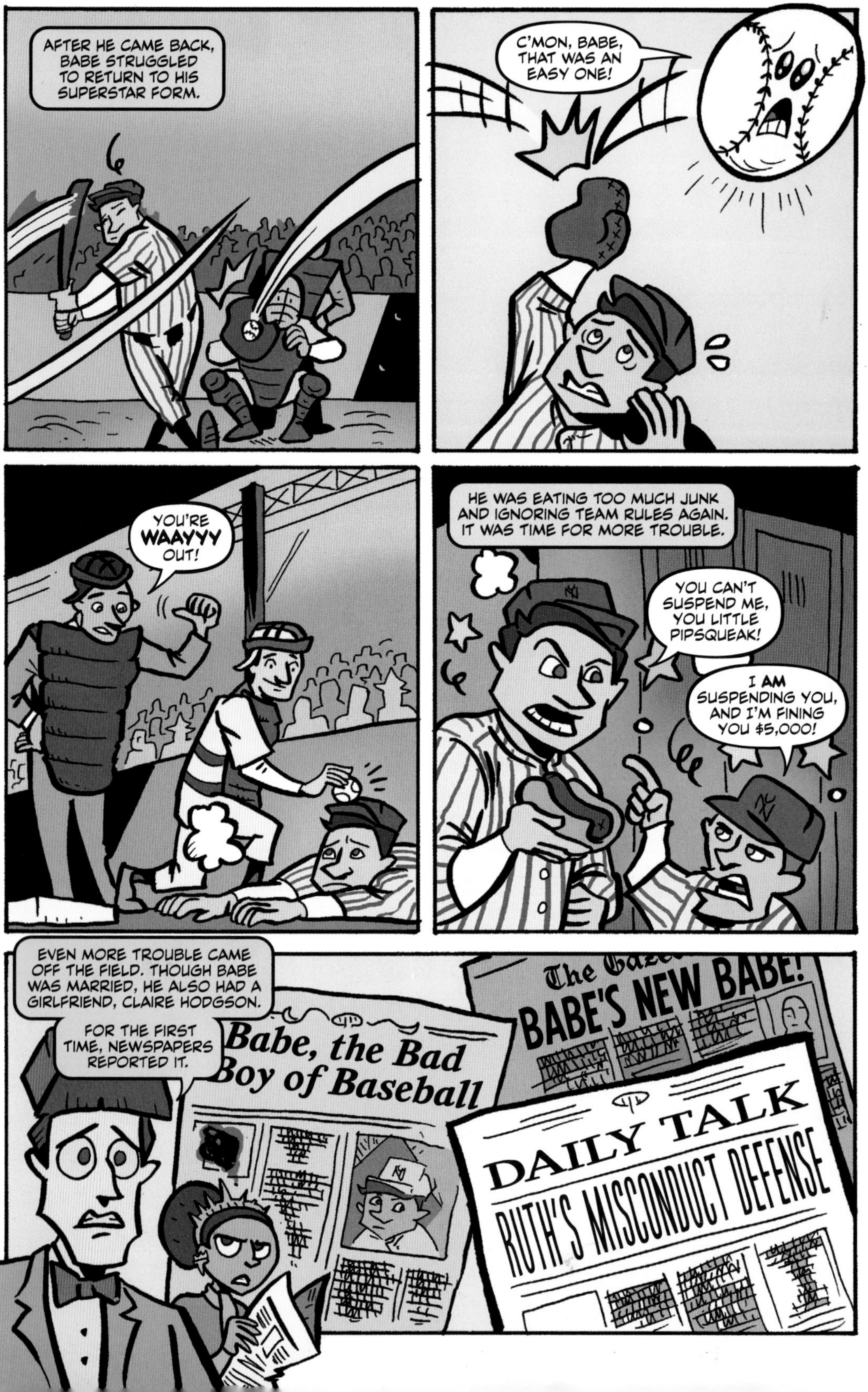

AFTER HE CAME BACK, BABE STRUGGLED TO RETURN TO HIS SUPERSTAR FORM.
C'MON, BABE, THAT WAS AN EASY ONE!
YOU'RE WAAYYY OUT!
HE WAS EATING TOO MUCH JUNK AND IGNORING TEAM RULES AGAIN. IT WAS TIME FOR MORE TROUBLE.
YOU CAN'T SUSPEND ME, YOU LITTLE PIPSQUEAK!
I AM SUSPENDING YOU, AND I'M FINING YOU $5,000!
EVEN MORE TROUBLE CAME OFF THE FIELD. THOUGH BABE WAS MARRIED, HE ALSO HAD A GIRLFRIEND, CLAIRE HODGSON.
FOR THE FIRST TIME, NEWSPAPERS REPORTED IT.
Babe, the Bad Boy of Baseball
BABE'S NEW BABE!
DAILY TALK
RUTH'S MISCONDUCT DEFENSE

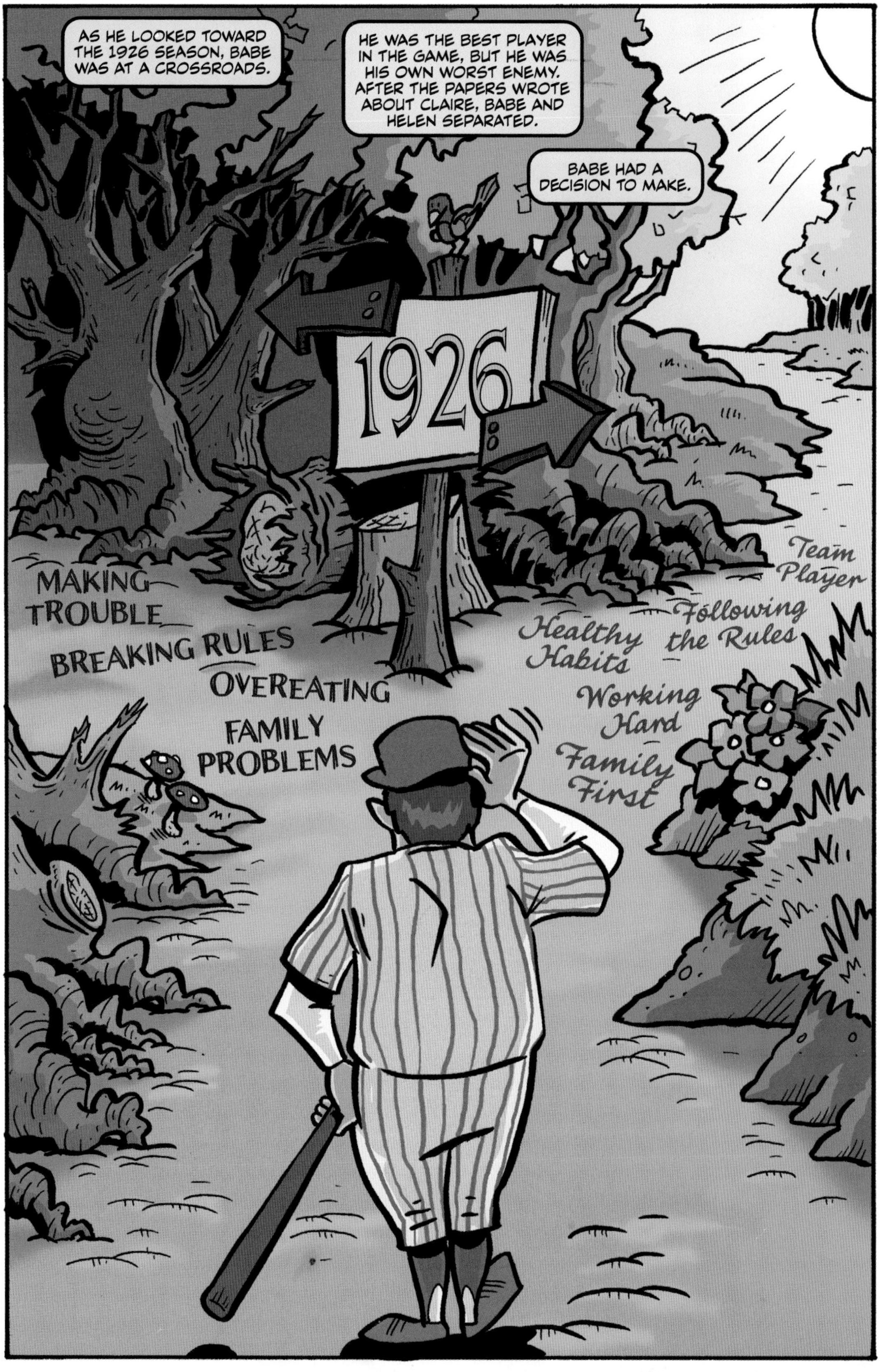
AS HE LOOKED TOWARD THE 1926 SEASON, BABE WAS AT A CROSSROADS.
HE WAS THE BEST PLAYER IN THE GAME, BUT HE WAS HIS OWN WORST ENEMY. AFTER THE PAPERS WROTE ABOUT CLAIRE, BABE AND HELEN SEPARATED.
BABE HAD A DECISION TO MAKE.
1926
MAKING TROUBLE
BREAKING RULES
OVEREATING
FAMILY PROBLEMS
Team Player
Following the Rules
Healthy Habits
Working Hard
Family First

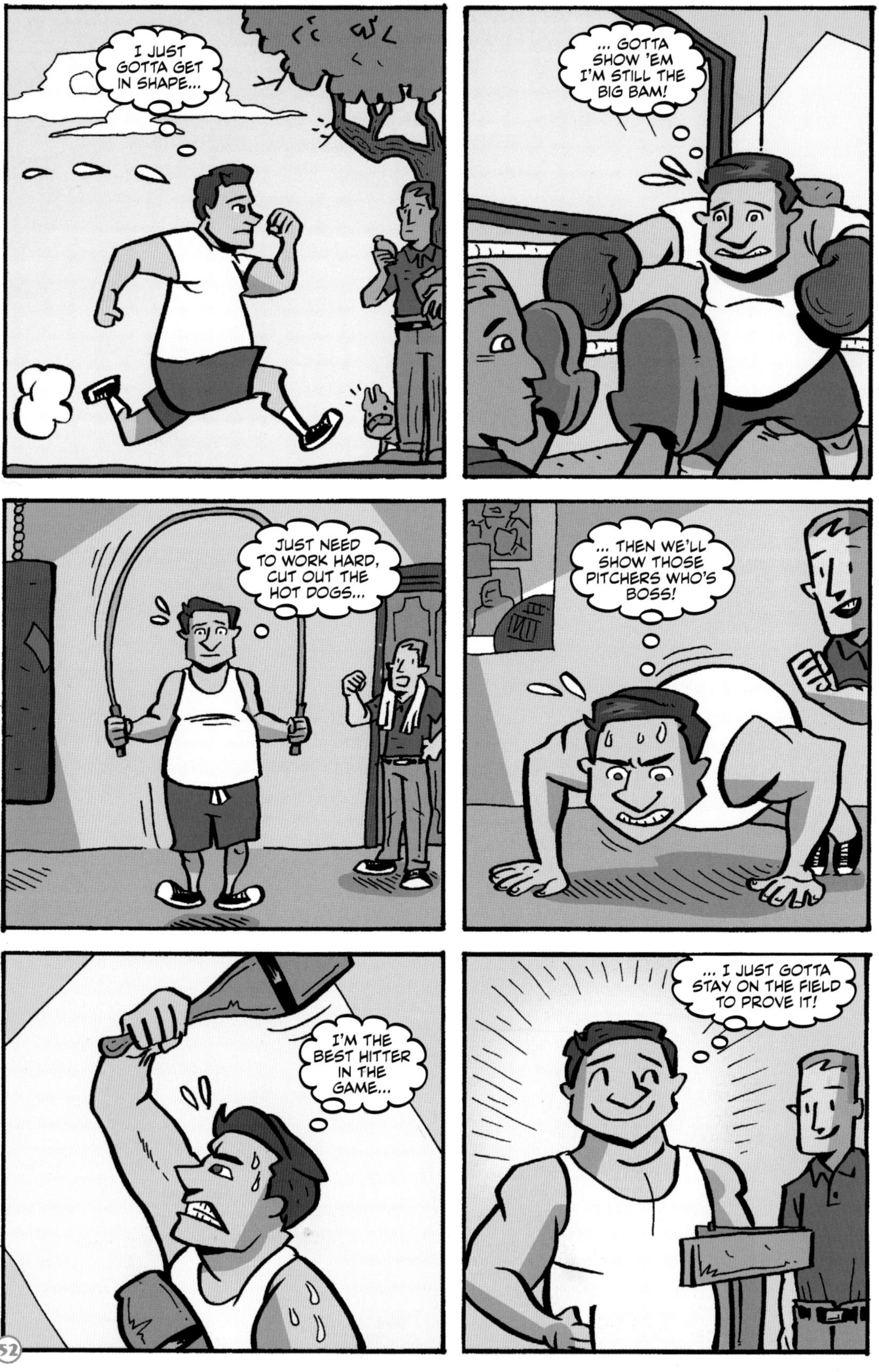
I JUST GOTTA GET IN SHAPE...
... GOTTA SHOW 'EM I'M STILL THE BIG BAM!
JUST NEED TO WORK HARD, CUT OUT THE HOT DOGS...
... THEN WE'LL SHOW THOSE PITCHERS WHO'S BOSS!
I'M THE BEST HITTER IN THE GAME...
... I JUST GOTTA STAY ON THE FIELD TO PROVE IT!

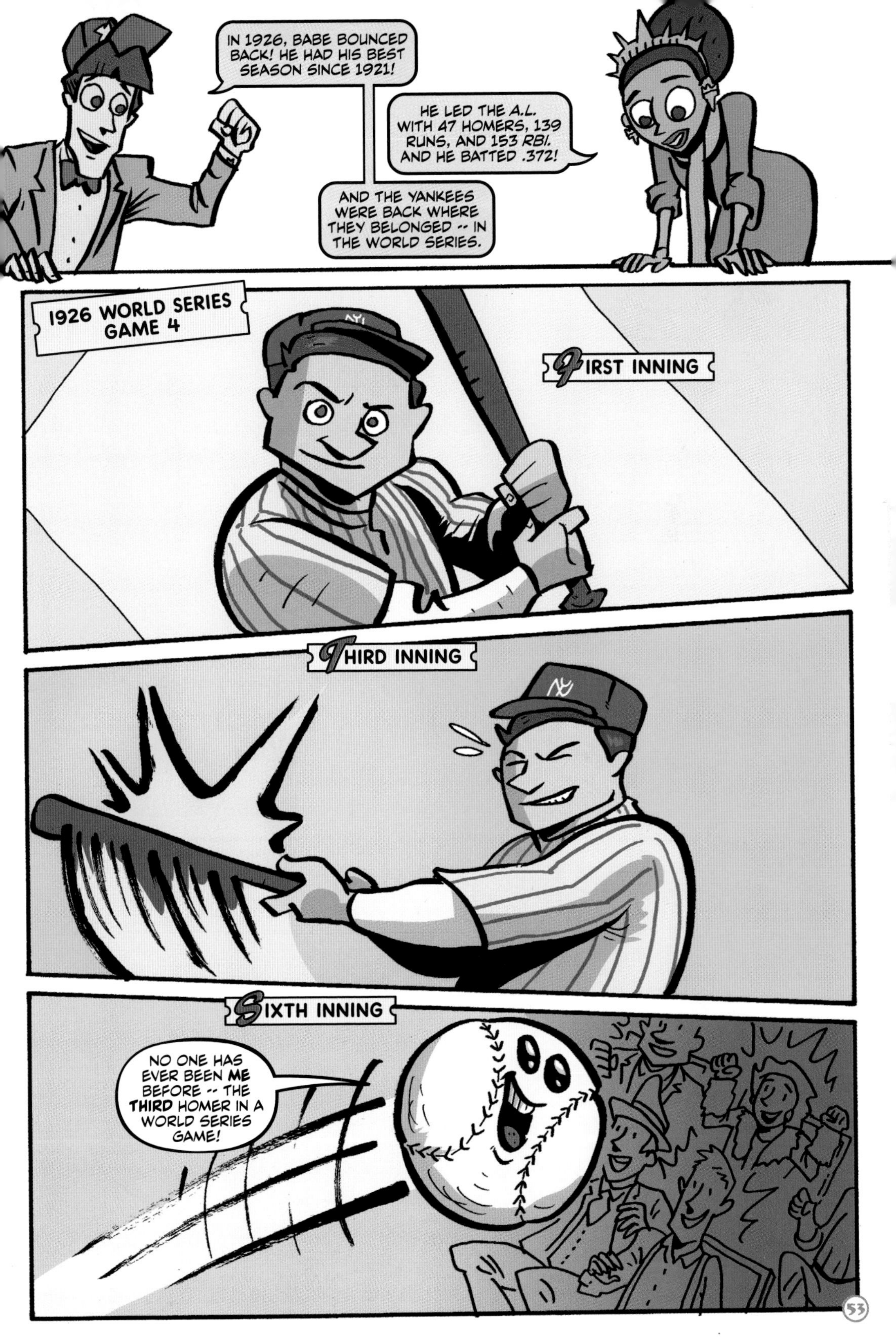

IN 1926, BABE BOUNCED BACK! HE HAD HIS BEST SEASON SINCE 1921!
HE LED THE A.L. WITH 47 HOMERS, 139 RUNS, AND 153 *RBI*. AND HE BATTED .372!
AND THE YANKEES WERE BACK WHERE THEY BELONGED -- IN THE WORLD SERIES.
1926 WORLD SERIES GAME 4
FIRST INNING
THIRD INNING
SIXTH INNING
NO ONE HAS EVER BEEN **ME** BEFORE -- THE **THIRD** HOMER IN A WORLD SERIES GAME!

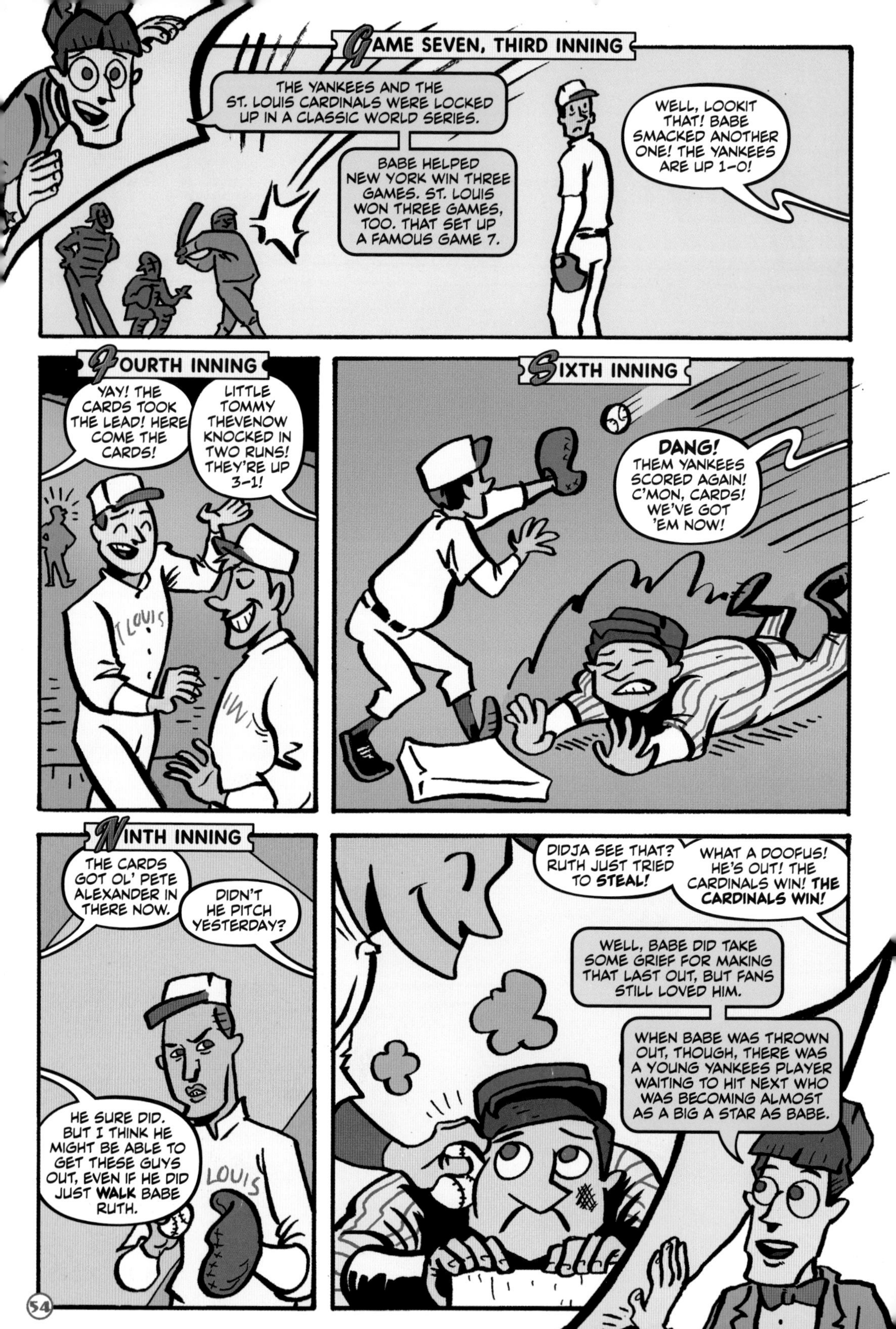
GAME SEVEN, THIRD INNING
THE YANKEES AND THE ST. LOUIS CARDINALS WERE LOCKED UP IN A CLASSIC WORLD SERIES.
BABE HELPED NEW YORK WIN THREE GAMES. ST. LOUIS WON THREE GAMES, TOO. THAT SET UP A FAMOUS GAME 7.
WELL, LOOKIT THAT! BABE SMACKED ANOTHER ONE! THE YANKEES ARE UP 1–0!
FOURTH INNING
YAY! THE CARDS TOOK THE LEAD! HERE COME THE CARDS!
LITTLE TOMMY THEVENOW KNOCKED IN TWO RUNS! THEY'RE UP 3–1!
SIXTH INNING
DANG! THEM YANKEES SCORED AGAIN! C'MON, CARDS! WE'VE GOT 'EM NOW!
NINTH INNING
THE CARDS GOT OL' PETE ALEXANDER IN THERE NOW.
DIDN'T HE PITCH YESTERDAY?
HE SURE DID. BUT I THINK HE MIGHT BE ABLE TO GET THESE GUYS OUT, EVEN IF HE DID JUST WALK BABE RUTH.
DIDJA SEE THAT? RUTH JUST TRIED TO STEAL!
WHAT A DOOFUS! HE'S OUT! THE CARDINALS WIN! THE CARDINALS WIN!
WELL, BABE DID TAKE SOME GRIEF FOR MAKING THAT LAST OUT, BUT FANS STILL LOVED HIM.
WHEN BABE WAS THROWN OUT, THOUGH, THERE WAS A YOUNG YANKEES PLAYER WAITING TO HIT NEXT WHO WAS BECOMING ALMOST AS A BIG A STAR AS BABE.

Meet LOU GEHRIG!

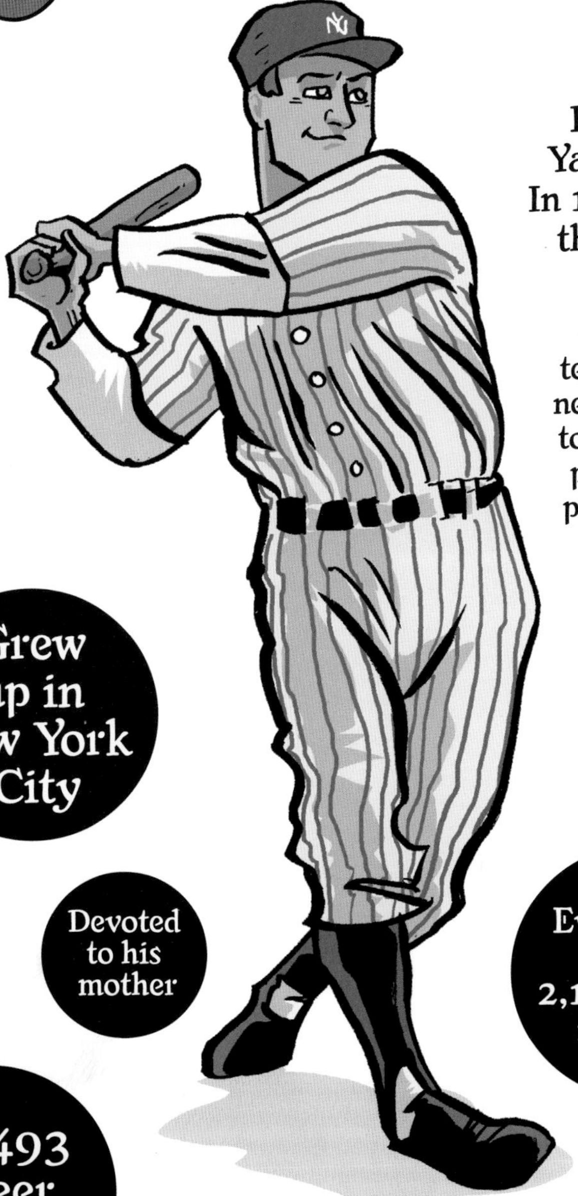

NY

Lou joined the Yankees in 1923. In 1925, he became the regular first baseman.

Gehrig and Ruth teamed up over the next several seasons to become the most powerful one-two punch baseball has ever seen.

- Grew up in New York City
- Played at Columbia University
- Devoted to his mother
- Eventually played 2,130 games in a row
- Hit 493 career homers
- Nickname: "The Iron Horse"

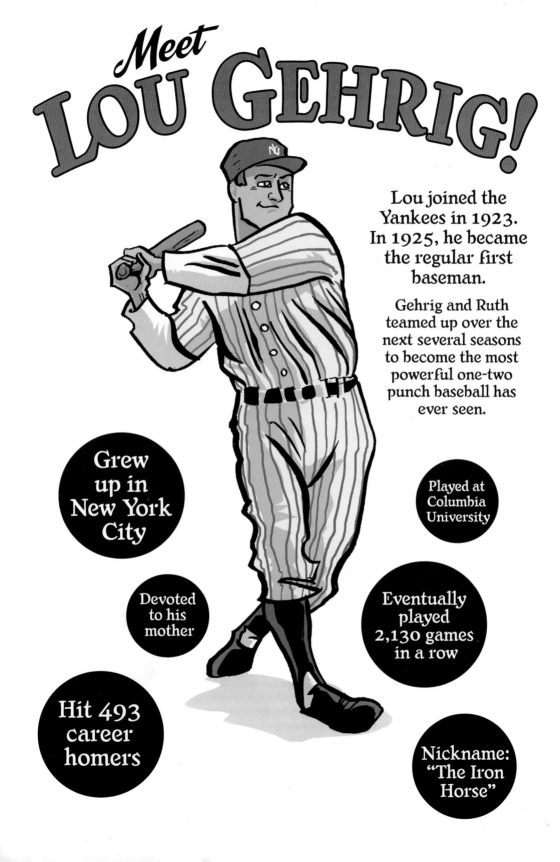

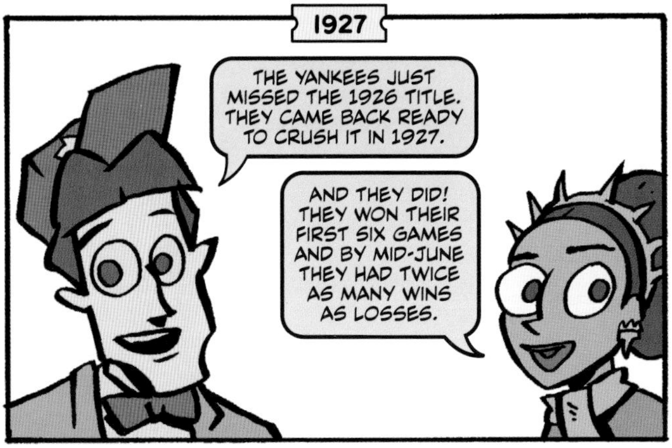
1927
THE YANKEES JUST MISSED THE 1926 TITLE. THEY CAME BACK READY TO CRUSH IT IN 1927.
AND THEY DID! THEY WON THEIR FIRST SIX GAMES AND BY MID-JUNE THEY HAD TWICE AS MANY WINS AS LOSSES.

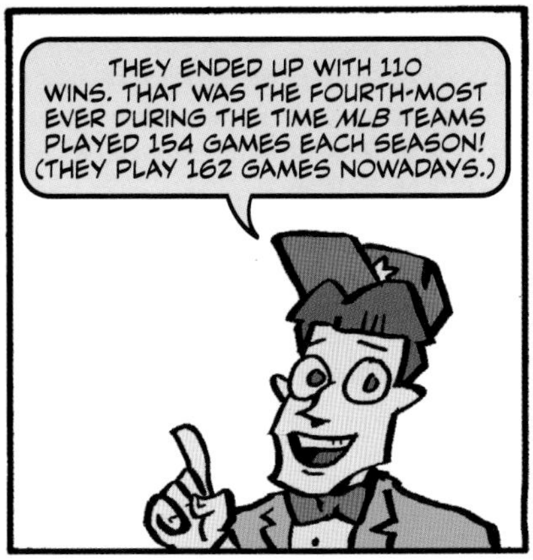
THEY ENDED UP WITH 110 WINS. THAT WAS THE FOURTH-MOST EVER DURING THE TIME *MLB* TEAMS PLAYED 154 GAMES EACH SEASON! (THEY PLAY 162 GAMES NOWADAYS.)

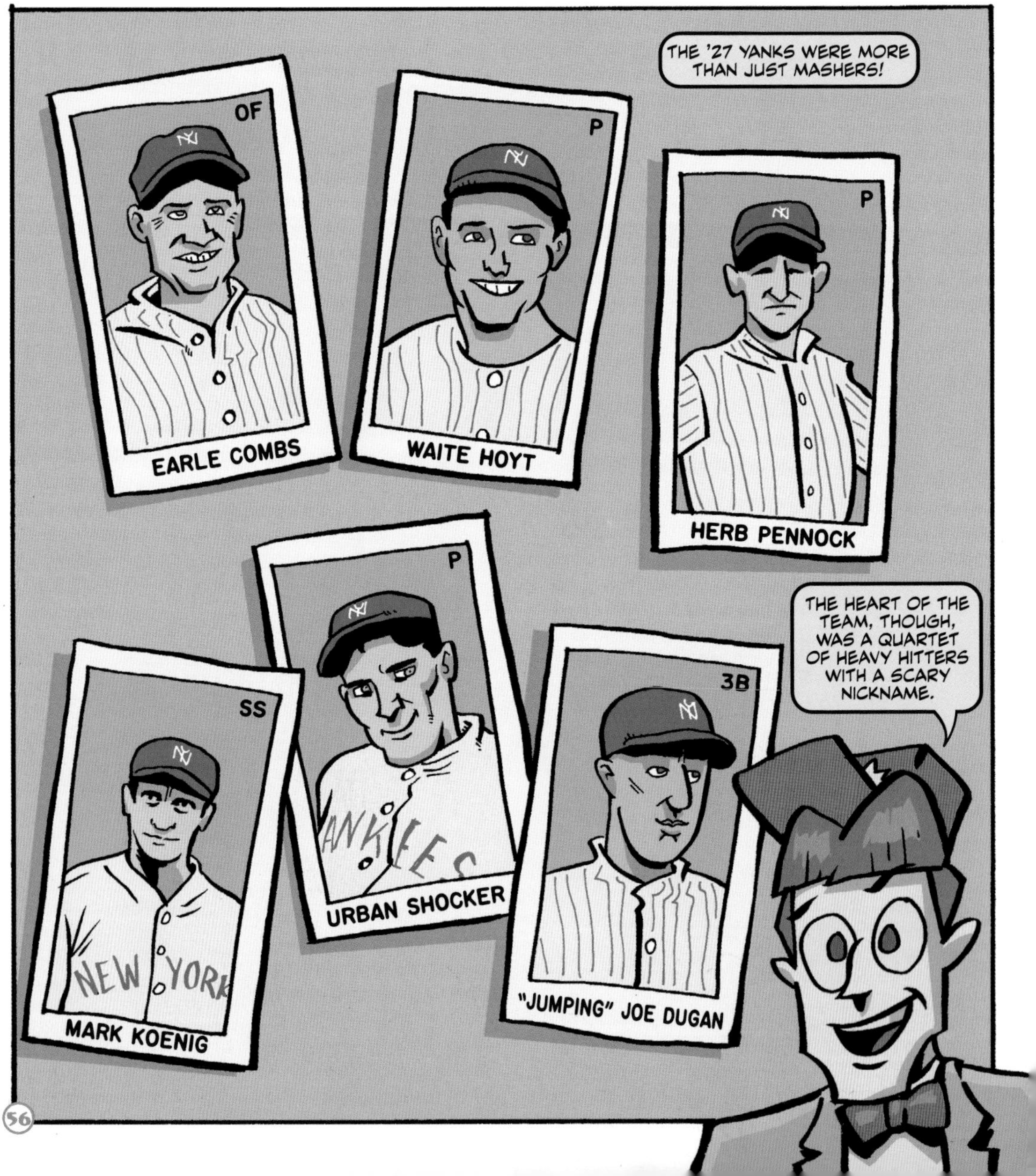
THE '27 YANKS WERE MORE THAN JUST MASHERS!
OF
EARLE COMBS
P
WAITE HOYT
P
HERB PENNOCK
P
URBAN SHOCKER
SS
MARK KOENIG
3B
"JUMPING" JOE DUGAN
THE HEART OF THE TEAM, THOUGH, WAS A QUARTET OF HEAVY HITTERS WITH A SCARY NICKNAME.

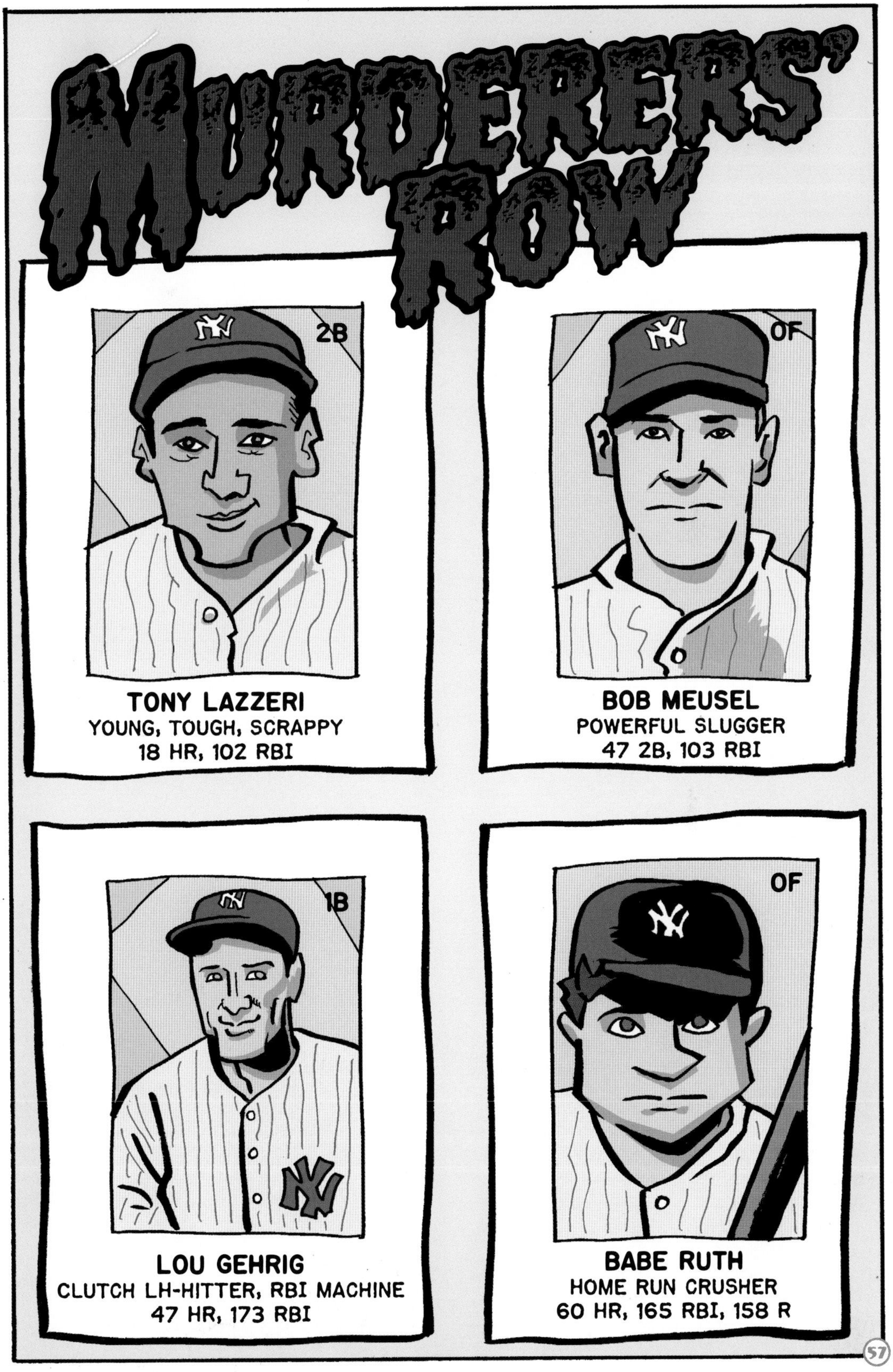

MURDERERS' ROW
2B
TONY LAZZERI
YOUNG, TOUGH, SCRAPPY
18 HR, 102 RBI
OF
BOB MEUSEL
POWERFUL SLUGGER
47 2B, 103 RBI
1B
LOU GEHRIG
CLUTCH LH-HITTER, RBI MACHINE
47 HR, 173 RBI
OF
BABE RUTH
HOME RUN CRUSHER
60 HR, 165 RBI, 158 R

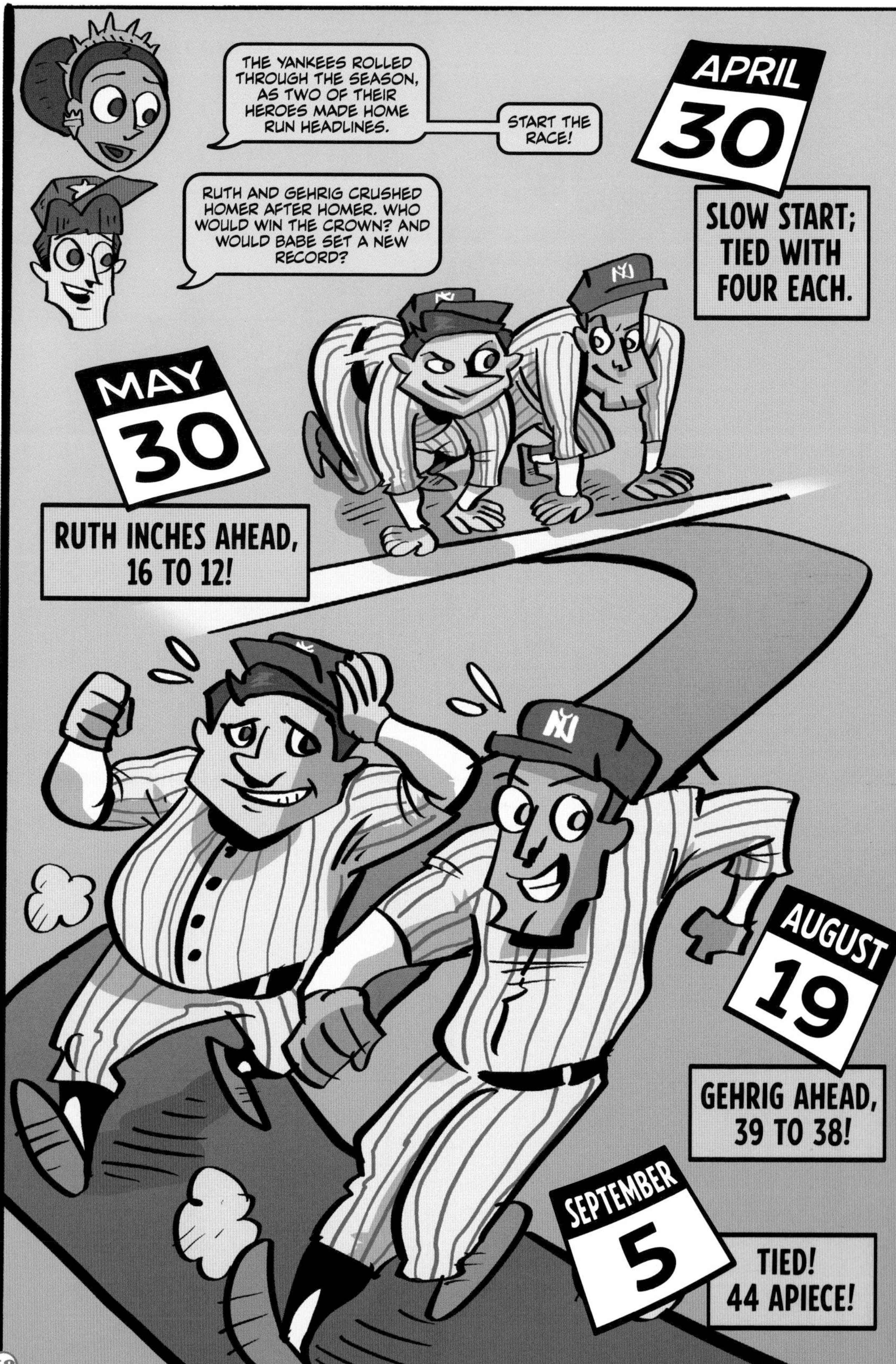
THE YANKEES ROLLED THROUGH THE SEASON, AS TWO OF THEIR HEROES MADE HOME RUN HEADLINES.
START THE RACE!
RUTH AND GEHRIG CRUSHED HOMER AFTER HOMER. WHO WOULD WIN THE CROWN? AND WOULD BABE SET A NEW RECORD?
APRIL 30
SLOW START; TIED WITH FOUR EACH.
MAY 30
RUTH INCHES AHEAD, 16 TO 12!
AUGUST 19
GEHRIG AHEAD, 39 TO 38!
SEPTEMBER 5
TIED! 44 APIECE!

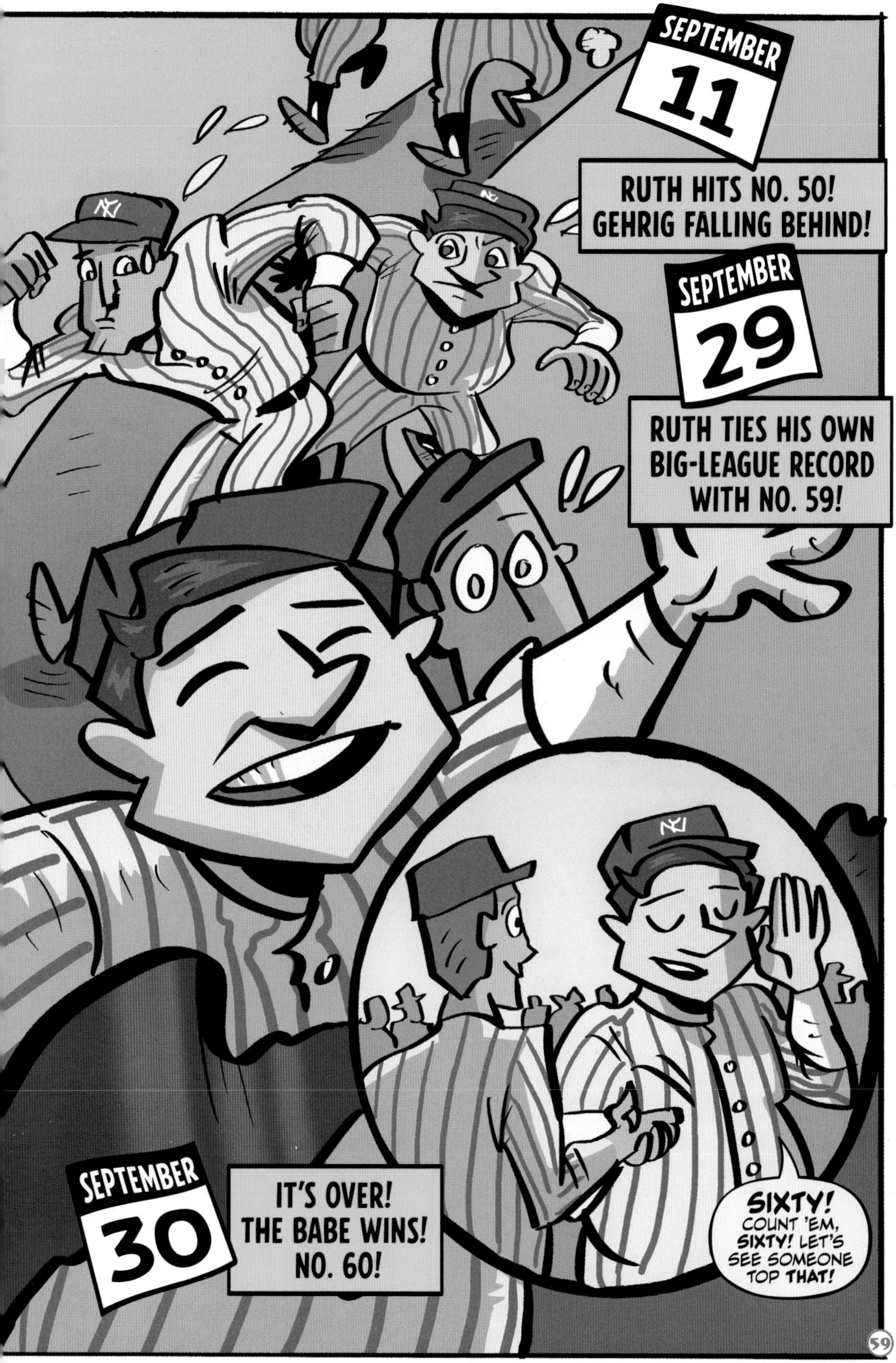

SEPTEMBER 11
RUTH HITS NO. 50! GEHRIG FALLING BEHIND!
SEPTEMBER 29
RUTH TIES HIS OWN BIG-LEAGUE RECORD WITH NO. 59!
SEPTEMBER 30
IT'S OVER! THE BABE WINS! NO. 60!
SIXTY! COUNT 'EM, SIXTY! LET'S SEE SOMEONE TOP THAT!

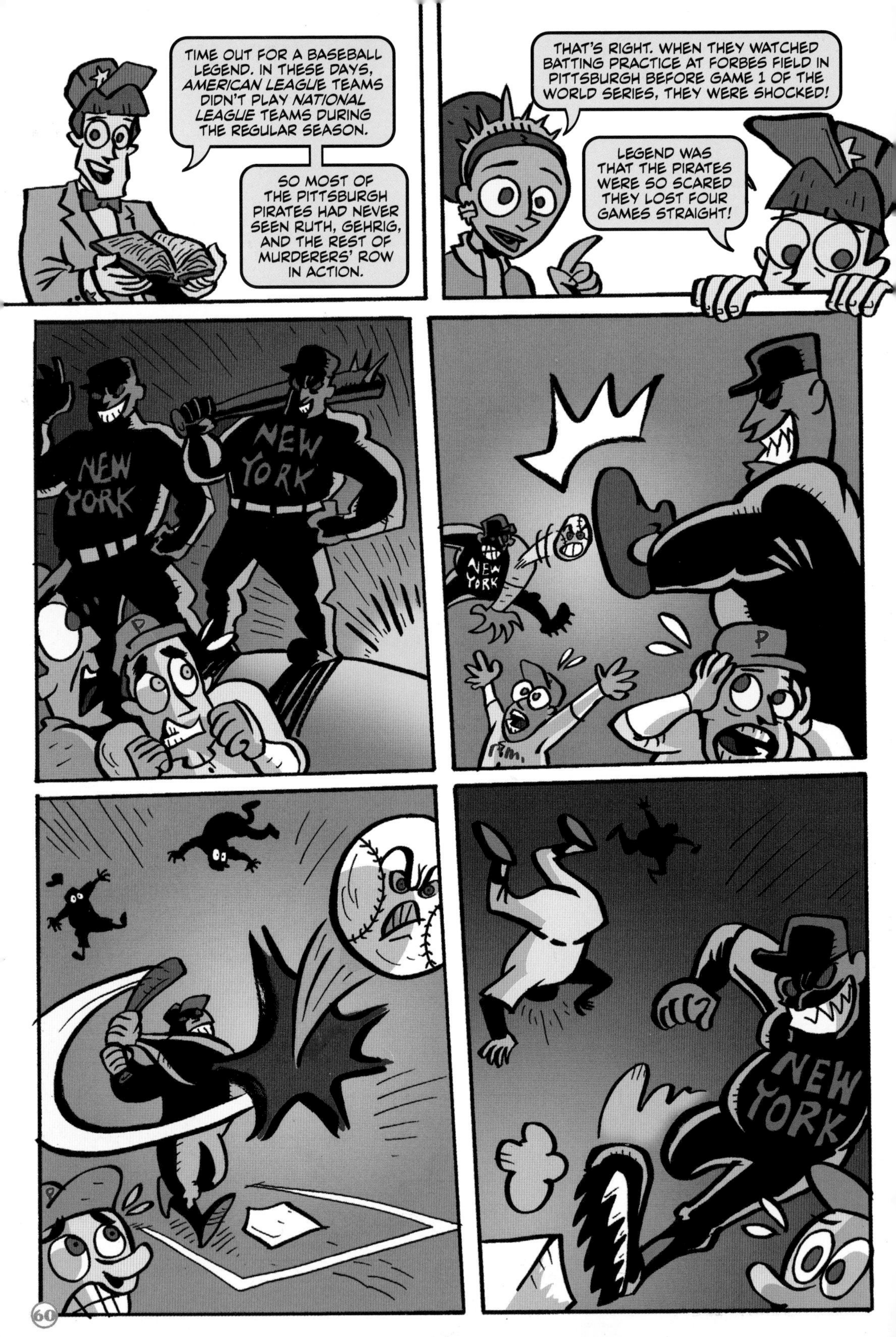
TIME OUT FOR A BASEBALL LEGEND. IN THESE DAYS, *AMERICAN LEAGUE* TEAMS DIDN'T PLAY *NATIONAL LEAGUE* TEAMS DURING THE REGULAR SEASON.
SO MOST OF THE PITTSBURGH PIRATES HAD NEVER SEEN RUTH, GEHRIG, AND THE REST OF MURDERERS' ROW IN ACTION.
THAT'S RIGHT. WHEN THEY WATCHED BATTING PRACTICE AT FORBES FIELD IN PITTSBURGH BEFORE GAME 1 OF THE WORLD SERIES, THEY WERE SHOCKED!
LEGEND WAS THAT THE PIRATES WERE SO SCARED THEY LOST FOUR GAMES STRAIGHT!
NEW YORK
NEW YORK
NEW YORK
NEW YORK

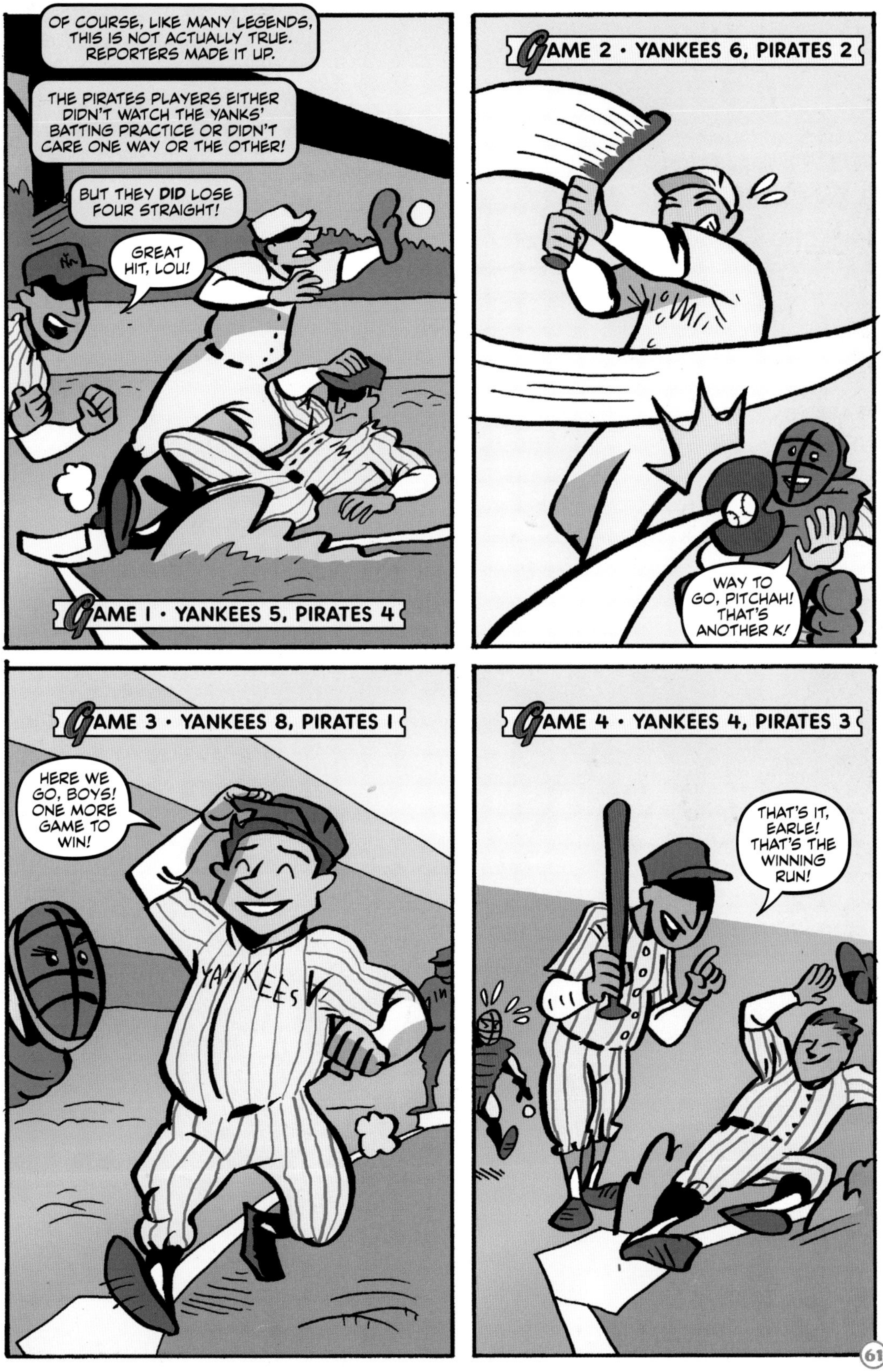

OF COURSE, LIKE MANY LEGENDS, THIS IS NOT ACTUALLY TRUE. REPORTERS MADE IT UP.
THE PIRATES PLAYERS EITHER DIDN'T WATCH THE YANKS' BATTING PRACTICE OR DIDN'T CARE ONE WAY OR THE OTHER!
BUT THEY DID LOSE FOUR STRAIGHT!
GREAT HIT, LOU!
GAME 1 · YANKEES 5, PIRATES 4
GAME 2 · YANKEES 6, PIRATES 2
WAY TO GO, PITCHAH! THAT'S ANOTHER K!
GAME 3 · YANKEES 8, PIRATES 1
HERE WE GO, BOYS! ONE MORE GAME TO WIN!
YANKEES
GAME 4 · YANKEES 4, PIRATES 3
THAT'S IT, EARLE! THAT'S THE WINNING RUN!

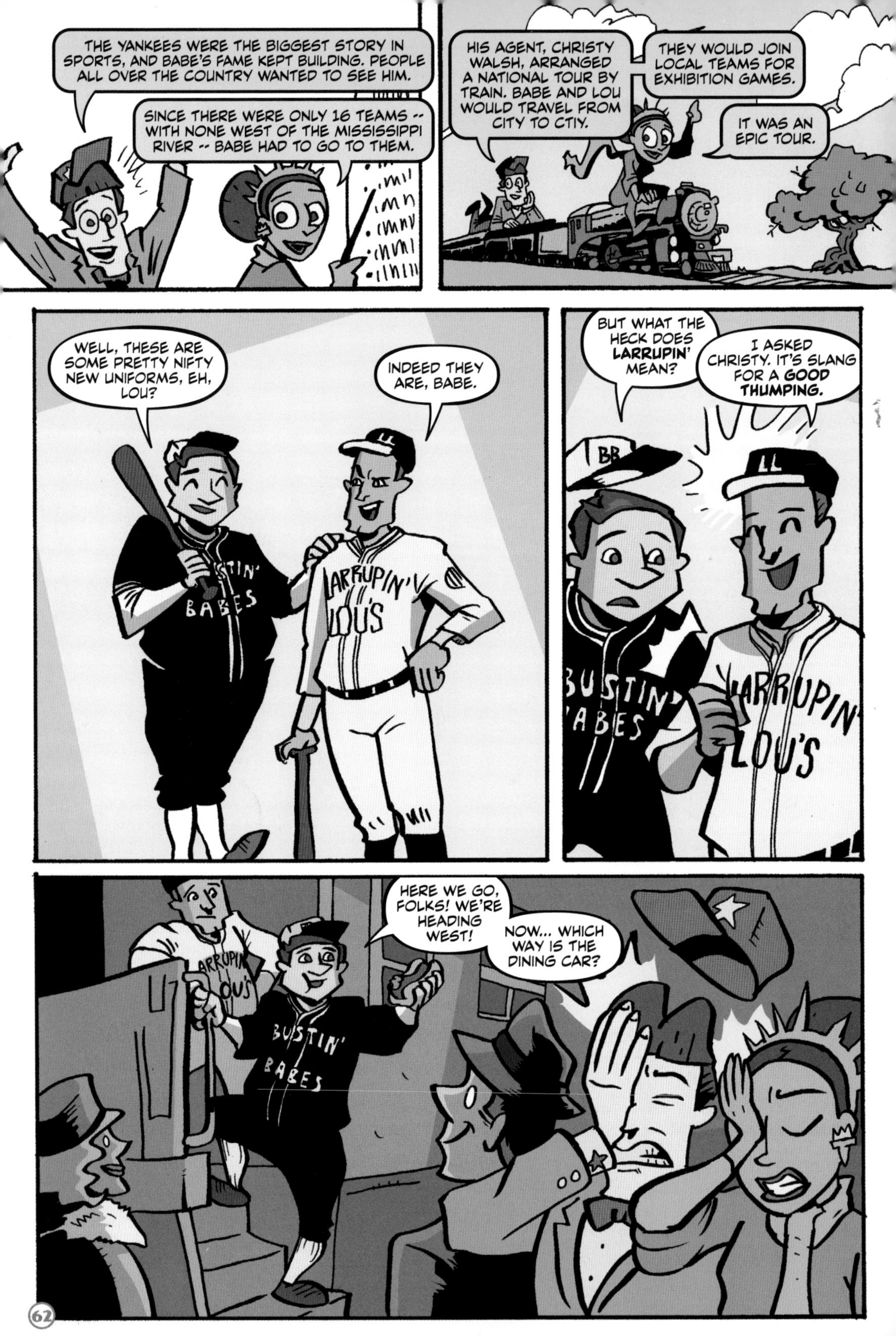
THE YANKEES WERE THE BIGGEST STORY IN SPORTS, AND BABE'S FAME KEPT BUILDING. PEOPLE ALL OVER THE COUNTRY WANTED TO SEE HIM.
SINCE THERE WERE ONLY 16 TEAMS -- WITH NONE WEST OF THE MISSISSIPPI RIVER -- BABE HAD TO GO TO THEM.
HIS AGENT, CHRISTY WALSH, ARRANGED A NATIONAL TOUR BY TRAIN. BABE AND LOU WOULD TRAVEL FROM CITY TO CTIY.
THEY WOULD JOIN LOCAL TEAMS FOR EXHIBITION GAMES.
IT WAS AN EPIC TOUR.
WELL, THESE ARE SOME PRETTY NIFTY NEW UNIFORMS, EH, LOU?
INDEED THEY ARE, BABE.
BUT WHAT THE HECK DOES **LARRUPIN'** MEAN?
I ASKED CHRISTY. IT'S SLANG FOR A **GOOD THUMPING.**
BUSTIN' BABES
LARRUPIN' LOU'S
HERE WE GO, FOLKS! WE'RE HEADING WEST!
NOW... WHICH WAY IS THE DINING CAR?

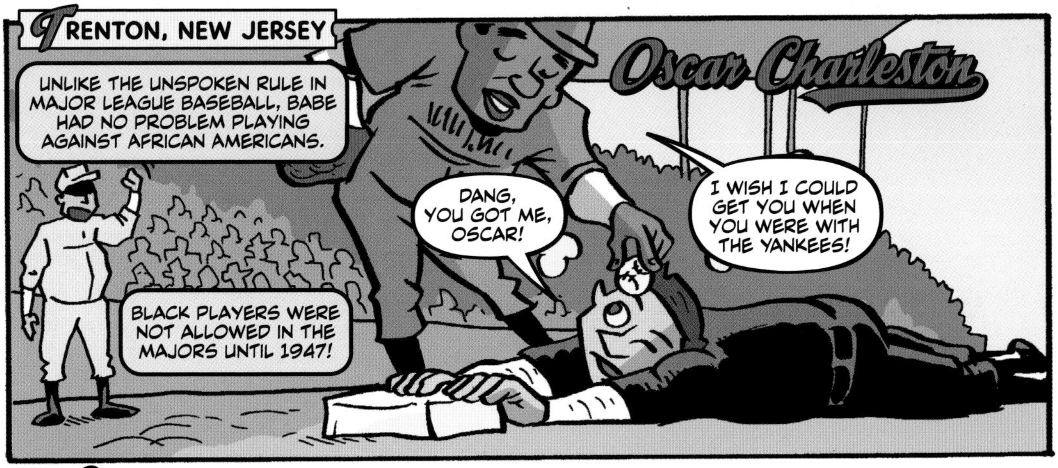
TRENTON, NEW JERSEY
UNLIKE THE UNSPOKEN RULE IN MAJOR LEAGUE BASEBALL, BABE HAD NO PROBLEM PLAYING AGAINST AFRICAN AMERICANS.
Oscar Charleston
I WISH I COULD GET YOU WHEN YOU WERE WITH THE YANKEES!
DANG, YOU GOT ME, OSCAR!
BLACK PLAYERS WERE NOT ALLOWED IN THE MAJORS UNTIL 1947!

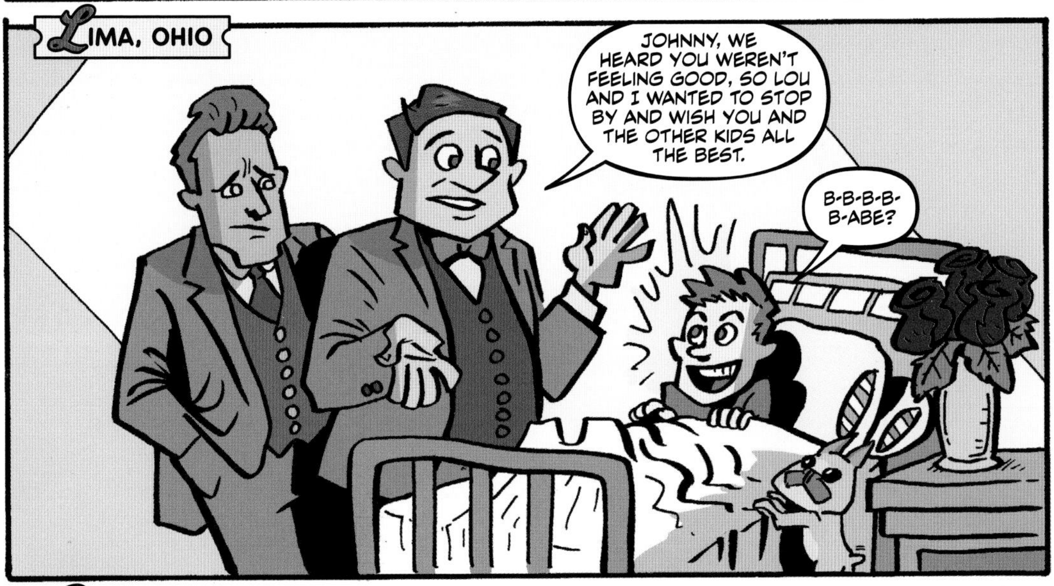
LIMA, OHIO
JOHNNY, WE HEARD YOU WEREN'T FEELING GOOD, SO LOU AND I WANTED TO STOP BY AND WISH YOU AND THE OTHER KIDS ALL THE BEST.
B-B-B-B-B-ABE?

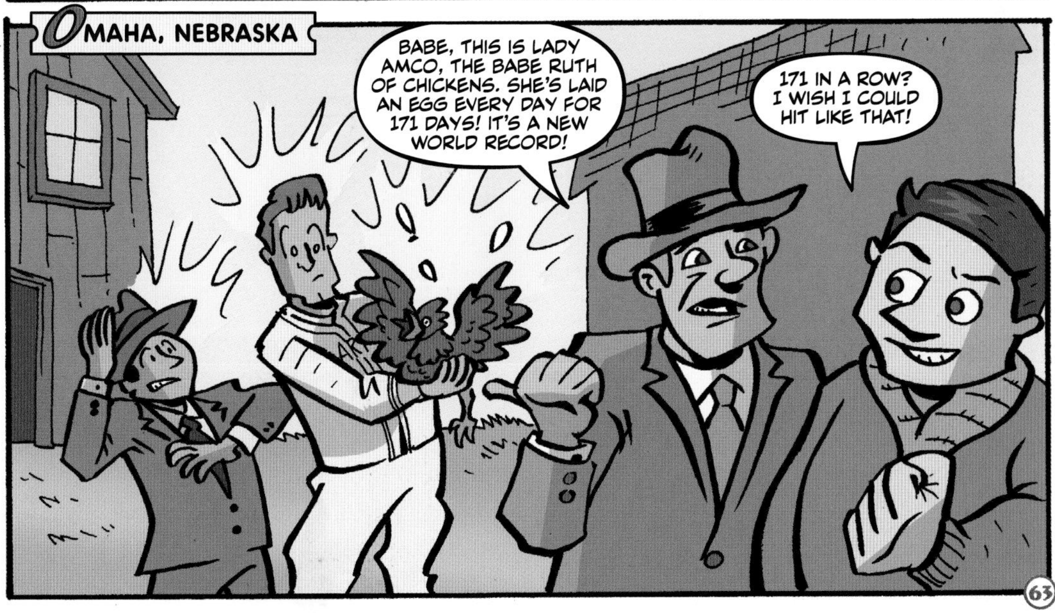
OMAHA, NEBRASKA
BABE, THIS IS LADY AMCO, THE BABE RUTH OF CHICKENS. SHE'S LAID AN EGG EVERY DAY FOR 171 DAYS! IT'S A NEW WORLD RECORD!
171 IN A ROW? I WISH I COULD HIT LIKE THAT!

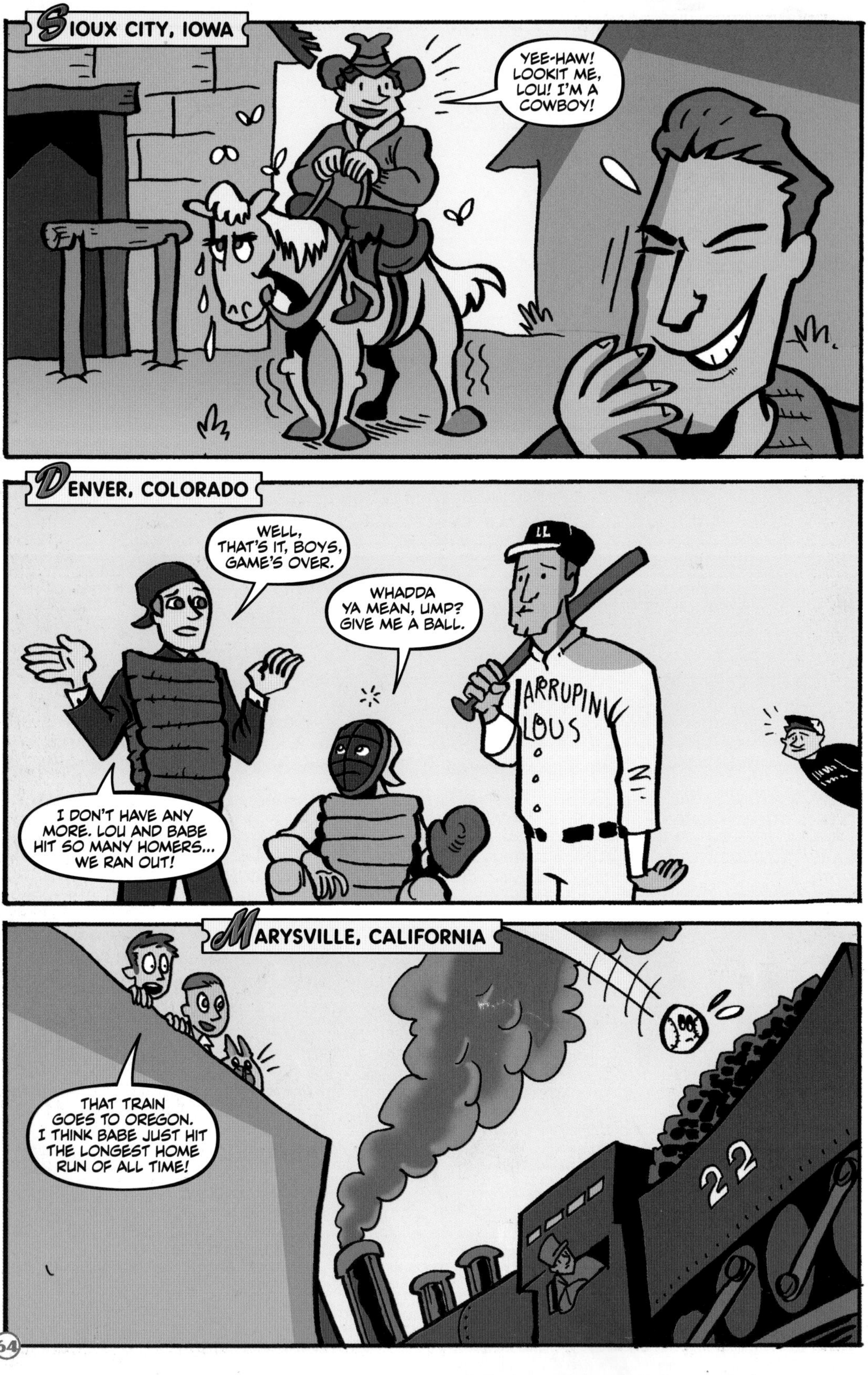
SIOUX CITY, IOWA
YEE-HAW! LOOKIT ME, LOU! I'M A COWBOY!
DENVER, COLORADO
WELL, THAT'S IT, BOYS, GAME'S OVER.
WHADDA YA MEAN, UMP? GIVE ME A BALL.
I DON'T HAVE ANY MORE. LOU AND BABE HIT SO MANY HOMERS... WE RAN OUT!
ARRUPIN LOUS
MARYSVILLE, CALIFORNIA
THAT TRAIN GOES TO OREGON. I THINK BABE JUST HIT THE LONGEST HOME RUN OF ALL TIME!
22

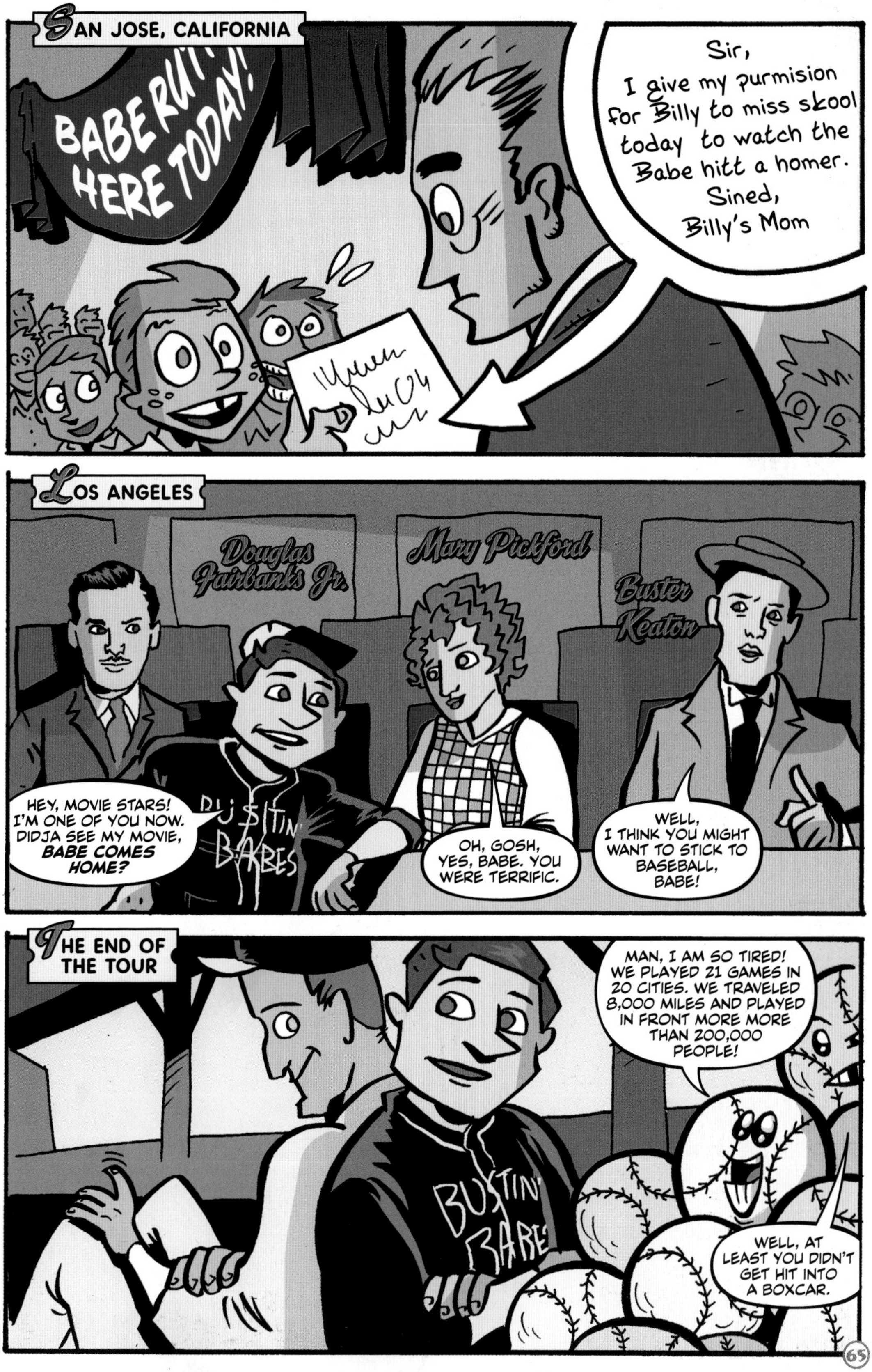

SAN JOSE, CALIFORNIA
BABE RUT[H] HERE TODAY!
Sir, I give my purmision for Billy to miss skool today to watch the Babe hitt a homer. Sined, Billy's Mom
LOS ANGELES
Douglas Fairbanks Jr.
Mary Pickford
Buster Keaton
HEY, MOVIE STARS! I'M ONE OF YOU NOW. DIDJA SEE MY MOVIE, *BABE COMES HOME?*
BUSTIN' BABES
OH, GOSH, YES, BABE. YOU WERE TERRIFIC.
WELL, I THINK YOU MIGHT WANT TO STICK TO BASEBALL, BABE!
THE END OF THE TOUR
MAN, I AM SO TIRED! WE PLAYED 21 GAMES IN 20 CITIES. WE TRAVELED 8,000 MILES AND PLAYED IN FRONT MORE MORE THAN 200,000 PEOPLE!
BUSTIN' BABES
WELL, AT LEAST YOU DIDN'T GET HIT INTO A BOXCAR.

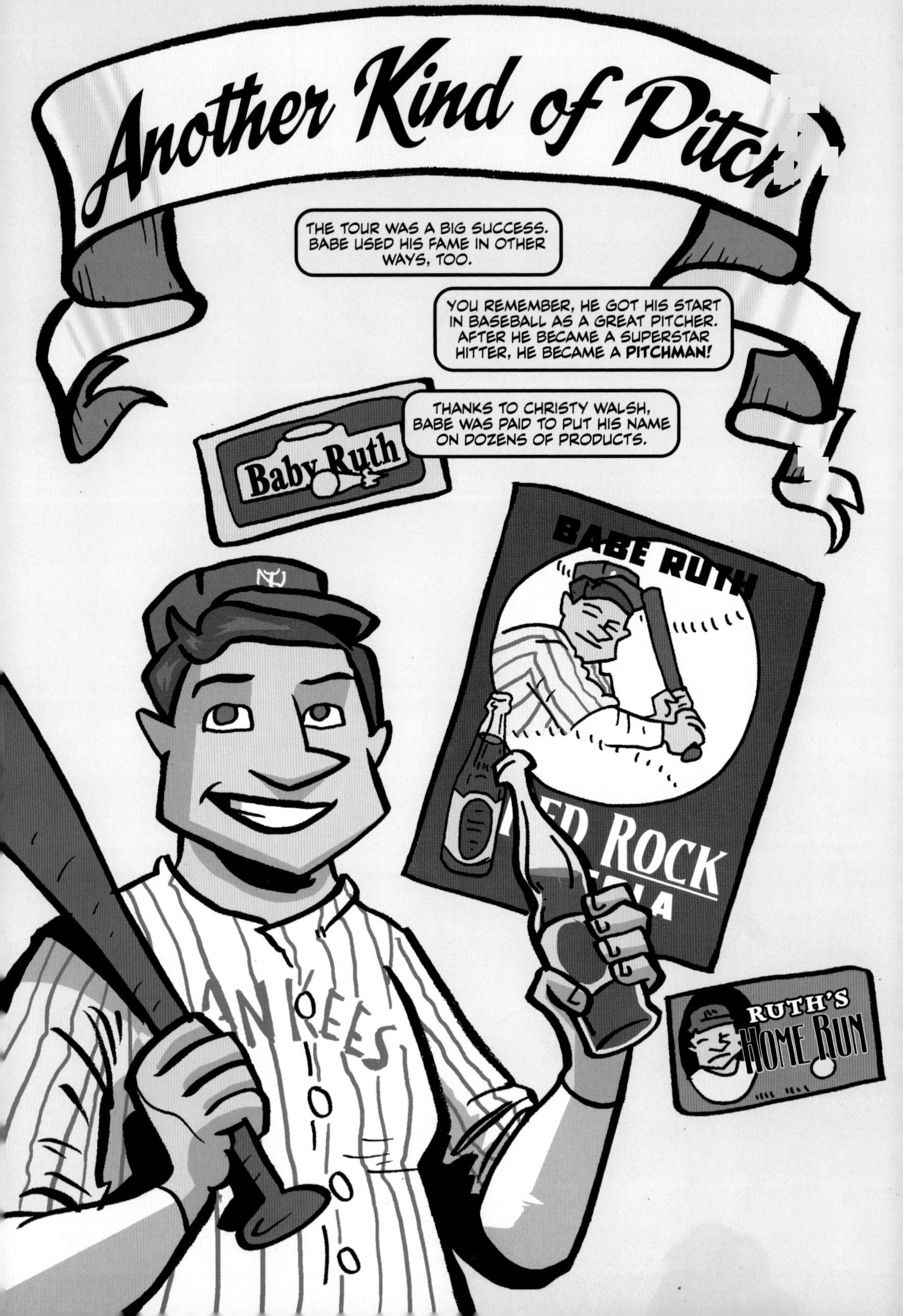

Another Kind of Pitch
THE TOUR WAS A BIG SUCCESS. BABE USED HIS FAME IN OTHER WAYS, TOO.
YOU REMEMBER, HE GOT HIS START IN BASEBALL AS A GREAT PITCHER. AFTER HE BECAME A SUPERSTAR HITTER, HE BECAME A **PITCHMAN!**
THANKS TO CHRISTY WALSH, BABE WAS PAID TO PUT HIS NAME ON DOZENS OF PRODUCTS.
Baby Ruth
BABE RUTH
RUTH'S HOME RUN

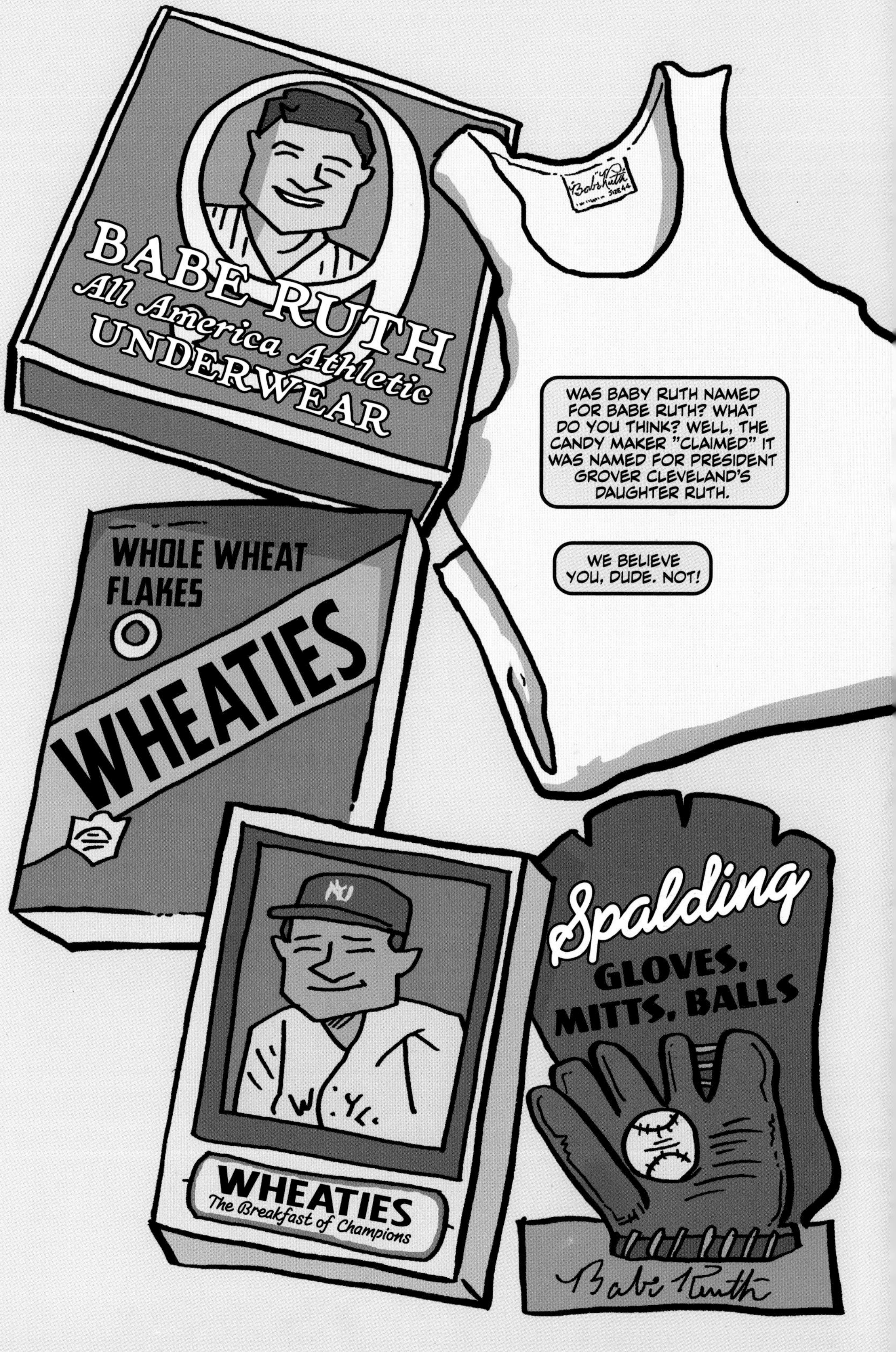
BABE RUTH
All America Athletic
UNDERWEAR
WAS BABY RUTH NAMED FOR BABE RUTH? WHAT DO YOU THINK? WELL, THE CANDY MAKER "CLAIMED" IT WAS NAMED FOR PRESIDENT GROVER CLEVELAND'S DAUGHTER RUTH.
WE BELIEVE YOU, DUDE. NOT!
WHOLE WHEAT FLAKES
WHEATIES
WHEATIES
The Breakfast of Champions
Spalding
GLOVES, MITTS, BALLS
Babe Ruth

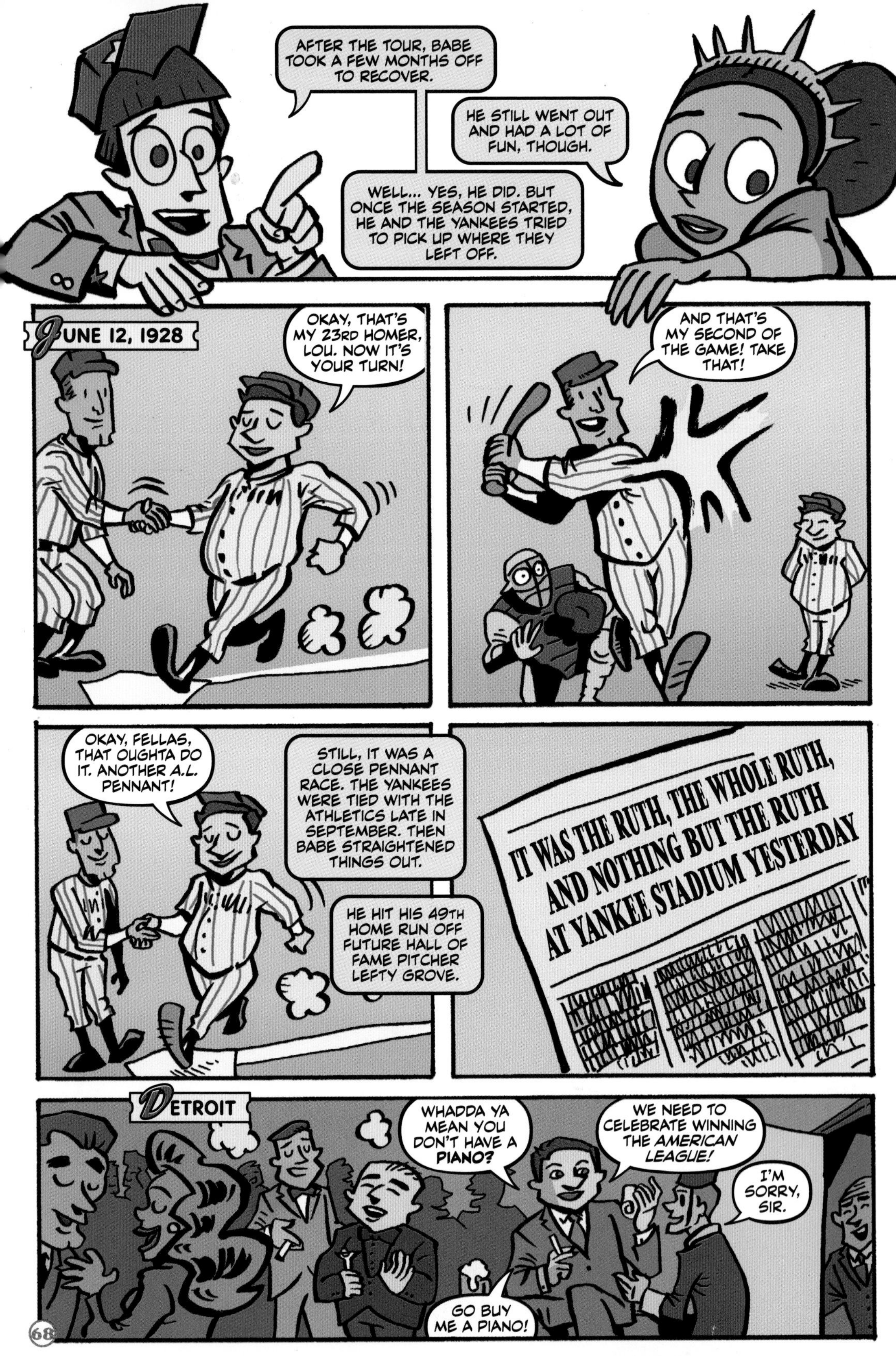

AFTER THE TOUR, BABE TOOK A FEW MONTHS OFF TO RECOVER.
HE STILL WENT OUT AND HAD A LOT OF FUN, THOUGH.
WELL... YES, HE DID. BUT ONCE THE SEASON STARTED, HE AND THE YANKEES TRIED TO PICK UP WHERE THEY LEFT OFF.
JUNE 12, 1928
OKAY, THAT'S MY 23RD HOMER, LOU. NOW IT'S YOUR TURN!
AND THAT'S MY SECOND OF THE GAME! TAKE THAT!
OKAY, FELLAS, THAT OUGHTA DO IT. ANOTHER A.L. PENNANT!
STILL, IT WAS A CLOSE PENNANT RACE. THE YANKEES WERE TIED WITH THE ATHLETICS LATE IN SEPTEMBER. THEN BABE STRAIGHTENED THINGS OUT.
HE HIT HIS 49TH HOME RUN OFF FUTURE HALL OF FAME PITCHER LEFTY GROVE.
IT WAS THE RUTH, THE WHOLE RUTH, AND NOTHING BUT THE RUTH AT YANKEE STADIUM YESTERDAY
DETROIT
WHADDA YA MEAN YOU DON'T HAVE A PIANO?
WE NEED TO CELEBRATE WINNING THE AMERICAN LEAGUE!
I'M SORRY, SIR.
GO BUY ME A PIANO!

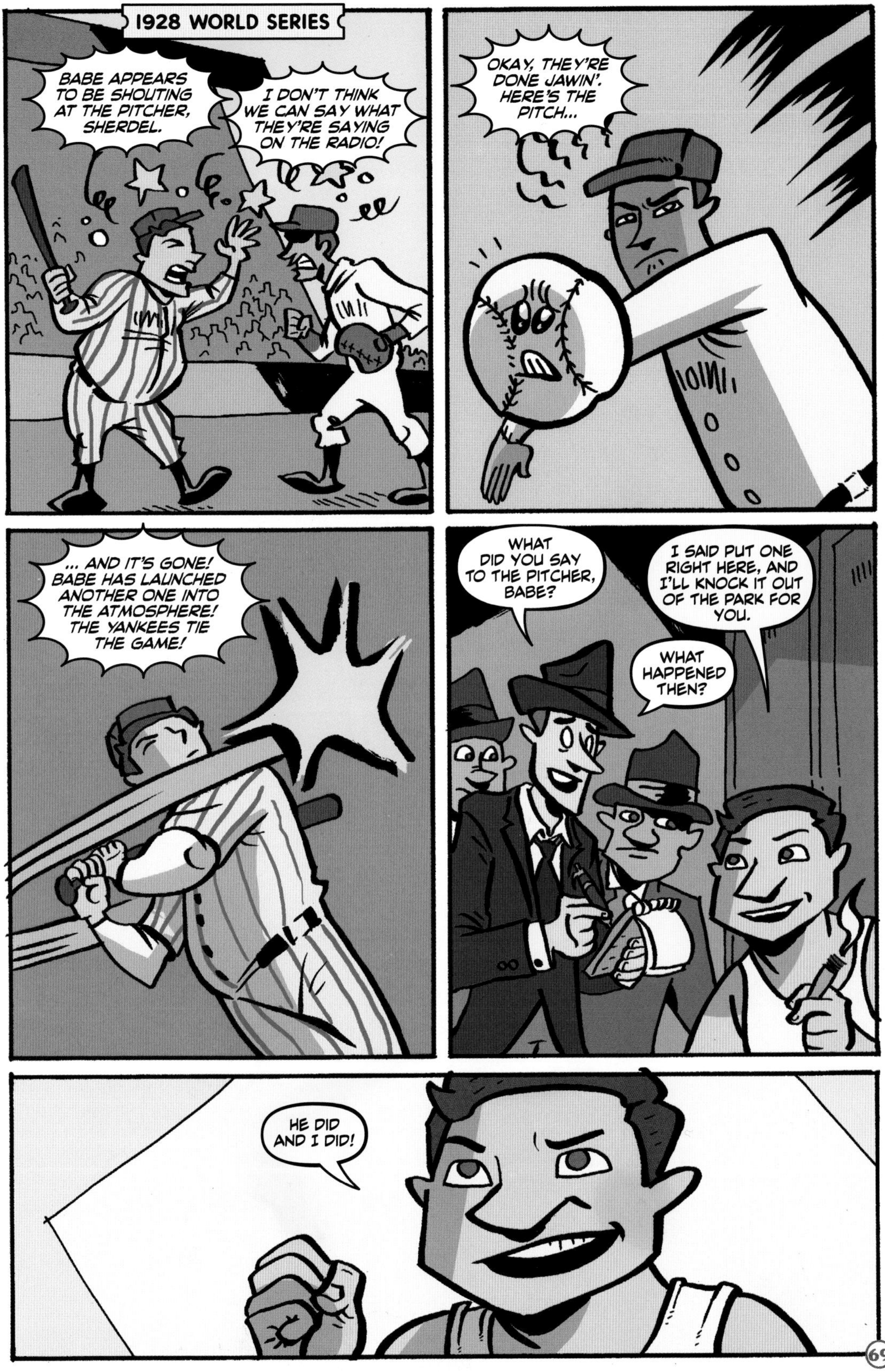
1928 WORLD SERIES
BABE APPEARS TO BE SHOUTING AT THE PITCHER, SHERDEL.
I DON'T THINK WE CAN SAY WHAT THEY'RE SAYING ON THE RADIO!
OKAY, THEY'RE DONE JAWIN'. HERE'S THE PITCH...
... AND IT'S GONE! BABE HAS LAUNCHED ANOTHER ONE INTO THE ATMOSPHERE! THE YANKEES TIE THE GAME!
WHAT DID YOU SAY TO THE PITCHER, BABE?
I SAID PUT ONE RIGHT HERE, AND I'LL KNOCK IT OUT OF THE PARK FOR YOU.
WHAT HAPPENED THEN?
HE DID AND I DID!

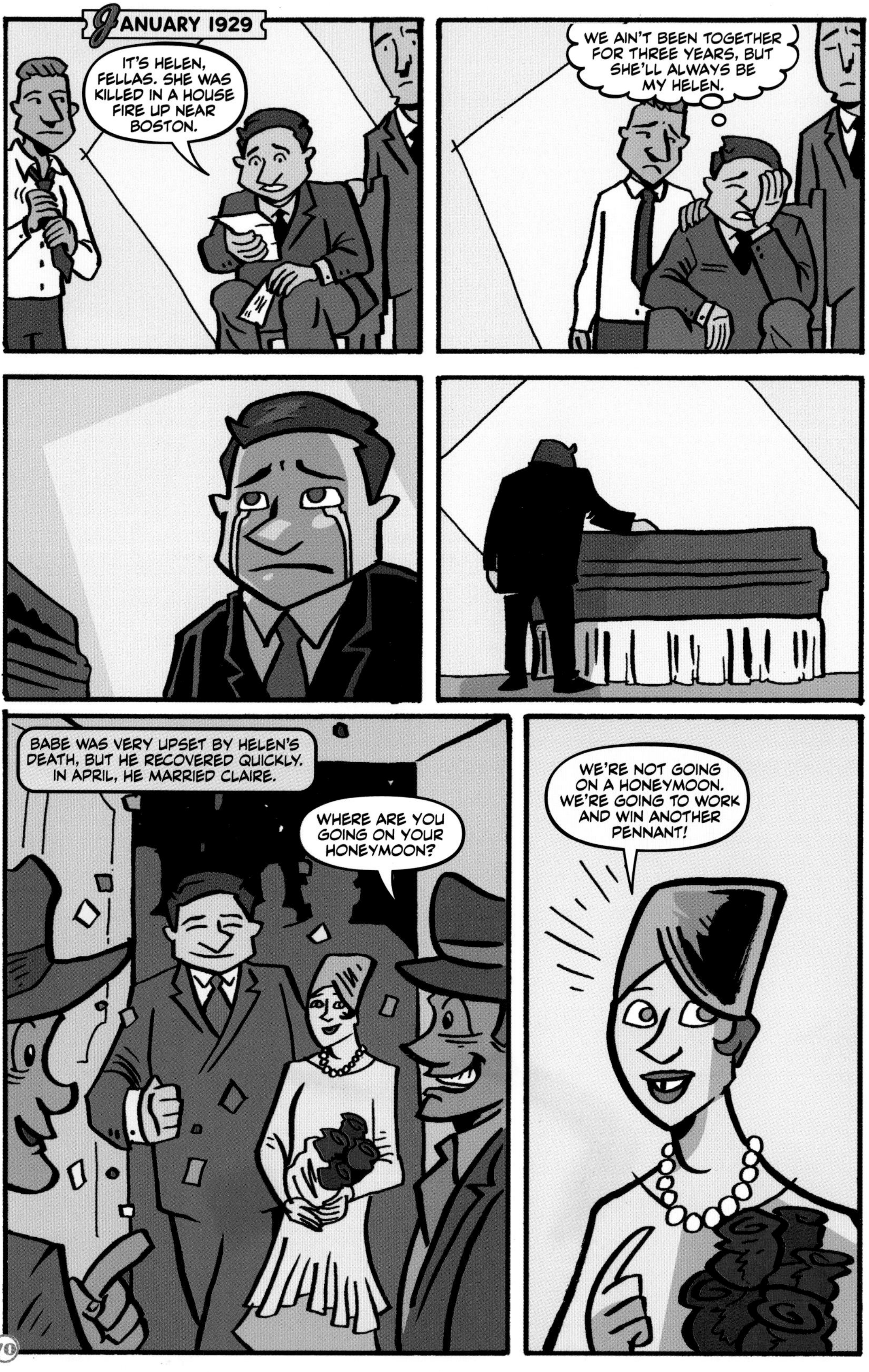
JANUARY 1929
IT'S HELEN, FELLAS. SHE WAS KILLED IN A HOUSE FIRE UP NEAR BOSTON.
WE AIN'T BEEN TOGETHER FOR THREE YEARS, BUT SHE'LL ALWAYS BE MY HELEN.
BABE WAS VERY UPSET BY HELEN'S DEATH, BUT HE RECOVERED QUICKLY. IN APRIL, HE MARRIED CLAIRE.
WHERE ARE YOU GOING ON YOUR HONEYMOON?
WE'RE NOT GOING ON A HONEYMOON. WE'RE GOING TO WORK AND WIN ANOTHER PENNANT!

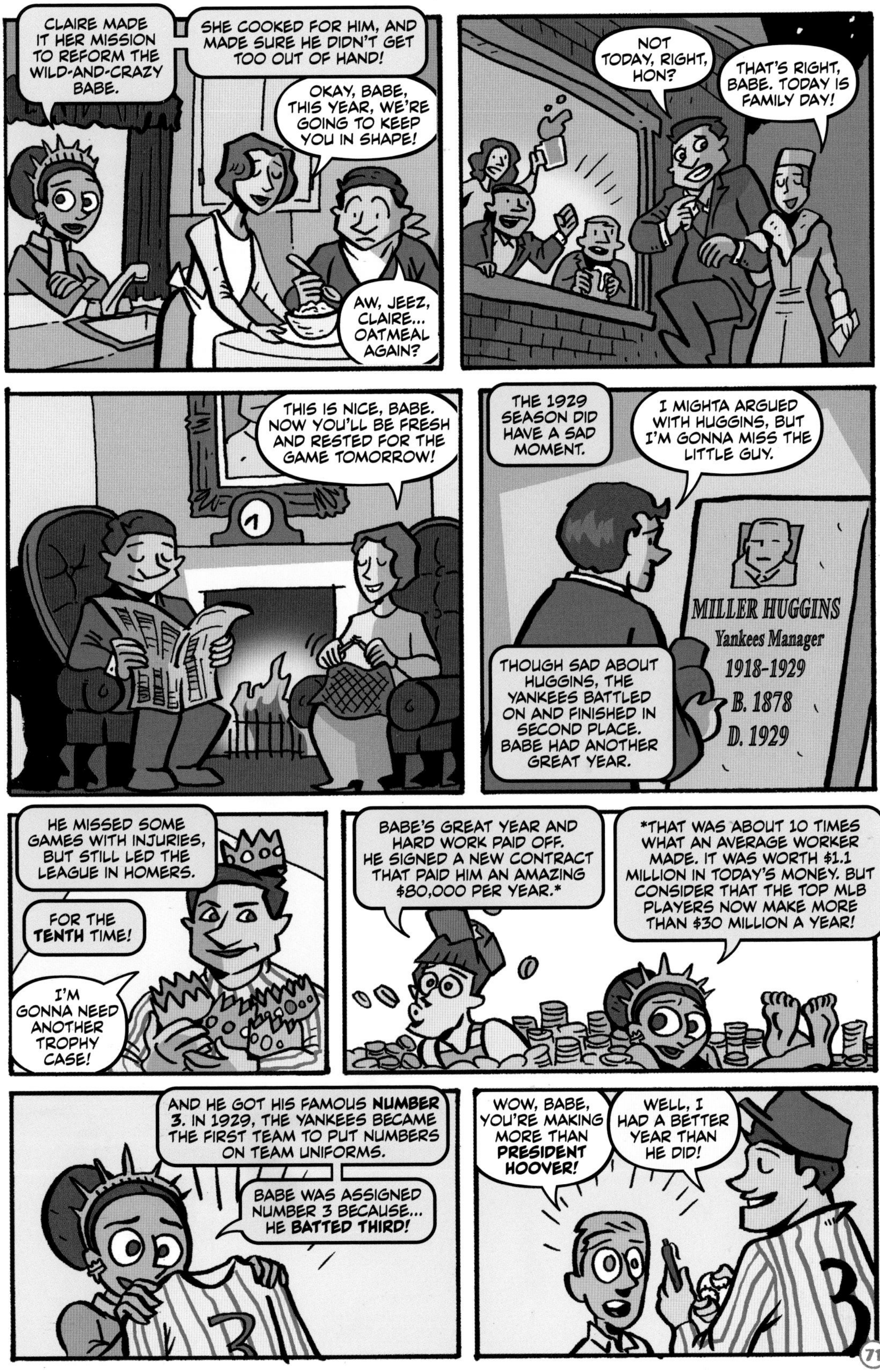
CLAIRE MADE IT HER MISSION TO REFORM THE WILD-AND-CRAZY BABE.
SHE COOKED FOR HIM, AND MADE SURE HE DIDN'T GET TOO OUT OF HAND!
OKAY, BABE, THIS YEAR, WE'RE GOING TO KEEP YOU IN SHAPE!
AW, JEEZ, CLAIRE... OATMEAL AGAIN?
NOT TODAY, RIGHT, HON?
THAT'S RIGHT, BABE. TODAY IS FAMILY DAY!
THIS IS NICE, BABE. NOW YOU'LL BE FRESH AND RESTED FOR THE GAME TOMORROW!
THE 1929 SEASON DID HAVE A SAD MOMENT.
I MIGHTA ARGUED WITH HUGGINS, BUT I'M GONNA MISS THE LITTLE GUY.
MILLER HUGGINS
Yankees Manager
1918-1929
B. 1878
D. 1929
THOUGH SAD ABOUT HUGGINS, THE YANKEES BATTLED ON AND FINISHED IN SECOND PLACE. BABE HAD ANOTHER GREAT YEAR.
HE MISSED SOME GAMES WITH INJURIES, BUT STILL LED THE LEAGUE IN HOMERS.
FOR THE **TENTH** TIME!
I'M GONNA NEED ANOTHER TROPHY CASE!
BABE'S GREAT YEAR AND HARD WORK PAID OFF. HE SIGNED A NEW CONTRACT THAT PAID HIM AN AMAZING $80,000 PER YEAR.*
*THAT WAS ABOUT 10 TIMES WHAT AN AVERAGE WORKER MADE. IT WAS WORTH $1.1 MILLION IN TODAY'S MONEY. BUT CONSIDER THAT THE TOP MLB PLAYERS NOW MAKE MORE THAN $30 MILLION A YEAR!
AND HE GOT HIS FAMOUS **NUMBER 3**. IN 1929, THE YANKEES BECAME THE FIRST TEAM TO PUT NUMBERS ON TEAM UNIFORMS.
BABE WAS ASSIGNED NUMBER 3 BECAUSE... HE **BATTED THIRD**!
WOW, BABE, YOU'RE MAKING MORE THAN **PRESIDENT HOOVER**!
WELL, I HAD A BETTER YEAR THAN HE DID!

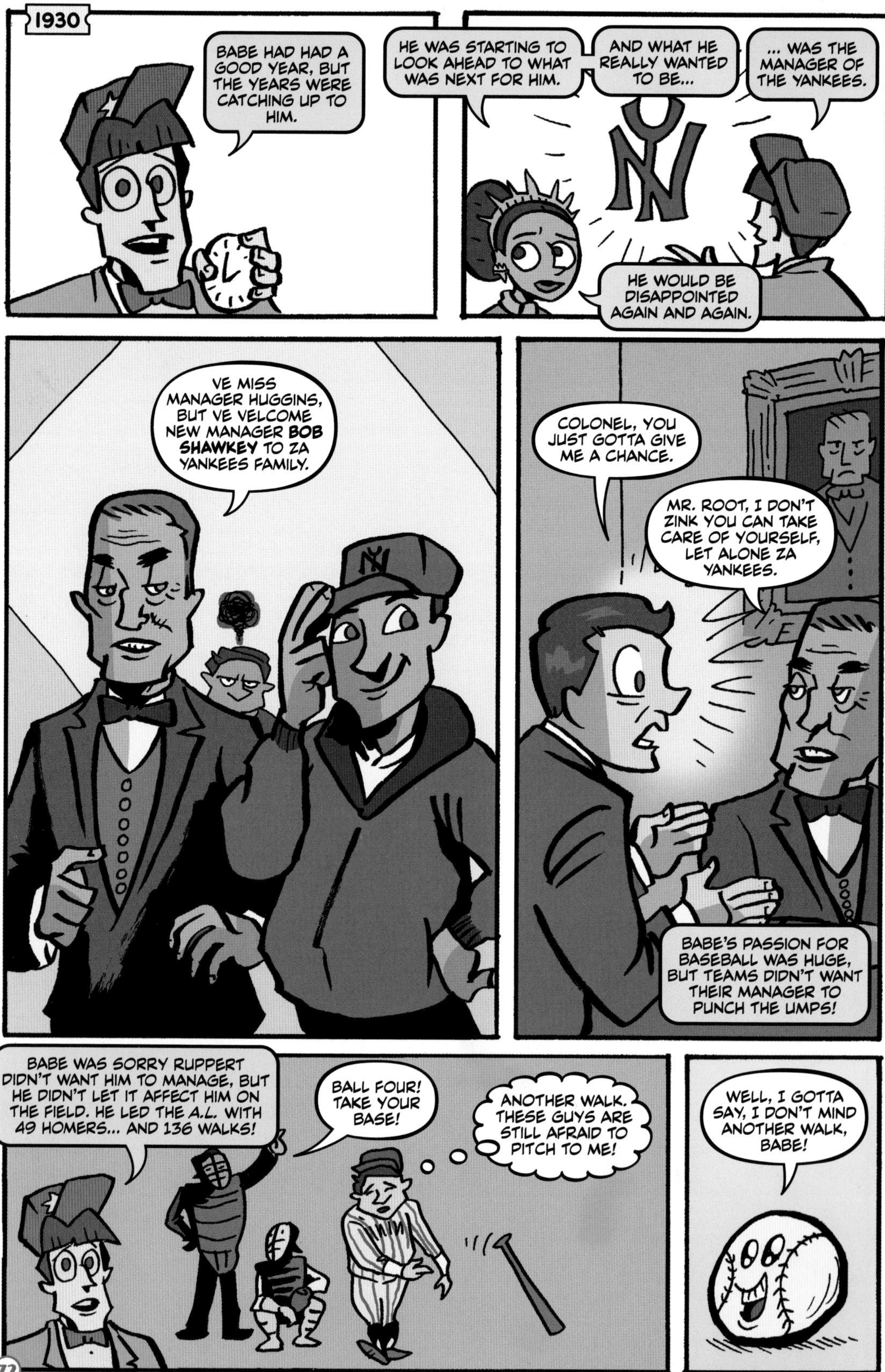

1930
BABE HAD HAD A GOOD YEAR, BUT THE YEARS WERE CATCHING UP TO HIM.
HE WAS STARTING TO LOOK AHEAD TO WHAT WAS NEXT FOR HIM.
AND WHAT HE REALLY WANTED TO BE...
... WAS THE MANAGER OF THE YANKEES.
HE WOULD BE DISAPPOINTED AGAIN AND AGAIN.
VE MISS MANAGER HUGGINS, BUT VE VELCOME NEW MANAGER **BOB SHAWKEY** TO ZA YANKEES FAMILY.
COLONEL, YOU JUST GOTTA GIVE ME A CHANCE.
MR. ROOT, I DON'T ZINK YOU CAN TAKE CARE OF YOURSELF, LET ALONE ZA YANKEES.
BABE'S PASSION FOR BASEBALL WAS HUGE, BUT TEAMS DIDN'T WANT THEIR MANAGER TO PUNCH THE UMPS!
BABE WAS SORRY RUPPERT DIDN'T WANT HIM TO MANAGE, BUT HE DIDN'T LET IT AFFECT HIM ON THE FIELD. HE LED THE A.L. WITH 49 HOMERS... AND 136 WALKS!
BALL FOUR! TAKE YOUR BASE!
ANOTHER WALK. THESE GUYS ARE STILL AFRAID TO PITCH TO ME!
WELL, I GOTTA SAY, I DON'T MIND ANOTHER WALK, BABE!

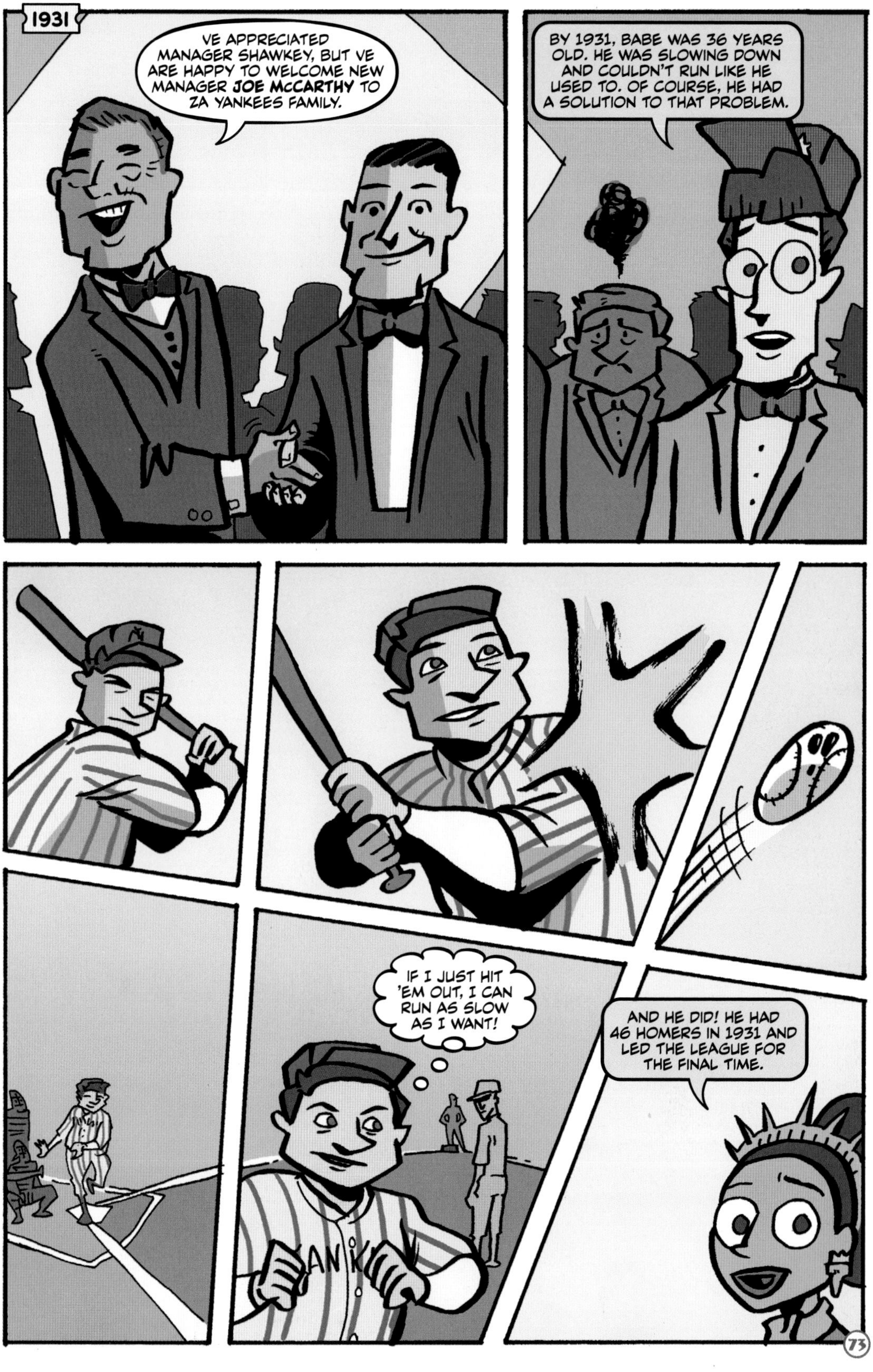
1931
VE APPRECIATED MANAGER SHAWKEY, BUT VE ARE HAPPY TO WELCOME NEW MANAGER **JOE McCARTHY** TO ZA YANKEES FAMILY.
BY 1931, BABE WAS 36 YEARS OLD. HE WAS SLOWING DOWN AND COULDN'T RUN LIKE HE USED TO. OF COURSE, HE HAD A SOLUTION TO THAT PROBLEM.
IF I JUST HIT 'EM OUT, I CAN RUN AS SLOW AS I WANT!
AND HE DID! HE HAD 46 HOMERS IN 1931 AND LED THE LEAGUE FOR THE FINAL TIME.

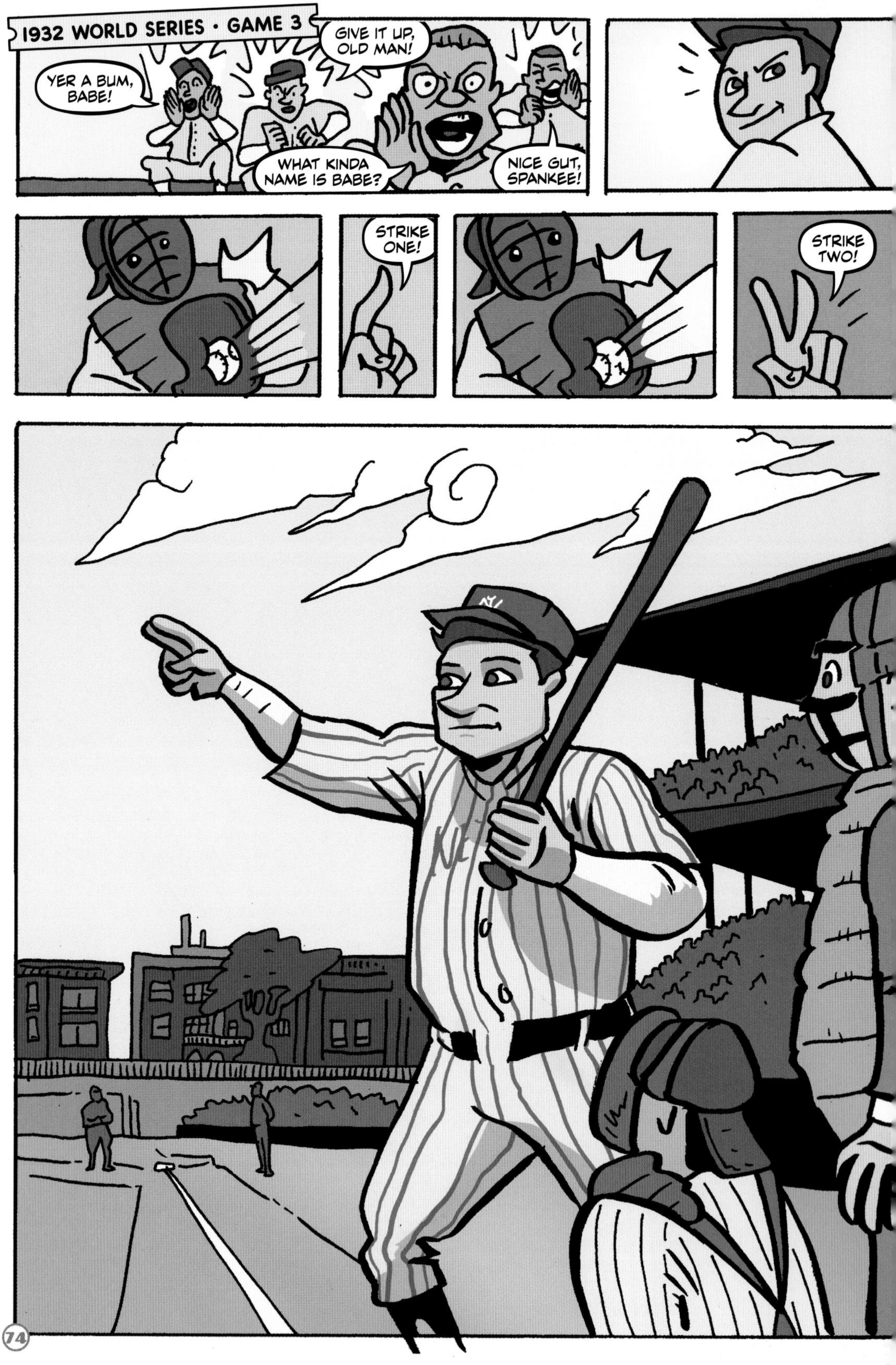
1932 WORLD SERIES • GAME 3
YER A BUM, BABE!
GIVE IT UP, OLD MAN!
WHAT KINDA NAME IS BABE?
NICE GUT, SPANKEE!
STRIKE ONE!
STRIKE TWO!

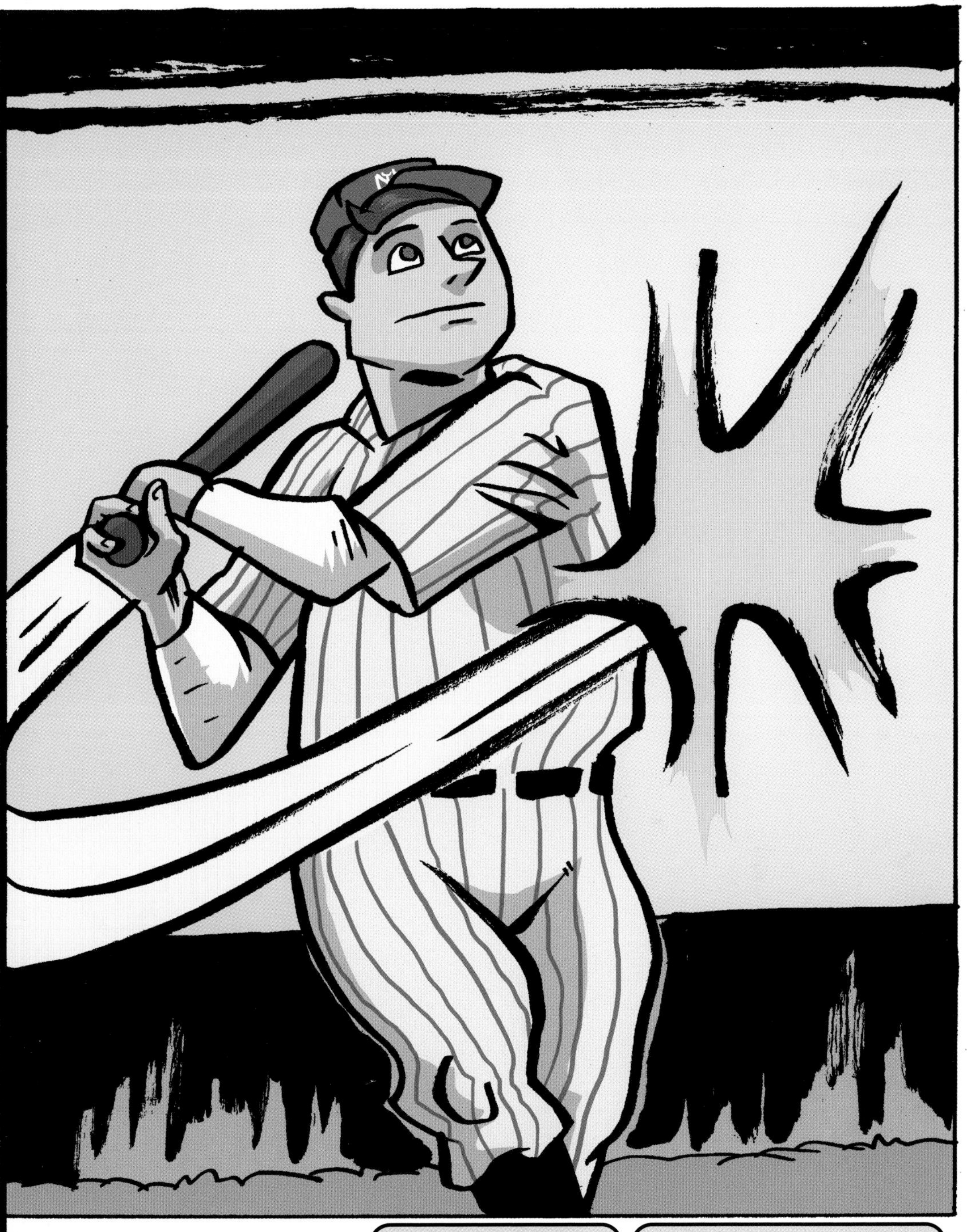

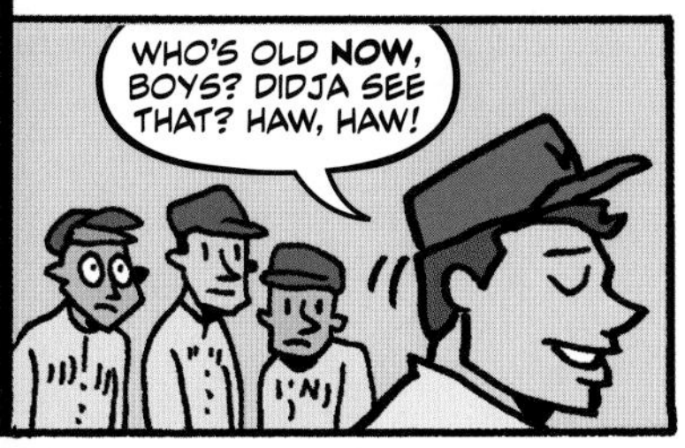

WHO'S OLD **NOW**, BOYS? DIDJA SEE THAT? HAW, HAW!

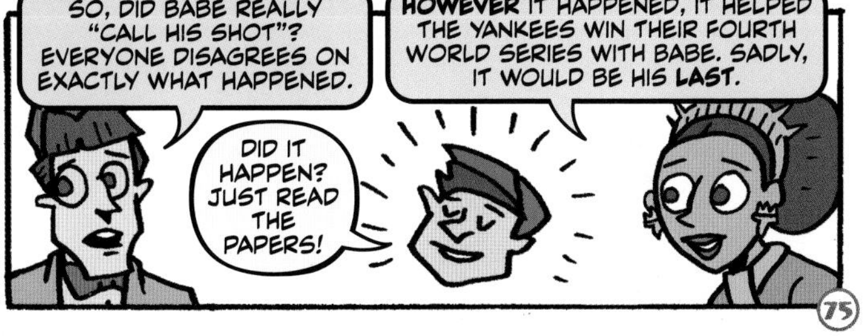

SO, DID BABE REALLY "CALL HIS SHOT"? EVERYONE DISAGREES ON EXACTLY WHAT HAPPENED.
DID IT HAPPEN? JUST READ THE PAPERS!
HOWEVER IT HAPPENED, IT HELPED THE YANKEES WIN THEIR FOURTH WORLD SERIES WITH BABE. SADLY, IT WOULD BE HIS **LAST**.

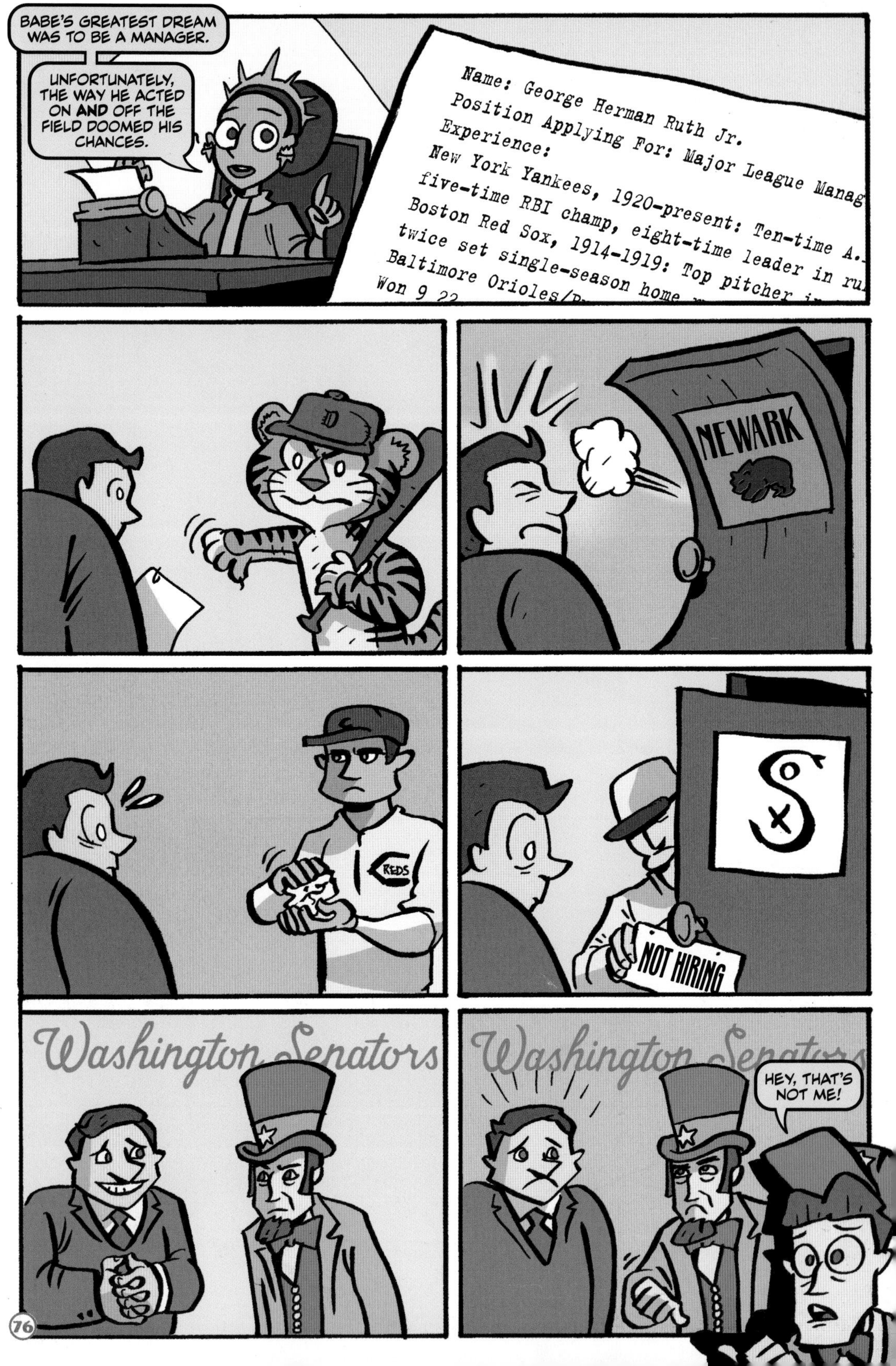
BABE'S GREATEST DREAM WAS TO BE A MANAGER.
UNFORTUNATELY, THE WAY HE ACTED ON AND OFF THE FIELD DOOMED HIS CHANCES.
Name: George Herman Ruth Jr.
Position Applying For: Major League Manag
Experience:
New York Yankees, 1920-present: Ten-time A
five-time RBI champ, eight-time leader in ru
Boston Red Sox, 1914-1919: Top pitcher in
twice set single-season home
Baltimore Orioles/
D
NEWARK
REDS
S
NOT HIRING
Washington Senators
Washington Senators
HEY, THAT'S NOT ME!

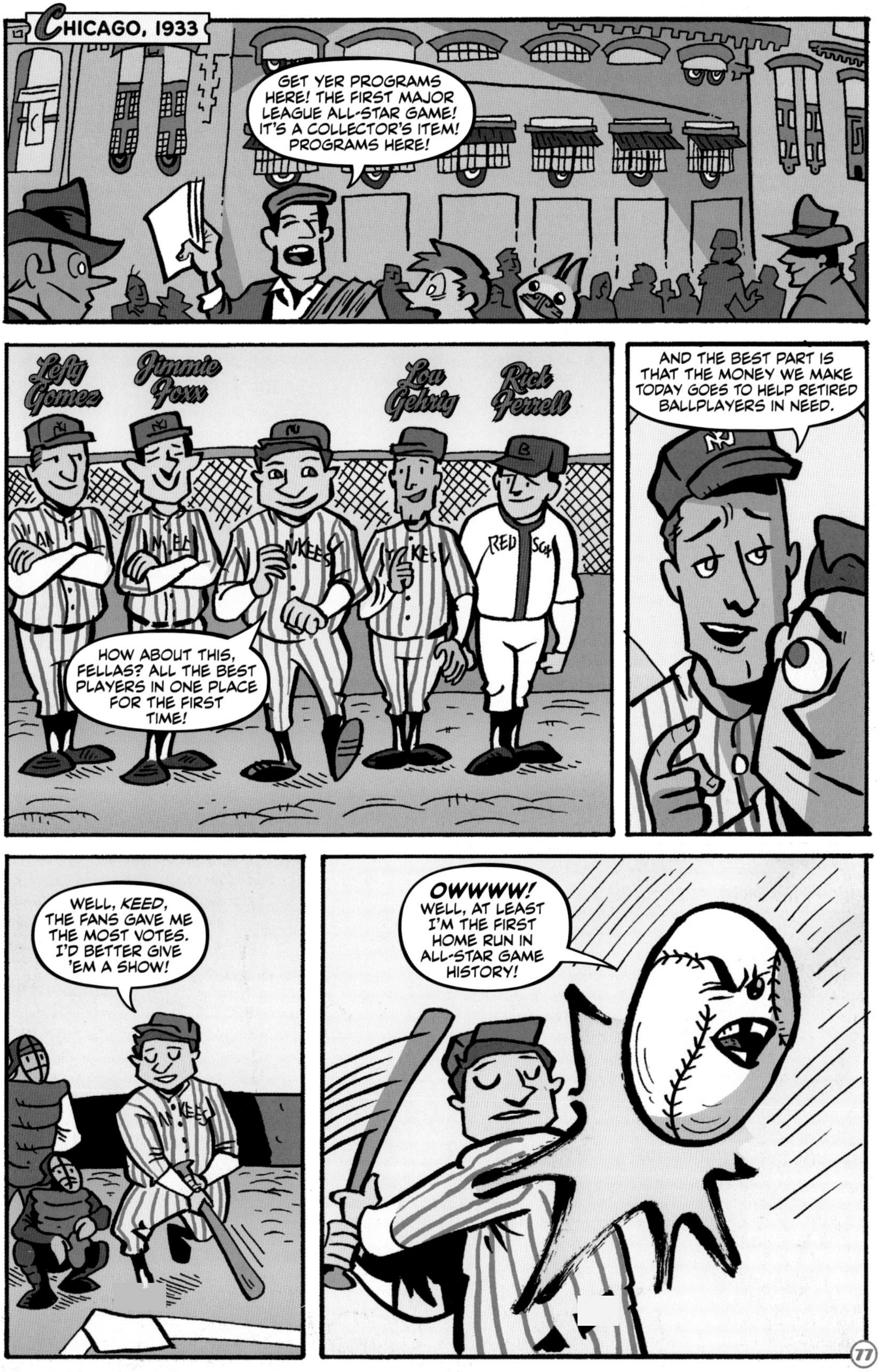
CHICAGO, 1933
GET YER PROGRAMS HERE! THE FIRST MAJOR LEAGUE ALL-STAR GAME! IT'S A COLLECTOR'S ITEM! PROGRAMS HERE!
Lefty Gomez
Jimmie Foxx
Lou Gehrig
Rick Ferrell
HOW ABOUT THIS, FELLAS? ALL THE BEST PLAYERS IN ONE PLACE FOR THE FIRST TIME!
AND THE BEST PART IS THAT THE MONEY WE MAKE TODAY GOES TO HELP RETIRED BALLPLAYERS IN NEED.
WELL, KEED, THE FANS GAVE ME THE MOST VOTES. I'D BETTER GIVE 'EM A SHOW!
OWWWW! WELL, AT LEAST I'M THE FIRST HOME RUN IN ALL-STAR GAME HISTORY!

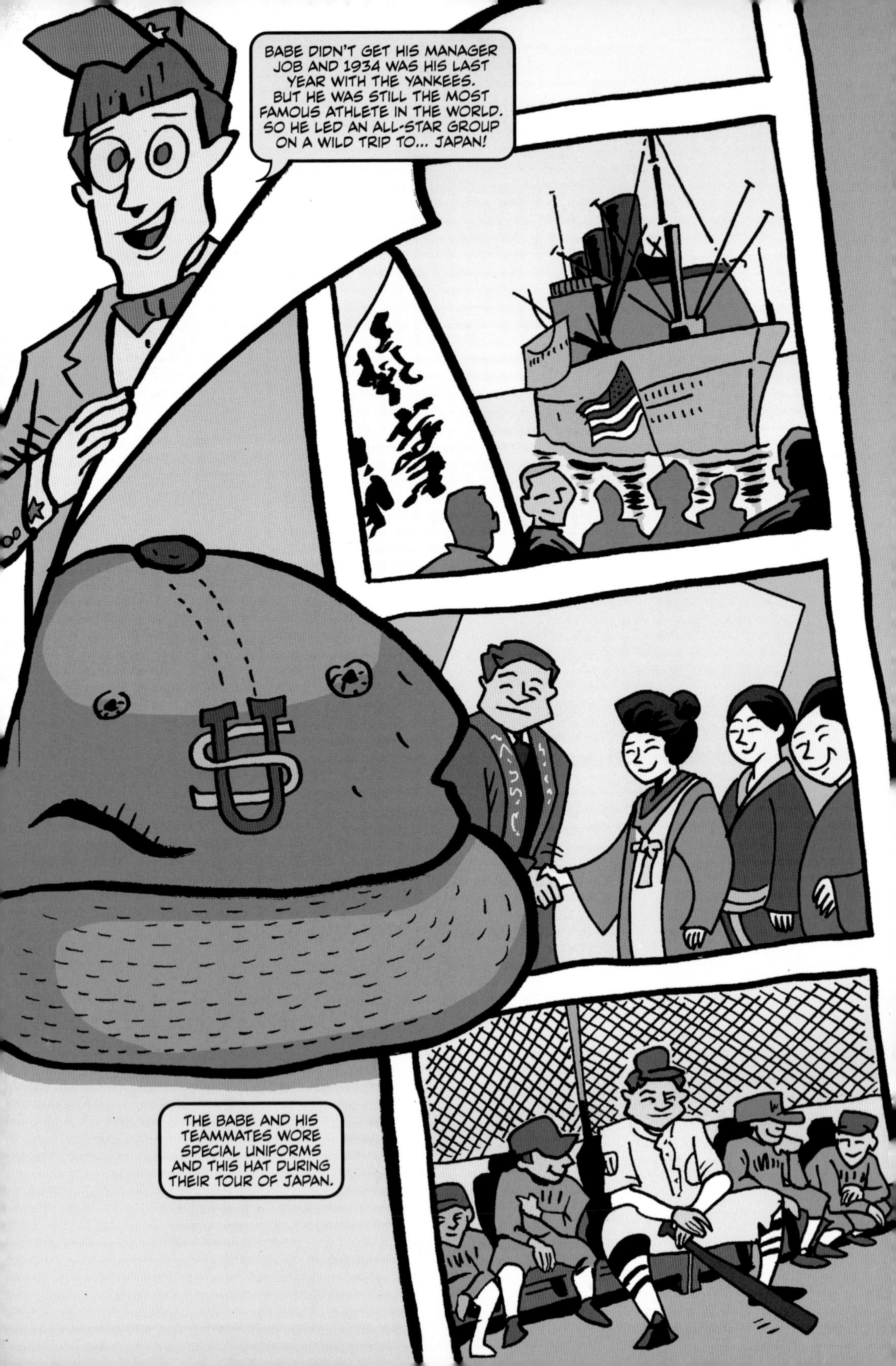
BABE DIDN'T GET HIS MANAGER JOB AND 1934 WAS HIS LAST YEAR WITH THE YANKEES. BUT HE WAS STILL THE MOST FAMOUS ATHLETE IN THE WORLD. SO HE LED AN ALL-STAR GROUP ON A WILD TRIP TO... JAPAN!
THE BABE AND HIS TEAMMATES WORE SPECIAL UNIFORMS AND THIS HAT DURING THEIR TOUR OF JAPAN.

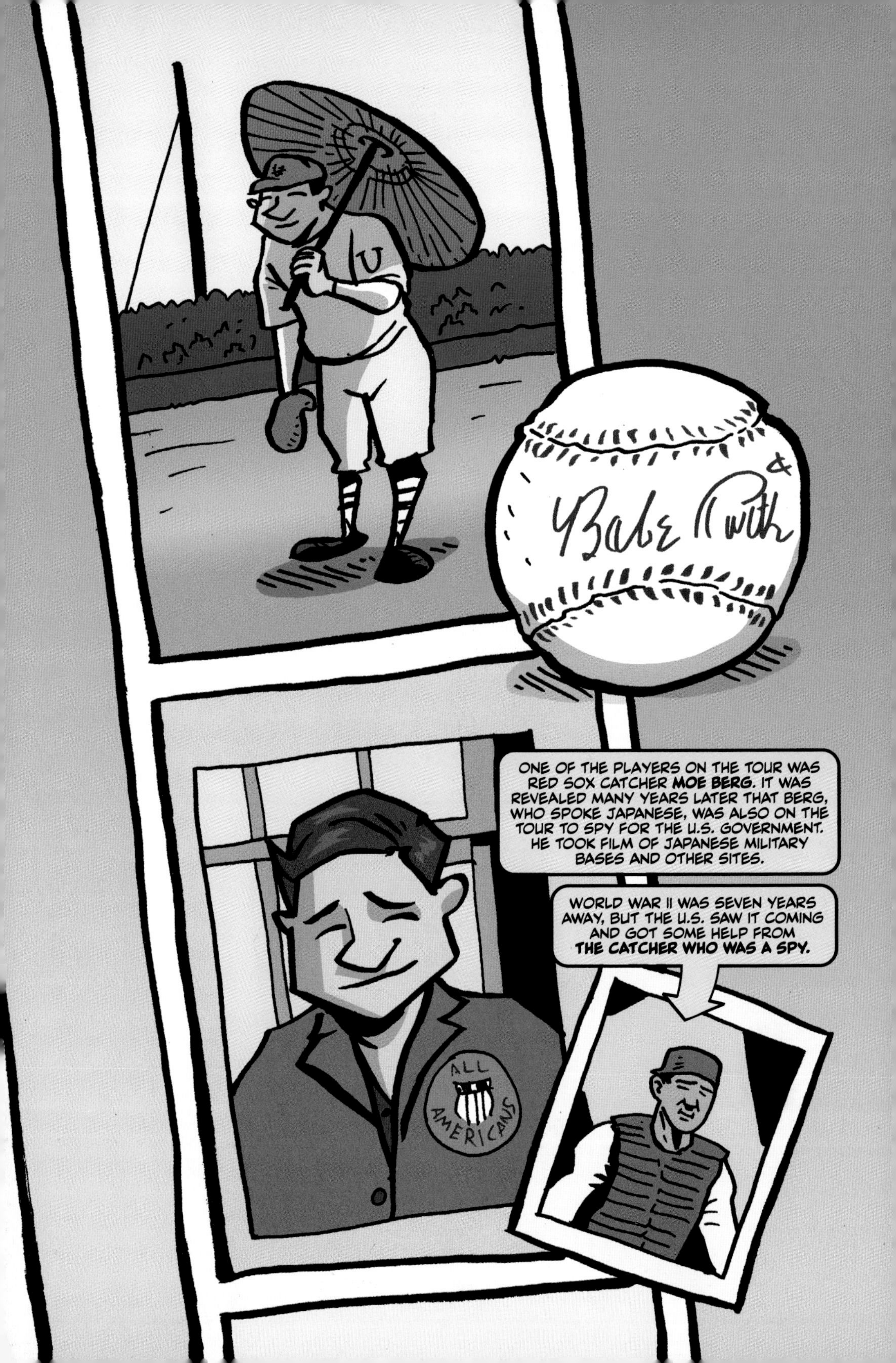
U
Babe Ruth
ONE OF THE PLAYERS ON THE TOUR WAS RED SOX CATCHER **MOE BERG**. IT WAS REVEALED MANY YEARS LATER THAT BERG, WHO SPOKE JAPANESE, WAS ALSO ON THE TOUR TO SPY FOR THE U.S. GOVERNMENT. HE TOOK FILM OF JAPANESE MILITARY BASES AND OTHER SITES.
ALL AMERICANS
WORLD WAR II WAS SEVEN YEARS AWAY, BUT THE U.S. SAW IT COMING AND GOT SOME HELP FROM **THE CATCHER WHO WAS A SPY.**

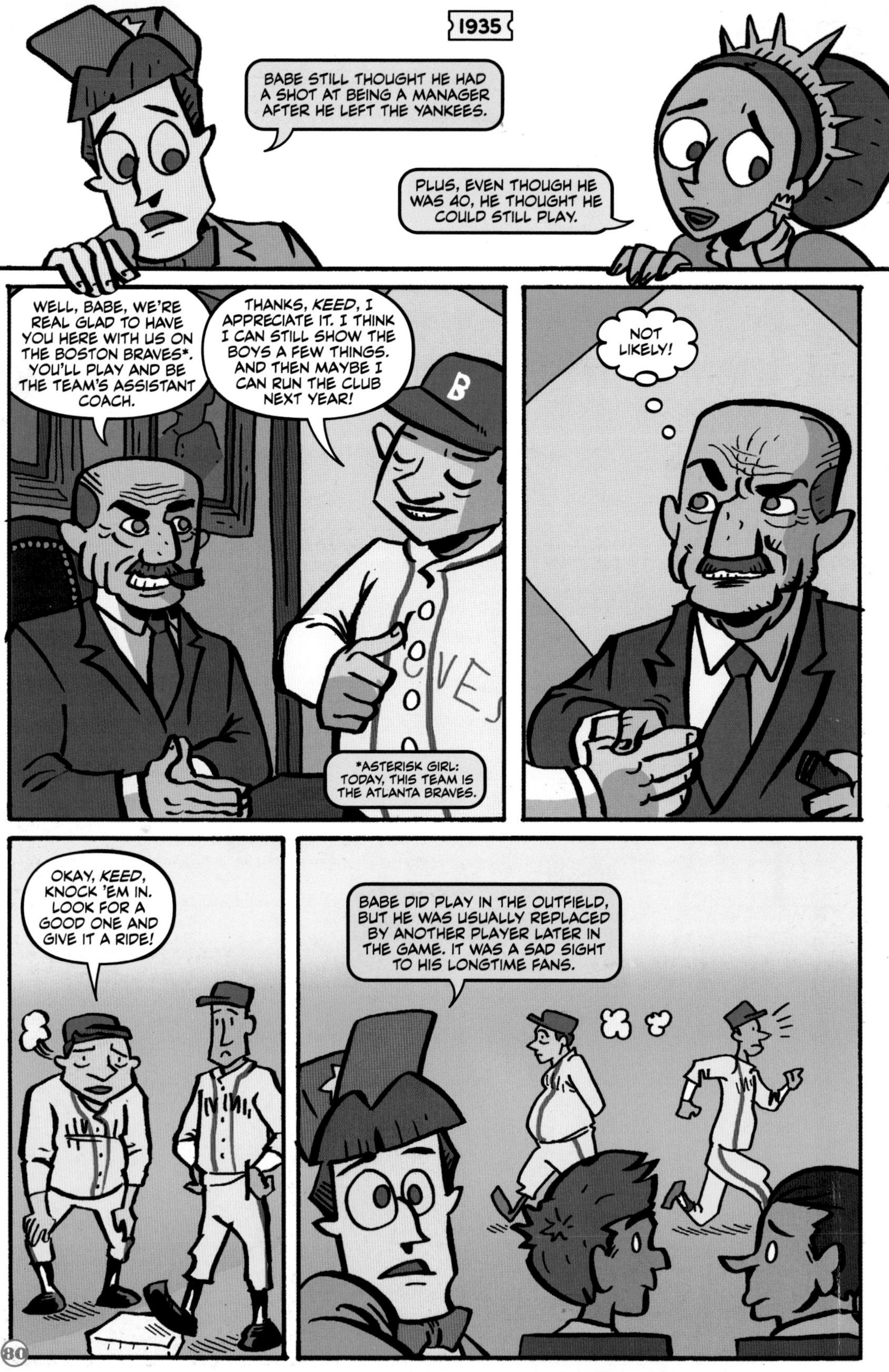
1935
BABE STILL THOUGHT HE HAD A SHOT AT BEING A MANAGER AFTER HE LEFT THE YANKEES.
PLUS, EVEN THOUGH HE WAS 40, HE THOUGHT HE COULD STILL PLAY.
WELL, BABE, WE'RE REAL GLAD TO HAVE YOU HERE WITH US ON THE BOSTON BRAVES*. YOU'LL PLAY AND BE THE TEAM'S ASSISTANT COACH.
THANKS, *KEED*, I APPRECIATE IT. I THINK I CAN STILL SHOW THE BOYS A FEW THINGS. AND THEN MAYBE I CAN RUN THE CLUB NEXT YEAR!
*ASTERISK GIRL: TODAY, THIS TEAM IS THE ATLANTA BRAVES.
NOT LIKELY!
OKAY, *KEED*, KNOCK 'EM IN. LOOK FOR A GOOD ONE AND GIVE IT A RIDE!
BABE DID PLAY IN THE OUTFIELD, BUT HE WAS USUALLY REPLACED BY ANOTHER PLAYER LATER IN THE GAME. IT WAS A SAD SIGHT TO HIS LONGTIME FANS.

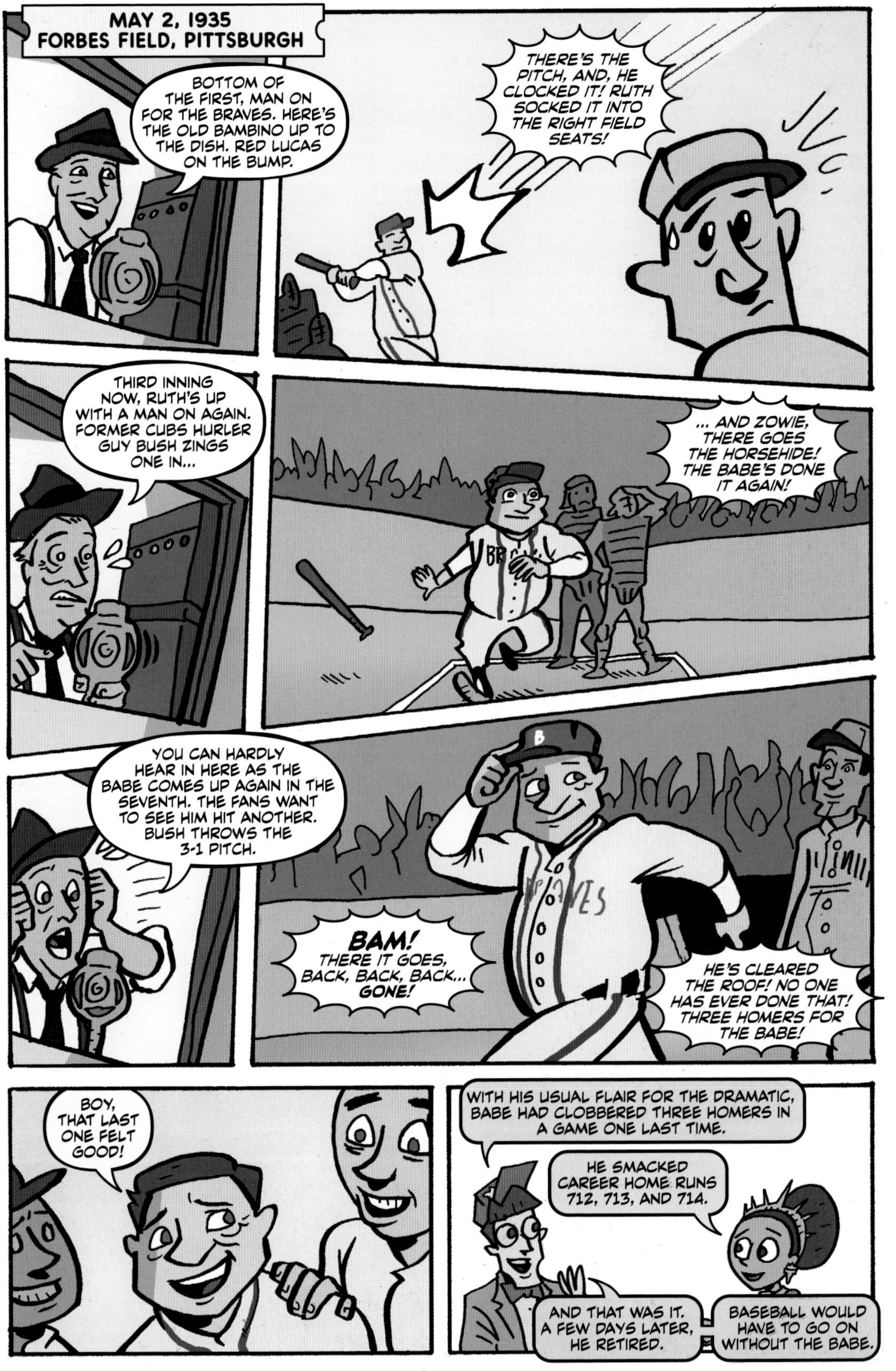
MAY 2, 1935
FORBES FIELD, PITTSBURGH
BOTTOM OF THE FIRST, MAN ON FOR THE BRAVES. HERE'S THE OLD BAMBINO UP TO THE DISH. RED LUCAS ON THE BUMP.
THERE'S THE PITCH, AND, HE CLOCKED IT! RUTH SOCKED IT INTO THE RIGHT FIELD SEATS!
THIRD INNING NOW, RUTH'S UP WITH A MAN ON AGAIN. FORMER CUBS HURLER GUY BUSH ZINGS ONE IN...
... AND ZOWIE, THERE GOES THE HORSEHIDE! THE BABE'S DONE IT AGAIN!
YOU CAN HARDLY HEAR IN HERE AS THE BABE COMES UP AGAIN IN THE SEVENTH. THE FANS WANT TO SEE HIM HIT ANOTHER. BUSH THROWS THE 3-1 PITCH.
BAM! THERE IT GOES, BACK, BACK, BACK... GONE!
HE'S CLEARED THE ROOF! NO ONE HAS EVER DONE THAT! THREE HOMERS FOR THE BABE!
BOY, THAT LAST ONE FELT GOOD!
WITH HIS USUAL FLAIR FOR THE DRAMATIC, BABE HAD CLOBBERED THREE HOMERS IN A GAME ONE LAST TIME.
HE SMACKED CAREER HOME RUNS 712, 713, AND 714.
AND THAT WAS IT. A FEW DAYS LATER, HE RETIRED.
BASEBALL WOULD HAVE TO GO ON WITHOUT THE BABE.

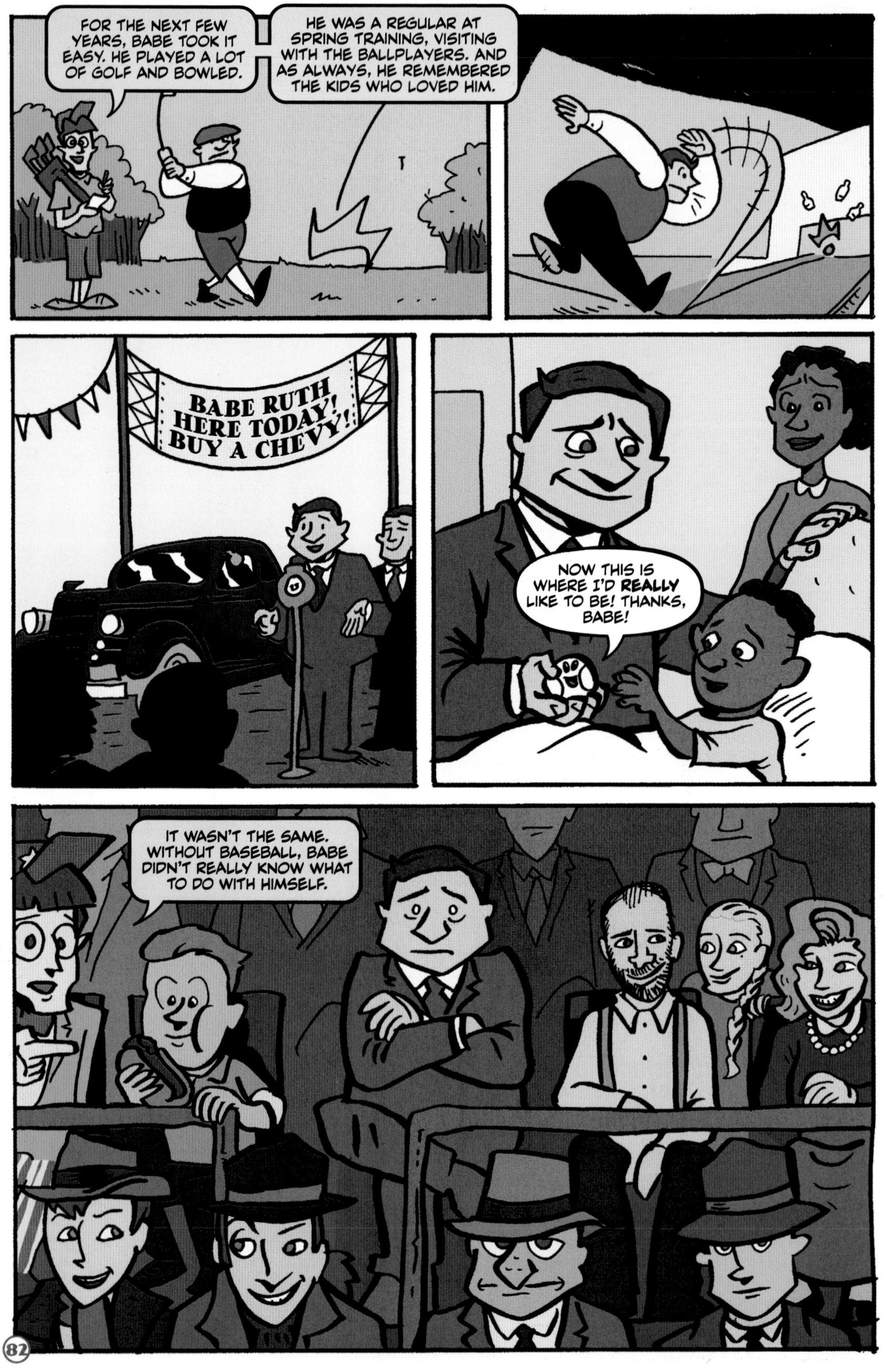
FOR THE NEXT FEW YEARS, BABE TOOK IT EASY. HE PLAYED A LOT OF GOLF AND BOWLED.
HE WAS A REGULAR AT SPRING TRAINING, VISITING WITH THE BALLPLAYERS. AND AS ALWAYS, HE REMEMBERED THE KIDS WHO LOVED HIM.
BABE RUTH HERE TODAY! BUY A CHEVY!
NOW THIS IS WHERE I'D **REALLY** LIKE TO BE! THANKS, BABE!
IT WASN'T THE SAME. WITHOUT BASEBALL, BABE DIDN'T REALLY KNOW WHAT TO DO WITH HIMSELF.

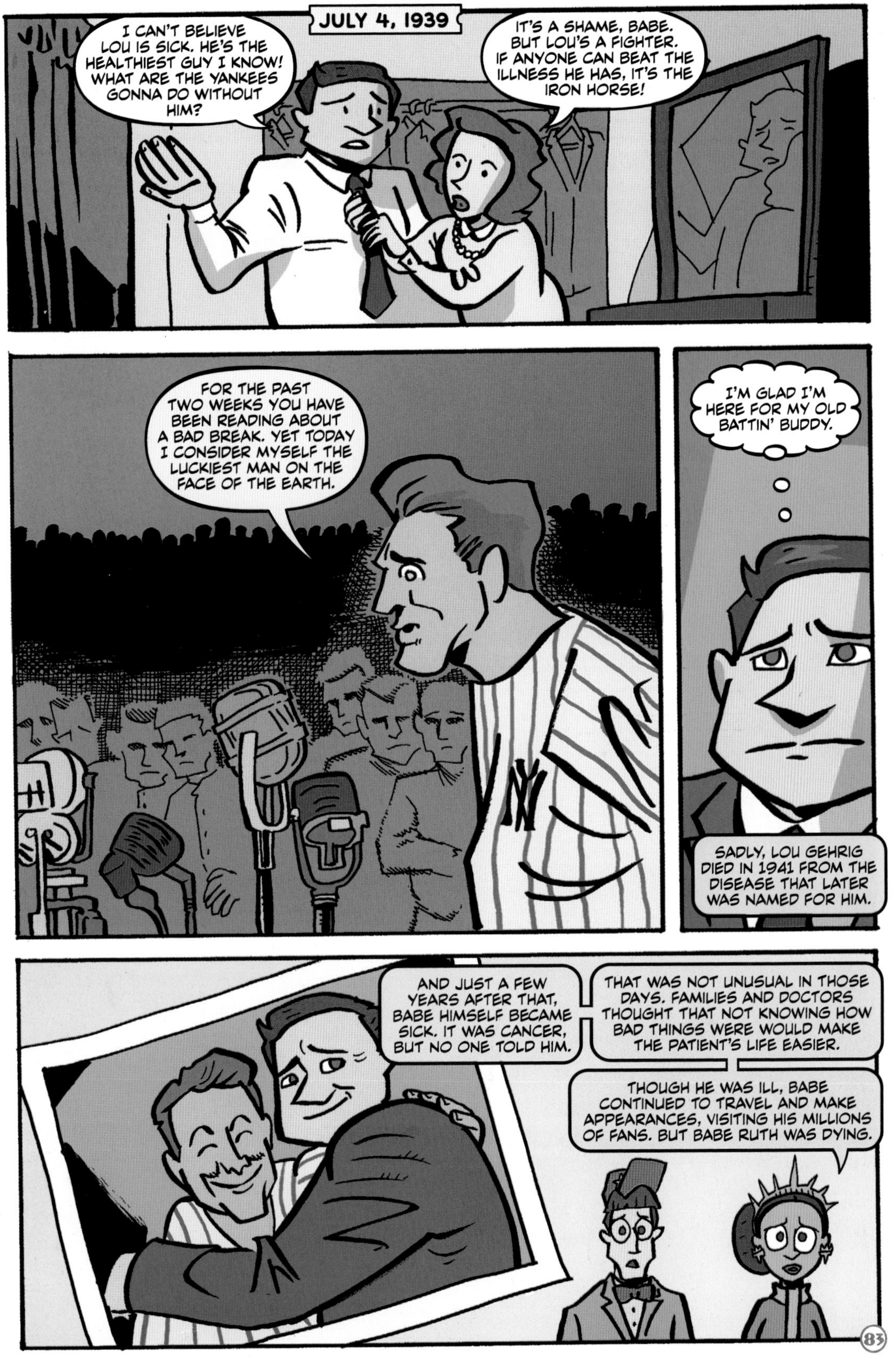

JULY 4, 1939
I CAN'T BELIEVE LOU IS SICK. HE'S THE HEALTHIEST GUY I KNOW! WHAT ARE THE YANKEES GONNA DO WITHOUT HIM?
IT'S A SHAME, BABE. BUT LOU'S A FIGHTER. IF ANYONE CAN BEAT THE ILLNESS HE HAS, IT'S THE IRON HORSE!
FOR THE PAST TWO WEEKS YOU HAVE BEEN READING ABOUT A BAD BREAK. YET TODAY I CONSIDER MYSELF THE LUCKIEST MAN ON THE FACE OF THE EARTH.
I'M GLAD I'M HERE FOR MY OLD BATTIN' BUDDY.
SADLY, LOU GEHRIG DIED IN 1941 FROM THE DISEASE THAT LATER WAS NAMED FOR HIM.
AND JUST A FEW YEARS AFTER THAT, BABE HIMSELF BECAME SICK. IT WAS CANCER, BUT NO ONE TOLD HIM.
THAT WAS NOT UNUSUAL IN THOSE DAYS. FAMILIES AND DOCTORS THOUGHT THAT NOT KNOWING HOW BAD THINGS WERE WOULD MAKE THE PATIENT'S LIFE EASIER.
THOUGH HE WAS ILL, BABE CONTINUED TO TRAVEL AND MAKE APPEARANCES, VISITING HIS MILLIONS OF FANS. BUT BABE RUTH WAS DYING.

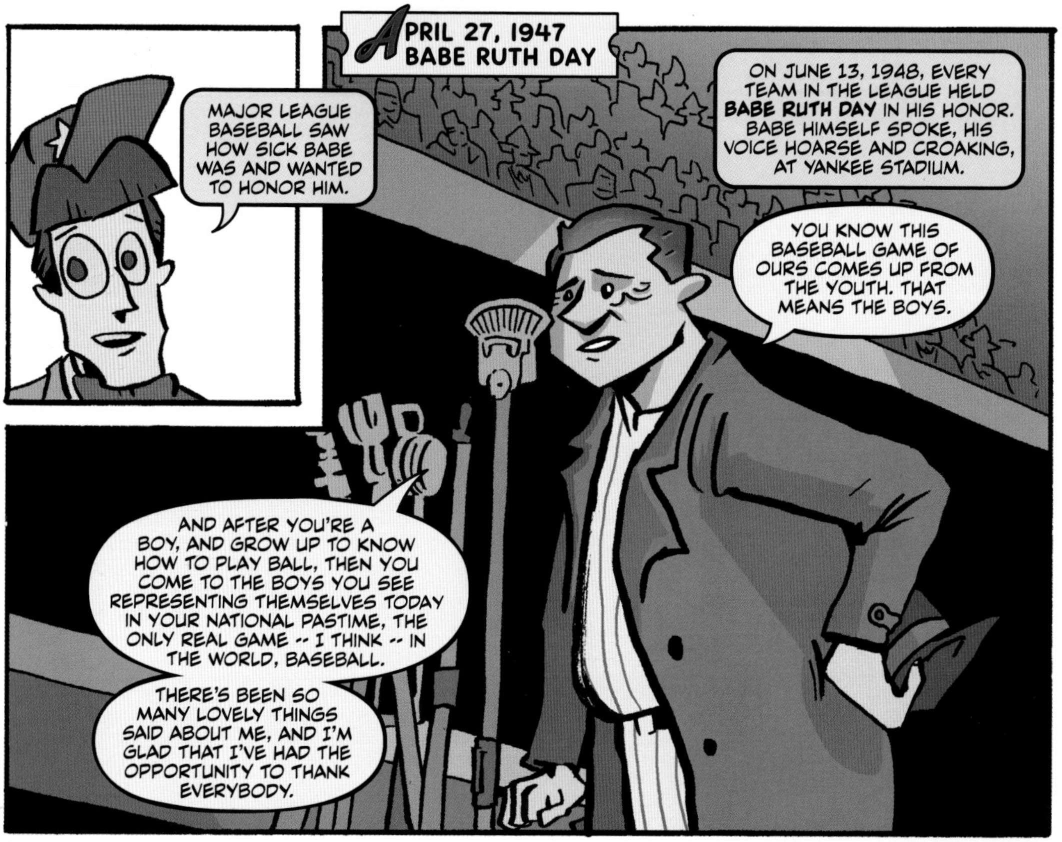

APRIL 27, 1947
BABE RUTH DAY
MAJOR LEAGUE BASEBALL SAW HOW SICK BABE WAS AND WANTED TO HONOR HIM.
ON JUNE 13, 1948, EVERY TEAM IN THE LEAGUE HELD **BABE RUTH DAY** IN HIS HONOR. BABE HIMSELF SPOKE, HIS VOICE HOARSE AND CROAKING, AT YANKEE STADIUM.
YOU KNOW THIS BASEBALL GAME OF OURS COMES UP FROM THE YOUTH. THAT MEANS THE BOYS.
AND AFTER YOU'RE A BOY, AND GROW UP TO KNOW HOW TO PLAY BALL, THEN YOU COME TO THE BOYS YOU SEE REPRESENTING THEMSELVES TODAY IN YOUR NATIONAL PASTIME, THE ONLY REAL GAME -- I THINK -- IN THE WORLD, BASEBALL.
THERE'S BEEN SO MANY LOVELY THINGS SAID ABOUT ME, AND I'M GLAD THAT I'VE HAD THE OPPORTUNITY TO THANK EVERYBODY.

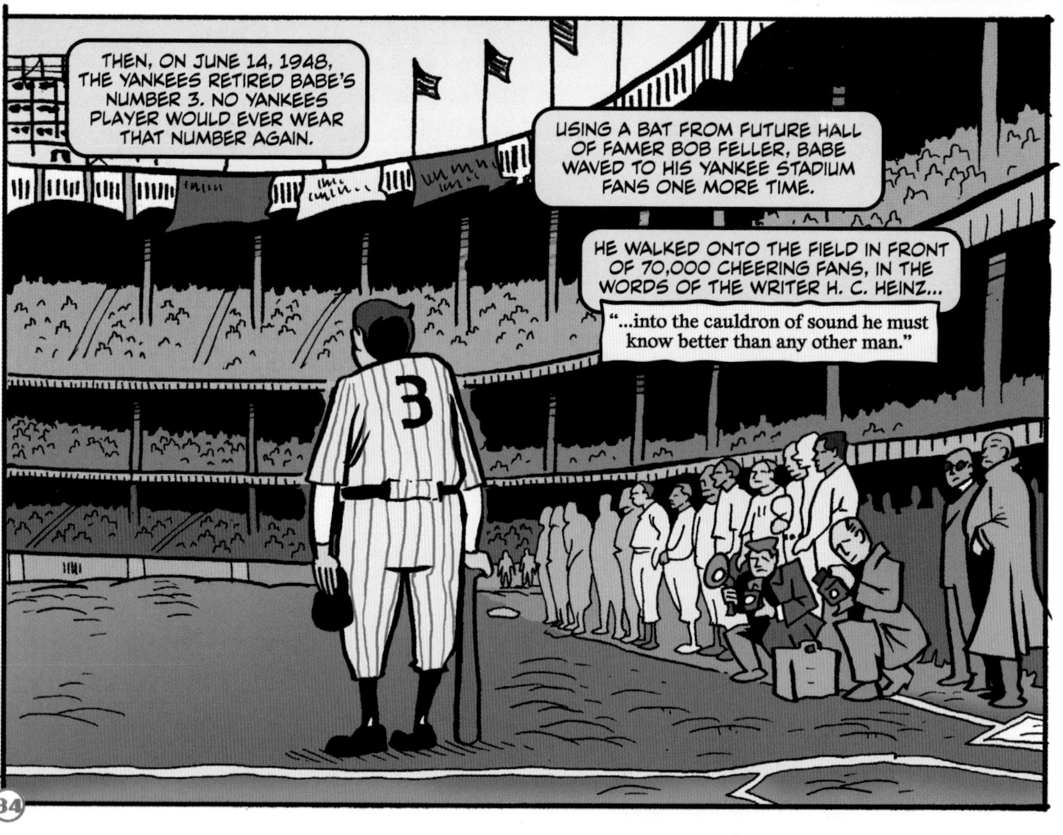

THEN, ON JUNE 14, 1948, THE YANKEES RETIRED BABE'S NUMBER 3. NO YANKEES PLAYER WOULD EVER WEAR THAT NUMBER AGAIN.
USING A BAT FROM FUTURE HALL OF FAMER BOB FELLER, BABE WAVED TO HIS YANKEE STADIUM FANS ONE MORE TIME.
HE WALKED ONTO THE FIELD IN FRONT OF 70,000 CHEERING FANS, IN THE WORDS OF THE WRITER H. C. HEINZ...
"...into the cauldron of sound he must know better than any other man."
3

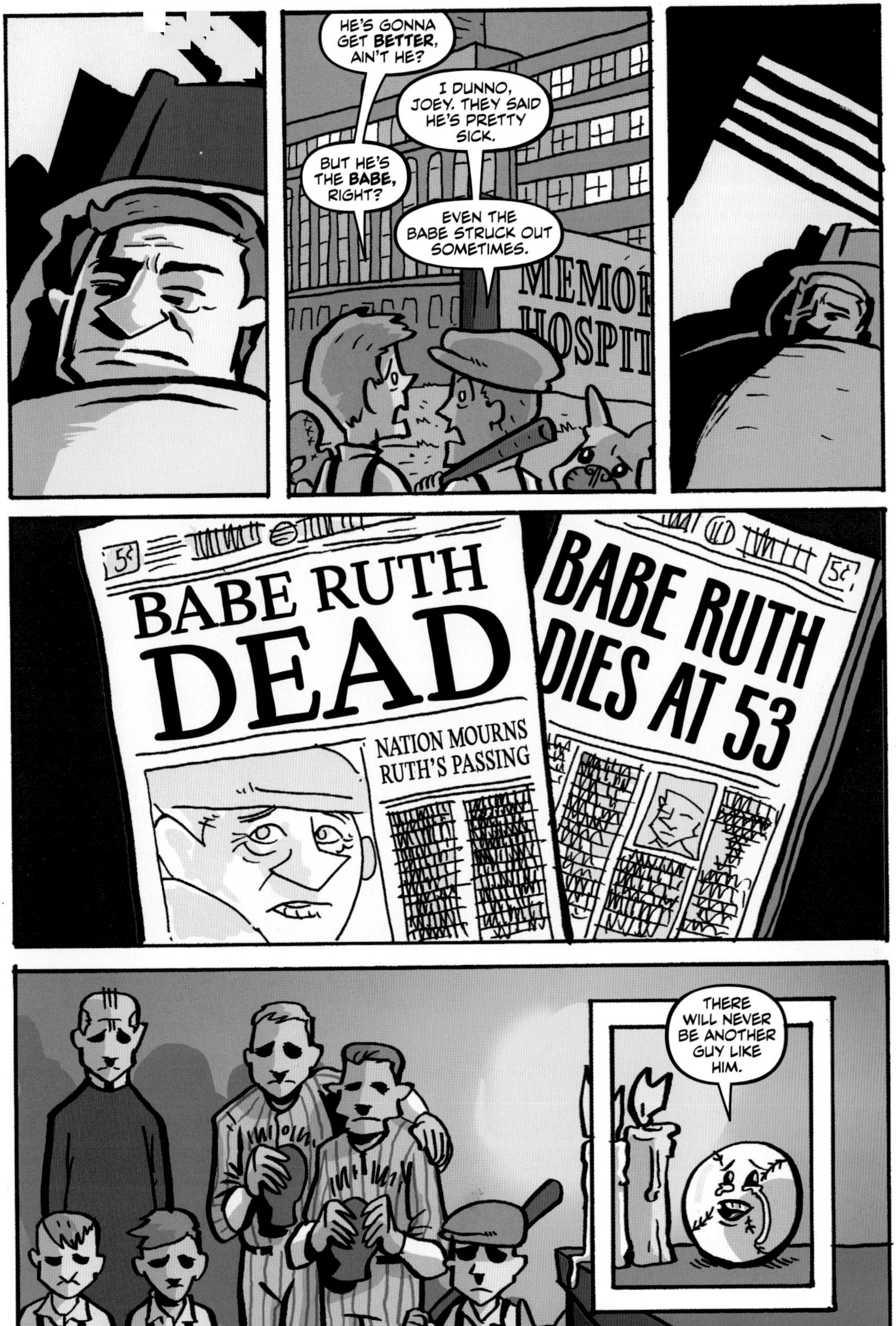

HE'S GONNA GET **BETTER**, AIN'T HE?
I DUNNO, JOEY. THEY SAID HE'S PRETTY SICK.
BUT HE'S THE **BABE**, RIGHT?
EVEN THE BABE STRUCK OUT SOMETIMES.
5¢
BABE RUTH DEAD
NATION MOURNS RUTH'S PASSING
5¢
BABE RUTH DIES AT 53
THERE WILL NEVER BE ANOTHER GUY LIKE HIM.

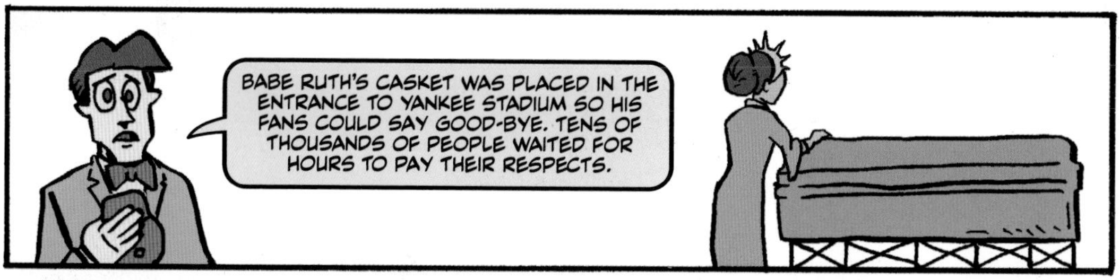
BABE RUTH'S CASKET WAS PLACED IN THE ENTRANCE TO YANKEE STADIUM SO HIS FANS COULD SAY GOOD-BYE. TENS OF THOUSANDS OF PEOPLE WAITED FOR HOURS TO PAY THEIR RESPECTS.

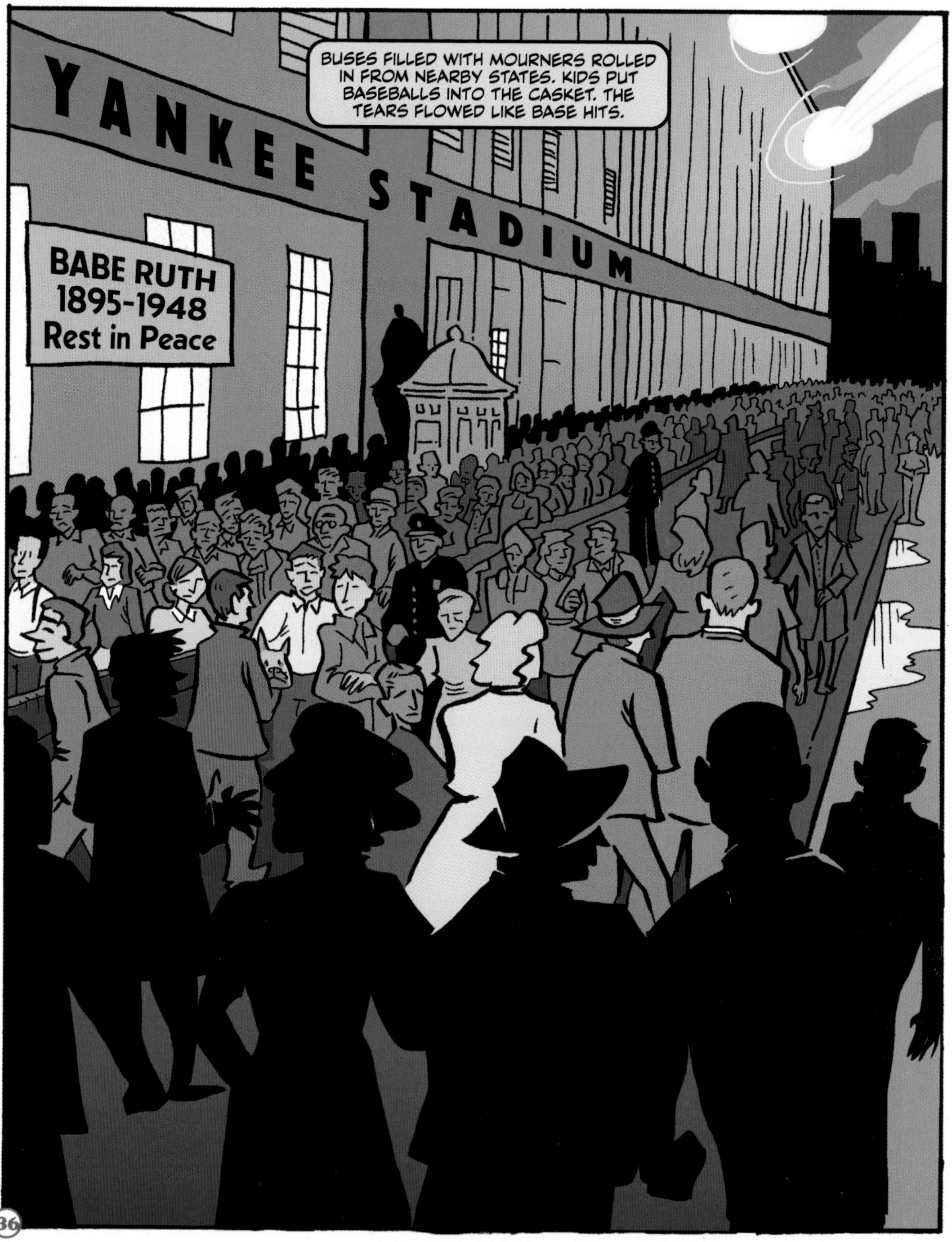
YANKEE STADIUM
BUSES FILLED WITH MOURNERS ROLLED IN FROM NEARBY STATES. KIDS PUT BASEBALLS INTO THE CASKET. THE TEARS FLOWED LIKE BASE HITS.
BABE RUTH
1895-1948
Rest in Peace

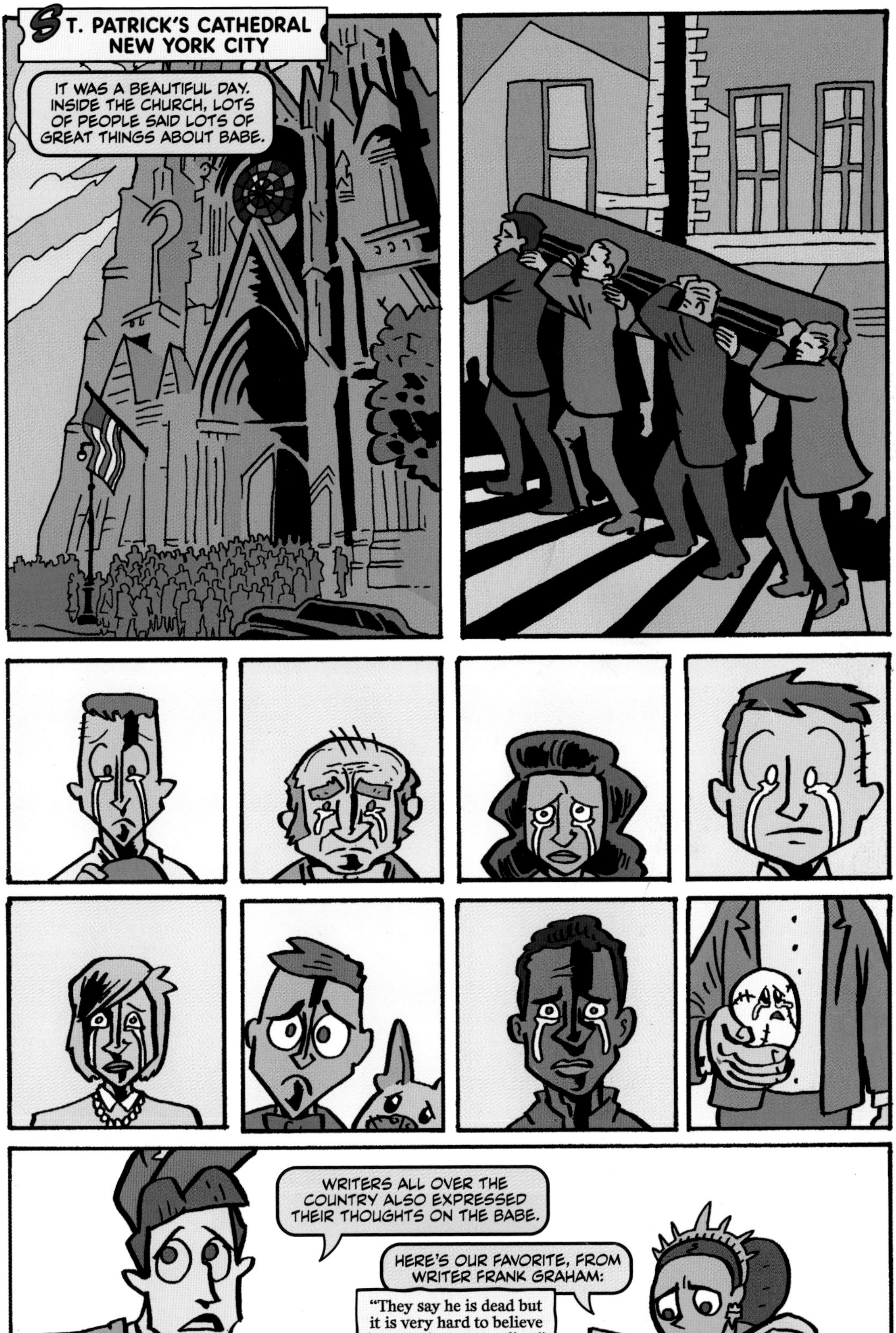
ST. PATRICK'S CATHEDRAL
NEW YORK CITY
IT WAS A BEAUTIFUL DAY. INSIDE THE CHURCH, LOTS OF PEOPLE SAID LOTS OF GREAT THINGS ABOUT BABE.
WRITERS ALL OVER THE COUNTRY ALSO EXPRESSED THEIR THOUGHTS ON THE BABE.
HERE'S OUR FAVORITE, FROM WRITER FRANK GRAHAM:
"They say he is dead but it is very hard to believe because he was so alive."

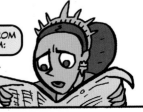

Baseball Since the Babe

	1932	2019
MLB Teams	16	30
MLB homers per team:	85	223
Avg. attendance per MLB game:	5,654	28,500
Yearly salary:	Babe Ruth $75,000 (worth $1.1 million today)	Mike Trout $36 million (for just **one season!**)

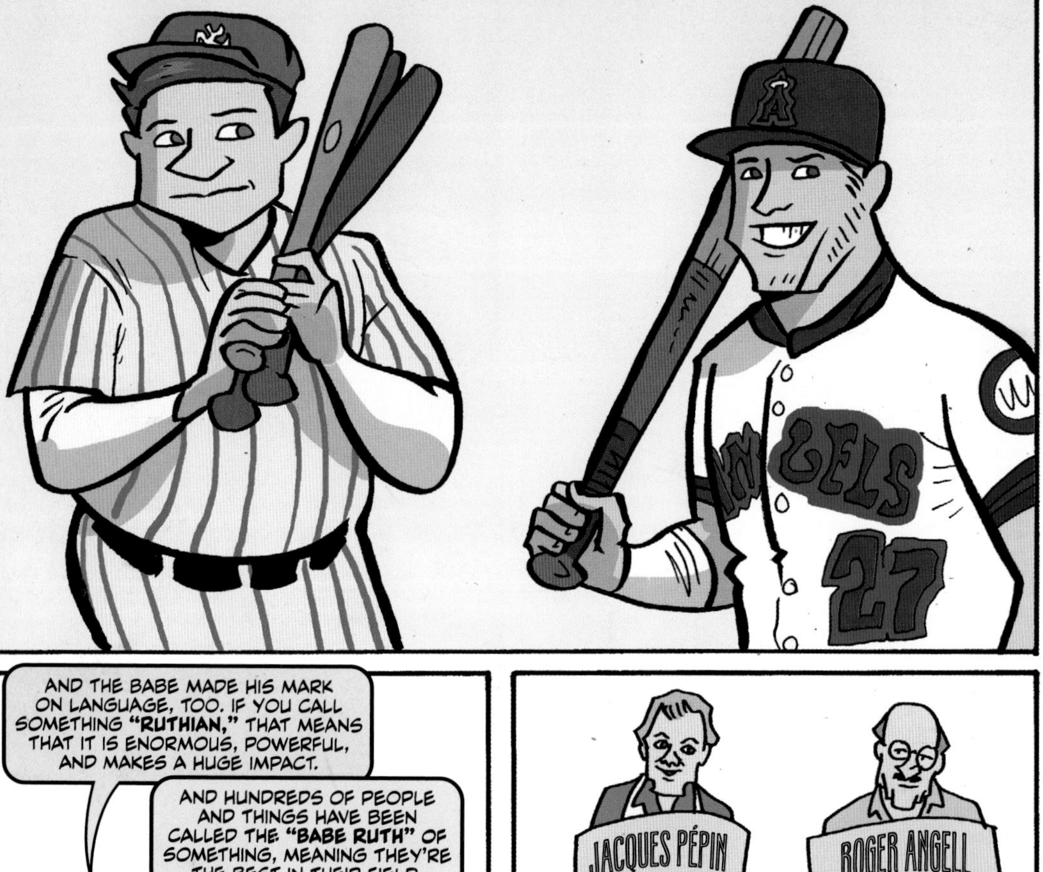

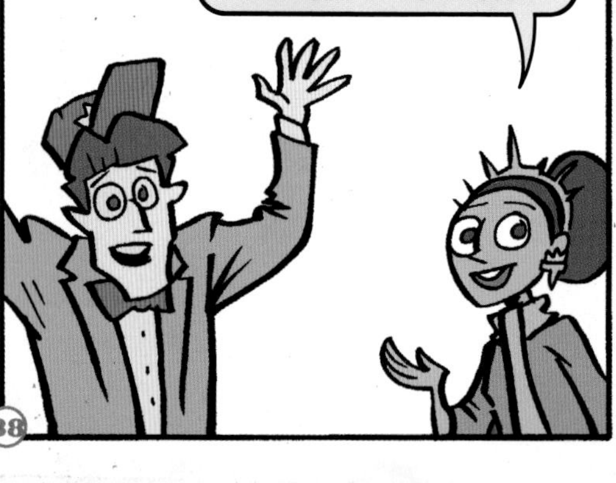
AND THE BABE MADE HIS MARK ON LANGUAGE, TOO. IF YOU CALL SOMETHING **"RUTHIAN,"** THAT MEANS THAT IT IS ENORMOUS, POWERFUL, AND MAKES A HUGE IMPACT.
AND HUNDREDS OF PEOPLE AND THINGS HAVE BEEN CALLED THE **"BABE RUTH"** OF SOMETHING, MEANING THEY'RE THE BEST IN THEIR FIELD.

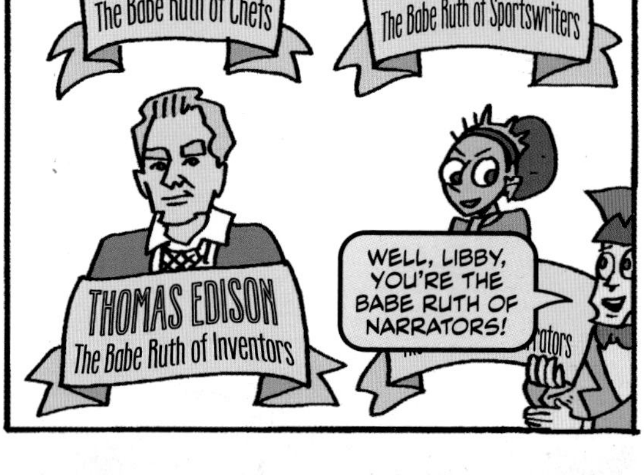
JACQUES PÉPIN
The Babe Ruth of Chefs
ROGER ANGELL
The Babe Ruth of Sportswriters
THOMAS EDISON
The Babe Ruth of Inventors
WELL, LIBBY, YOU'RE THE BABE RUTH OF NARRATORS!

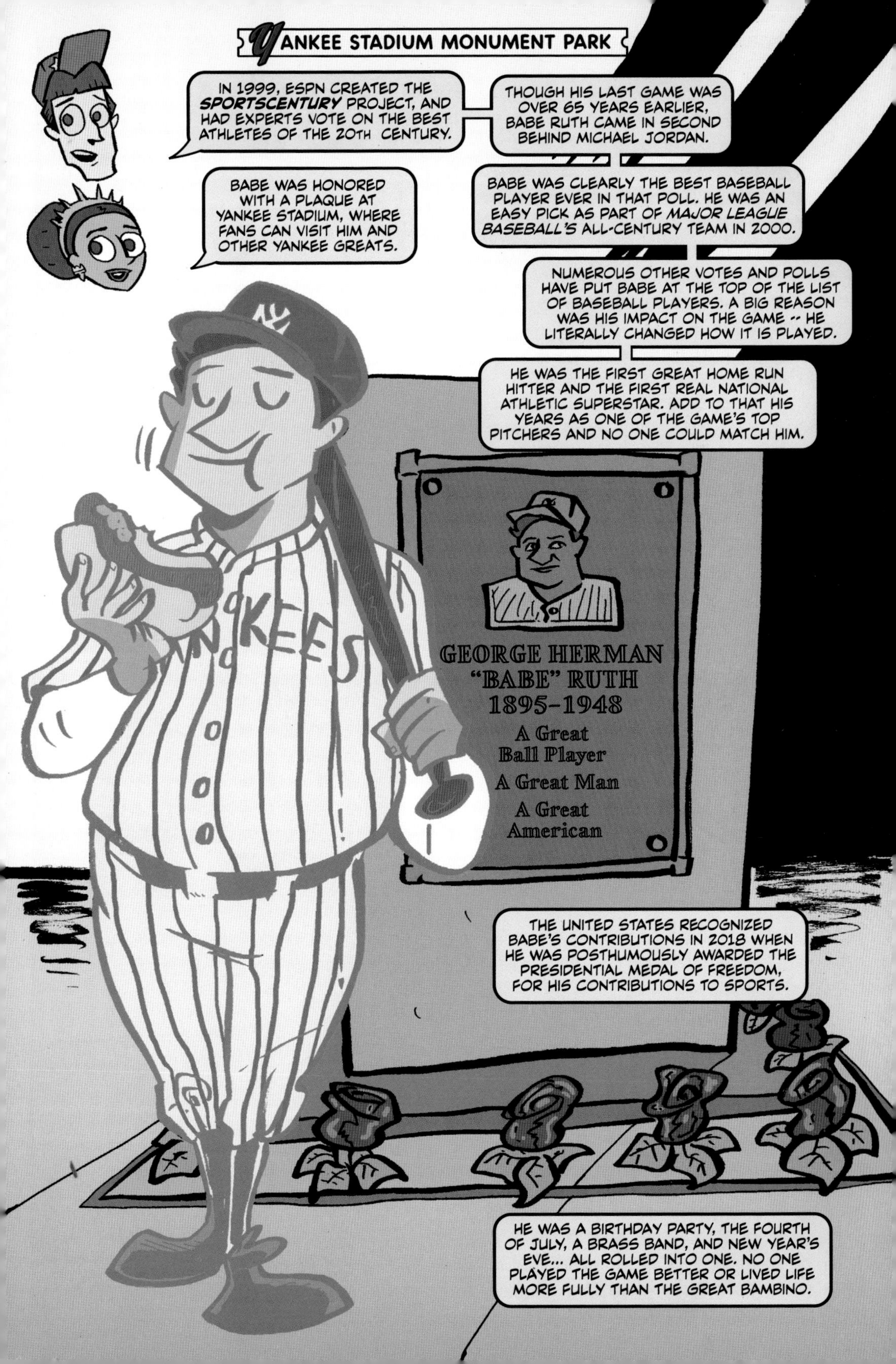
YANKEE STADIUM MONUMENT PARK
IN 1999, ESPN CREATED THE SPORTSCENTURY PROJECT, AND HAD EXPERTS VOTE ON THE BEST ATHLETES OF THE 20TH CENTURY.
THOUGH HIS LAST GAME WAS OVER 65 YEARS EARLIER, BABE RUTH CAME IN SECOND BEHIND MICHAEL JORDAN.
BABE WAS HONORED WITH A PLAQUE AT YANKEE STADIUM, WHERE FANS CAN VISIT HIM AND OTHER YANKEE GREATS.
BABE WAS CLEARLY THE BEST BASEBALL PLAYER EVER IN THAT POLL. HE WAS AN EASY PICK AS PART OF MAJOR LEAGUE BASEBALL'S ALL-CENTURY TEAM IN 2000.
NUMEROUS OTHER VOTES AND POLLS HAVE PUT BABE AT THE TOP OF THE LIST OF BASEBALL PLAYERS. A BIG REASON WAS HIS IMPACT ON THE GAME -- HE LITERALLY CHANGED HOW IT IS PLAYED.
HE WAS THE FIRST GREAT HOME RUN HITTER AND THE FIRST REAL NATIONAL ATHLETIC SUPERSTAR. ADD TO THAT HIS YEARS AS ONE OF THE GAME'S TOP PITCHERS AND NO ONE COULD MATCH HIM.
GEORGE HERMAN "BABE" RUTH 1895–1948
A Great Ball Player
A Great Man
A Great American
THE UNITED STATES RECOGNIZED BABE'S CONTRIBUTIONS IN 2018 WHEN HE WAS POSTHUMOUSLY AWARDED THE PRESIDENTIAL MEDAL OF FREEDOM, FOR HIS CONTRIBUTIONS TO SPORTS.
HE WAS A BIRTHDAY PARTY, THE FOURTH OF JULY, A BRASS BAND, AND NEW YEAR'S EVE... ALL ROLLED INTO ONE. NO ONE PLAYED THE GAME BETTER OR LIVED LIFE MORE FULLY THAN THE GREAT BAMBINO.

OTHER HOME RUN HEROES

JIMMIE FOXX: In 1940, Ol' Double X became the second player after Ruth to reach 500 career homers. He ended up with 534.

TED WILLIAMS: Called "the greatest hitter who ever lived," Teddy Ballgame had 521 homers in 19 seasons along with posting the highest on-base percentage ever.

WILLIE MAYS: Fifth all-time in homers, the Say-Hey Kid was the second player after Ruth to reach 600 homers, finally ending with 660.

FRANK ROBINSON: This slugging outfielder with 586 career homers was the first player to be named Most Valuable Player in each league: Cincinnati (1961) and Baltimore (1966).

REGGIE JACKSON: Known as Mr. October, like Ruth once hit three homers in a single World Series game -- on three pitches! Jackson ended with 563 dingers.

HANK AARON: Hammerin' Hank was the first person to top Babe's amazing total of 714 career homers. He hit the historic blast on April 8, 1974, and finished with 755 career home runs.

KEN GRIFFEY JR.: One of baseball's most recent slugging stars, The Kid blasted 630 homers with a sweet left-handed swing.

BABE RUTH WAS THE FIRST, OF COURSE, BUT IN THE YEARS SINCE, SLUGGERS HAVE BEEN AMONG BASEBALL'S BIGGEST STARS. HERE ARE JUST A FEW LEGENDARY LONGBALLERS!

DID THEY OR DIDN'T THEY? Three players with huge home run totals are under a cloud. Barry Bonds (762), Sammy Sosa (609), and Mark McGwire (583) are suspected of or were caught using performance-enhancing drugs. Do some research on their careers and see what you think.

BABE RUTH TIMELINE

1895 George Herman Ruth Jr. is born on February 6 in Baltimore.

1902 George's parents sent him to live at St. Mary's Industrial School.

1914 After a great sports career at St. Mary's, George joins the Baltimore Orioles, a minor league team. He gets a new nickname: The Babe. The O's trade him to the Major League Boston Red Sox that summer. He meets, and marries, Helen Woodford.

1918 Babe helps the Red Sox win their third World Series in four seasons. He sets a pitching record for consecutive scoreless World Series innings.

1920 In his first season with the New York Yankees, he sets a record with 54 homers.

1923 Babe hits a home run on Opening Day at the brand-new Yankee Stadium. The Yankees win their first World Series that October.

1927- Babe and the Yankees win back-to-back
1928 World Series.

1929 Helen Ruth dies in a fire. Babe marries Claire Hodgson, who has been his girlfriend for several years.

1934 Babe plays his final game for the Yankees.

1935 After 28 games with the Boston Braves, Babe retires at the age of 40.

1936 Babe is one of the first five people named to the new Baseball Hall of Fame.

1948 Babe dies of throat cancer at the age of 53.

GLOSSARY

BARNSTORMING: Traveling from place to place putting on performances or athletic events.

BATTING AVERAGE: A measure of hitting success -- divide total hits by total official at-bats.

CURFEW: Deadline for returning at the end of the day.

DETENTION: Temporary confinement or punishment.

EARMARKS: Indications of having a particular skill.

GREENSWARD: A fancy term for a large area of grass.

INCORRIGIBLE: Impossible to tame or deal with, very unruly.

MINOR LEAGUE: Professional teams a step below Major League Baseball.

PENNANT: A triangular cloth awarded to a league champion, also symbolic of the championship itself.

SHUTOUT: A baseball game in which one team does not allow the other team to score a run.

SLUGGING PERCENTAGE: A measure of power-hitting success -- divide total bases by official at-bats.

HORSEHIDE: An old-time nickname for a baseball (though balls are made from cow leather, not horsehide).

NATIONAL PASTIME: A nickname for the game of baseball.

RETIRED: As in a "retired number," means that a team will never reuse the number of a great player, in their honor.

FIND OUT MORE

BOOKS

Burleigh, Robert. *Home Run: The Story of Babe Ruth.* Boston: HMH Books for Young Readers, 2003.

Christopher, Matt. *Babe Ruth* Great Americans in Sports. New York: Little Brown, 2015.

Holub, Joan. *Who Was Babe Ruth?* Who Was? Series. New York: Penguin Workshop, 2012.

Montville, Leigh. *The Big Bam: The Life and Times of Babe Ruth.* New York: Doubleday, 2006.

Tavares, Matt. *Becoming Babe Ruth* Candlewick Biographies. Boston: Candlewick, 2016.

WEBSITES

www.baseball-reference.com

Babe Ruth Birthplace Museum
baberuthmuseum.org

Babe Ruth official Web site
www.baberuth.com

Major League Baseball: Glossary of Terms
www.mlb.com/glossary

National Baseball Hall of Fame and Museum
baseballhall.org

New York Yankees: Monument Park
www.mlb.com/yankees/news/history-of-monument-park/c-263612104
You can see plaques for Babe Ruth, Lou Gehrig, Miller Huggins, and other Yankee greats in deep center field.

VIDEOS

American Hercules: Babe Ruth. New York: Major League Baseball Productions, 2015.

Babe Ruth. Sports of the 20th Century. New York: HBO Sports, 1998.

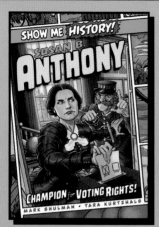
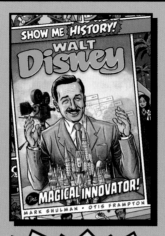

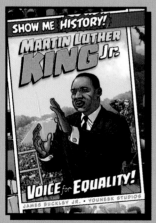

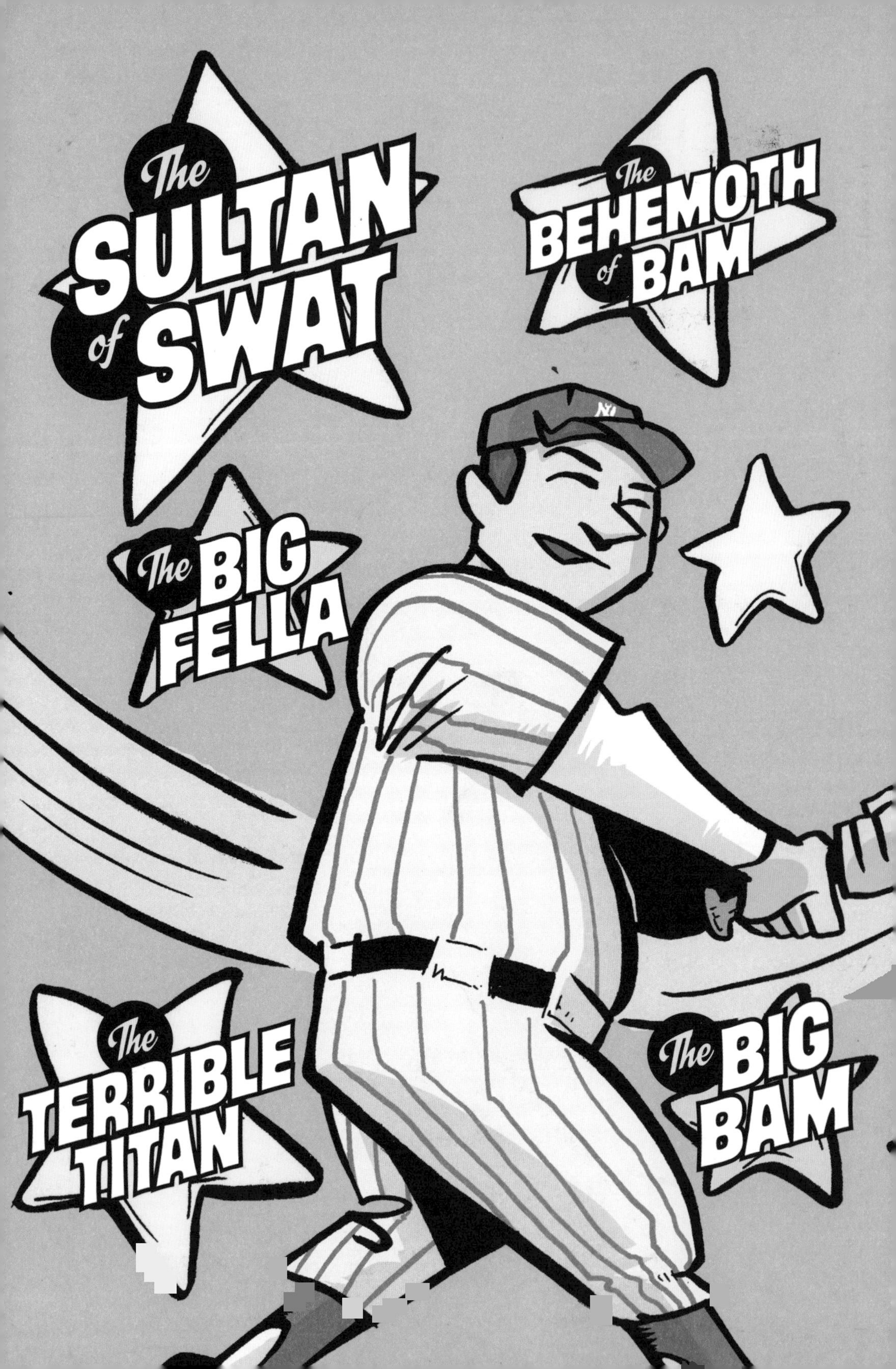
The SULTAN of SWAT
The BEHEMOTH of BAM
The BIG FELLA
The TERRIBLE TITAN
The BIG BAM